ENHANCING PRIMARY MATHEMATICS TEACHING

ENHANCING PRIMARY MATHEMATICS TEACHING

Edited by
Ian Thompson

Open University Press
Maidenhead · Philadelphia

Open University Press
McGraw-Hill Education
McGraw-Hill House
Shoppenhangers Road
Maidenhead
Berkshire
England
SL6 2QL

email: enquiries@openup.co.uk
world wide web: www.openup.co.uk

First published 2003

A catalogue record of this book is available from the British Library

ISBN 0 335 21375 8 (pb)   0 335 21376 6 (hb)

Library of Congress Cataloging-in-Publication Data
CIP data applied for

Typeset by RefineCatch Limited, Bungay, Suffolk
Printed in Great Britain by Bell and Bain Ltd, Glasgow

For my wife, Barbara, my children, John and Anna (my mathematical guinea-pigs) and the 7000 children, trainees and teachers I have taught over the last 40 years.

Contents

Notes on contributors

Mundher Adhami studied geophysics at Moscow and Durham universities, and worked in computer dynamic modelling before switching to teaching mathematics in London schools in 1974. Interest in open tasks and pupils' conceptual progression in the classroom led him to join the Graded Assessment in Mathematics (GAIM) project at King's College London. He became subject officer at the London board for the GAIM 100 per cent coursework GCSE based on collaboratively moderated teacher assessment. Since 1993 he has been a King's College research worker in the Cognitive Acceleration in Mathematics Education (CAME) series of research, and coordinator of associated professional development programmes across Key Stages 1 to 3.

Mike Askew is Reader in Mathematics Education at King's College, University of London. A former primary teacher, he now researches, lectures and writes on teaching primary mathematics. He directed the Teacher Training Agency funded 'Effective Teachers of Numeracy in Primary Schools', and the Nuffield Foundation funded 'Raising Attainment in Numeracy' and 'Mental Calculations: Interpretations and Implementation' projects. He was deputy director of the five-year Leverhulme Numeracy Research Programme looking at teaching, learning and progression from Reception to Year 7. When he is not writing up research he enjoys being a conjuror.

Carol Aubrey is currently Professor of Early Childhood Studies in the Institute of Education at the University of Warwick and leads the Childhood Research Group. She trained first as a primary school teacher, as a researcher in applied psychology and then as an educational psychologist. Later, she spent a number of years in primary teacher education with a particular focus on the early years, first at University College Cardiff and later at the University of Durham. A long-term interest has been children's early mathematical development, from the preschool period into Reception and through Key Stage 1, in the national and European context.

Margaret Brown is Professor of Mathematics Education at King's College London. After teaching in primary and secondary schools and teacher training, Margaret directed over 20 research projects in the teaching, learning and assessment of mathematics, including the *Leverhulme Numeracy Research Programme*. These have concerned all age groups. She was a member of the Numeracy Task Force, and has also been Chair of the Joint Mathematical Council of the UK, President of the Mathematical Association and President of the British Educational Research Association.

Ann Dowker is University Research Lecturer in the Department of Experimental Psychology at Oxford University, and Research Fellow for the Organization for Economic Cooperation and Development (OECD) Network on Brain, Development and Numeracy. Her interests include mathematical development and cognition; individual differences in arithmetic in children and adults; attitudes to mathematics and mathematics anxiety; and interventions to help children with numeracy difficulties. She has worked in collaboration with several Oxford primary schools to set up and pilot the Numeracy Recovery intervention project, funded by the Esmee Fairbairn Charitable Trust. She is joint editor with Arthur Baroody of *The Development of Arithmetic Concepts and Skills* (Erlbaum 2003).

Rosemary Hafeez taught in four different inner London boroughs. She then became Mathematics Adviser for Croydon local education authority where she wrote *Starting from Big Numbers* and *Calculating Dominoes* published by BEAM, and initiated the BEAM calendar. She worked jointly with King's College London, developing primary CAME. She moved to the Mathematics Test Development Team in the Assessment Division at the Qualifications and Curriculum Authority (QCA), having responsibility for using and applying mathematics, tasks for the less able, the year progress test and computer mediated testing. She is currently Inspector for Mathematics and Numeracy for the Royal Borough of Kingston upon Thames.

Steve Higgins is a senior lecturer in primary education at Newcastle University. His research interests are in the areas of effective teaching and learning with a particular focus on mathematics and the use of information and communication technology. He is a member of the Thinking Skills Research Centre at the university which investigates the impact of a range of thinking skills approaches on teachers, pupils and classroom interaction. As a former primary teacher he is particularly interested in the practical application of research in classrooms and the development of collaborative research projects.

Keith Jones is Director of the Centre for Research in Mathematics Education at the University of Southampton. Before taking up posts in higher education, he spent over ten years teaching in multi-ethnic inner-city schools where he was actively involved in curriculum development and classroom based research. His areas of research expertise, on which he has published widely, include the teaching and learning of geometry, the development of mathematical reasoning and proof and the use of technology in mathematics teaching. He was a member of the Royal Society inquiry into the teaching and learning of geometry and he organizes the geometry working group of the British Society for Research into Learning Mathematics (see www.soton.ac.uk/~dkj/bsrlmgeom/index.html).

Lesley Jones taught in schools in Birmingham, became a member of a team working with gifted and talented children, then an advisory teacher before moving into initial teacher training at Goldsmiths College, London. She has many years' experience of providing in-service education and training (INSET). She has researched children's reasoning skills and presented her findings at conferences in the UK and abroad, and has written numerous articles for *Junior Education* and *The Times Educational Supplement*. She is the editor of *Mathematics in School* and has jointly authored numerous books including, *Enriching Early Mathematical Learning* published by Open University Press.

Valsa Koshy is a reader in education and director of the Able Children's Education Centre at Brunel University. She worked as a class teacher and advisory teacher for mathematics prior to joining the university, where she is the Director of Academic and Professional Development programmes. She has written a substantial number of books on teaching mathematics and on provision for gifted education. Her research interests include the identification of gifted mathematicians, mathematics education, assessment and the development of talents in children aged 4–7. She works as a consultant to a wide network of local education authorities and is currently directing two Department for Education and skills (DfES) funded research projects on provision for gifted pupils.

Alison Millett is Senior Research Fellow at King's College London. She has considerable experience in primary teaching and management, and in research. She held the post of Research Fellow on the *'Evaluation of the Implementation of National Curriculum Mathematics' (1991–3)*; directed an ESRC-funded project *'Ofsted and Primary Maths' (1996–7)*; worked as Senior Research Fellow on the *Leverhulme Numeracy Research Programme (1997–2002)* and is currently principal investigator on the Nuffield-funded *'The Impact of the NNS; Comparing Pupils' Attainment and Teaching in Year 4 Before and After the Strategy's Introduction'*.

Claire Mooney is Director of the primary Postgraduate Certificate of Education (PGCE) course at the University of Southampton and its course leader for mathematics. She is an experienced mathematics teacher and educator and the author of several key texts on teaching mathematics at the primary level. Her research interests are in the teaching and learning of geometry, especially how teachers acquire and use geometrical knowledge.

Laurie Rousham was a primary teacher for 17 years and head teacher of a school involved in the 'Calculator-Aware Number' (CAN) project between 1984–9, before taking up a post in the mathematics department at Homerton College, Cambridge. An initial research interest in calculator use with young children developed into a wider concern with subtraction and the use of the empty number line. For some years he was a member of the National Curriculum Council's B Committee, which dealt with mathematics. In 1997 he returned to the classroom, getting to grips with the two strategies in a Year 4 class before becoming a Numeracy Consultant for Suffolk local education authority in 2000.

Malcolm Swan works at the School of Education, University of Nottingham, and with the Shell Centre/Mathematics Assessment Resource Service (MARS) team based in the university. His major interests are in curriculum, assessment and teacher education research and development, and he continues to work on projects in these areas both nationally and internationally. His current activities include designing problem solving curriculum and assessment material for 9- and 13-year-olds as part of the World Class Arena (a QCA project) and in developing a discussion-based approach to learning algebra for GCSE students in further education (with the Learning and Skills Development Agency).

Ian Thompson taught for 19 years before moving into teacher education. During his time working on secondary and primary PGCE courses at Newcastle University he began researching children's mental and written calculation strategies and their understanding of place value. He has edited two books for Open University Press: *Teaching and Learning Early Number* and *Issues in Teaching Numeracy in Primary Schools*. He was seconded to the National Numeracy Strategy for two years as a Regional Director for Initial Teacher Training, and in 2002 became an independent mathematics consultant and researcher. In 2003 he became Visiting Professor at Northumbria University.

Helen J. Williams is a freelance educational consultant with a particular interest in early years mathematics. She has been an advisory teacher for mathematics, involved in QCA consultation groups and in initial teacher training. Helen is a member of the Association of Teachers of Mathematics and jointly edits *Mathematics Teaching*, one of the Association's journals. Current work also involves teaching mathematics alongside colleagues in schools, organizing and leading INSET courses, contributing to conferences and writing, reviewing and trialing mathematics materials.

Editor's preface

Any book that attempts to make suggestions for improving the teaching and learning of mathematics in England in the early part of the twenty-first century must inevitably engage in a discussion, either explicitly or implicitly, of the National Numeracy Strategy (NNS). This government-backed project, adopted by the vast majority of schools in the country, was introduced in September 1999 and later became an integral part of the Primary Strategy in 2003. The purpose of the NNS' *Framework for Teaching Mathematics from Reception to Year 6* was to help schools set appropriately high expectations for their children and to help teachers understand how their pupils should progress through the primary years. It had a substantial influence on the teaching and learning of mathematics in almost every primary school in England.

This book is the third in a set of three edited collections concerned with the teaching and learning of mathematics in primary schools. The first, *Teaching and Learning Early Number* (Open University Press 1997), looked at research findings concerned with children's early number acquisition and the implications of this research for classroom practice. Some of this research had a substantial influence on the structure of those sections of the *Framework* dealing with early years numeracy. The second book, *Issues in Teaching Numeracy in Primary Schools* (Open University Press 1999) provided background and details to many of the issues which led to the development of the NNS. This third book makes a considered attempt to assess how the teaching of mathematics might be enhanced in the wake of the influence of the NNS.

Enhancing Primary Mathematics Teaching comprises 17 chapters arranged in six loosely-structured sections covering issues relating to the following areas: subject content, pedagogy, assessment, intervention, information and communication technology (ICT) and research. Chapters in all sections discuss theory in relation to practice, and some chapters contain cross-references to other chapters where this is deemed relevant. Each chapter, however, has been written to be read as a free-standing unit.

Acknowledgements

Every reasonable effort has been made to clear copyright permissions with the holders of materials reproduced in this book, but in some instances this has proved impossible. Figure 1.1 is copyright Pixar Animation Studios. Figure 1.2 is by Ludwig Abache, used by permission. Figure 1.4 is by Heiner Thiel, used by permission. Figure 1.5 is adapted from de Villiers, M. (1996) 'The future of secondary school geometry', paper presented at the 'Geometry Imperfect' conference, University of South Africa, Pretoria, South Africa. Figure 1.6 is adapted from Battista, M.T. and Clements, D.H. (1995) *3-D Geometry: Seeing Solids and Silhouettes, Grade 4* (Palo Alto, CA: Dale Seymour Publications, p. 61). Permission has been given by United Features Syndicate Inc. to reproduce Figure 5.1.

Section 1

SUBJECT CONTENT ISSUES

At the turn of the century major attempts were being made to improve the teaching of numeracy in English primary schools. The National Numeracy Project (NNP) was launched in September 1996; this then metamorphosed into the National Numeracy Strategy (NNS) three years later; and this in its turn was subsumed by the National Primary Strategy (NPS) in 2003. Given that the original focus of the NNP was numeracy rather than mathematics, it is not surprising that 'shape and space' was not initially included in the NNP handbook. However, by the time the NNS was launched in 1999, the *Framework for Teaching Mathematics from Reception to Year 6* incorporated all the mathematics strands of the National Curriculum. The first section of this book focuses specifically on subject content, and begins with a chapter on geometry in the primary school.

Chapter 1 is by Keith Jones, who was a member of the Royal Society/Joint Mathematical Council inquiry into the teaching and learning of geometry, and Claire Mooney, a primary mathematics education lecturer whose research interests include investigating how teachers acquire and use geometrical knowledge. Their chapter provides a brief background to 'the renaissance in geometry' before looking in some detail at the place of the subject in primary school mathematics and, in particular, in the NNS. The authors make a comparison between the number of Key Objectives devoted to the teaching of number and those allocated to shape, space and measures, and discuss the implications of this situation. They look briefly at some evidence from research into geometrical reasoning, and consider the importance of geometrical problem solving. They describe some activities they feel might compensate for opportunities missed in the *Framework* by providing an intuitive visual foundation for geometric topics that will be treated more deductively at a later stage.

The second and third chapters deal with the teaching of number, with a specific focus on the 'four rules'. Ian Thompson has carried out research on young children's idiosyncratic mental and written strategies for two decades.

In Chapter 2 he unpicks the NNS' approach to calculation. Progression from mental to written calculation within each of the four basic operations is scrutinized, and questions are raised whenever the author believes that the recommendations conflict with research findings and/or experience of working in the field. The chapter has been written with extra information (for the enthusiast!) in note form at the end. This is in order not to disrupt the flow of a chapter that demands that the reader work through several calculations whilst attempting to articulate their thought processes. The author notes a shift in philosophy as the NNS moves from mental to written calculation, and discusses what he believes to be some of the inconsistencies in the NNS' approach, particularly with respect to two-digit mental calculation and the informal to formal progression within written methods.

No mention is made of *jottings* – a key term used by the NNS – in Chapter 2 as this, in the form of the Empty Number Line (ENL) is the major focus of Chapter 3. Laurie Rousham had the good fortune to work with Meindert Beishuizen, a Dutch educator who has done a substantial amount of research on the ENL in Holland. In his chapter he attempts to clarify the many misconceptions that English mathematics educators have about this form of support for mental calculation. The chapter sets the scene by providing a thumbnail sketch, with an accompanying commentary, that captures the atmosphere of a typical lesson in a Dutch classroom. This is followed by a lucid explanation of the range of ENL strategies used and discussed by the children and their teacher. The author then argues that what appears to be missing from the English approach to using the ENL is a coherent account of how to merge several disparate elements into a clear and unified teaching strategy.

1

Making space for geometry in primary mathematics

Keith Jones and Claire Mooney

The movie *Toy Story*, released in 1995, was the first full-length, fully computer animated feature film. What may be surprising is that most of the *Toy Story* characters (see Figure 1.1) began life as collections of simple geometrical shapes, like spheres and cylinders, created on computers. These basic shapes were then transformed geometrically to produce each final figure. Once all the characters had been created, the challenge was to get them to move in what looked like realistic ways. This involved even more geometry. The final result was an award-winning film.

Figure 1.1 Some of the cast of *Toy Story*

Figure 1.2 The Great Court at the British Museum: classical and modern geometry combined

While much of the sophisticated geometry used in the making of films like *Toy Story* is very new (getting the shading right is apparently the most difficult part), the roots of this new geometry are very old. Nevertheless, by the middle of the twentieth century geometry was in danger of becoming eclipsed by the inexorable rise in the sophistication of algebraic techniques. These advances in algebra strongly influenced the curricular reforms that began in the 1960s, one of the results of which was that the amount of geometry included in school curricula around the world was reduced, sometimes severely so, especially for pupils aged 11–19.

Recently, however, there has begun a renaissance in geometry. Fuelled to a large extent by technological developments, it is now becoming possible to model situations visually/geometrically with quite astonishing sophistication. Computer animation, used to great effect in many popular films (such as *Toy Story*), is one manifestation of these advances. Medical imaging such as MRI (magnetic resonance imaging), global positioning systems and developments in many other areas, from architecture to robotics, all use advanced geometrical ideas. If anything, with the advent of new materials and new technologies, such as those used in the design and construction illustrated in Figure 1.2, the emphasis on everything visual is increasing. All this means that it is becoming increasingly vital to reassess our approach to the teaching and learning of geometrical ideas at all levels.

An inquiry by the Royal Society (RS) and Joint Mathematical Council (JMC) found that the current specification of the mathematics National Curriculum at primary school level is reasonable, arguing that: 'provided that this curriculum is effectively implemented, then pupils transferring from primary schools to Year 7 in secondary schools should have a suitable basis on which to develop their study of geometry' (RS/JMC 2001: 13).

Nevertheless, while the RS/JMC report contains many very useful recommendations, the fact that the inquiry was largely restricted to the needs of students in the 11–19 age range reinforces the impression that geometry at the primary school level is, and remains, the poor relation in comparison to work on number. Indeed, as Fielker (1986: 124) describes, up to the 1960s the mathematics curriculum at primary level was almost entirely devoted to work on number.

While, as mentioned above, the curricular reforms of the 1960s reduced the amount of geometry in the secondary school curriculum, some efforts were made to provide an appropriate geometry curriculum for primary age pupils. In many respects, the current specification of the National Curriculum for mathematics (DfEE 1999a) could be said to continue these efforts by including 'shape, space and measures' as one of the three content areas of mathematics at the upper primary level (along with number/algebra and handling data) and as one of only two areas (with handling data included as part of number) at Key Stage 1. From this specification, it might be surmised that geometry could constitute as much as one third of the primary mathematics curriculum, yet the National Curriculum documentation provides little guidance on its implementation with respect to the relative importance of the specified content areas. This leaves the National Numeracy Strategy (NNS) free to specify the relative emphasis given to the various aspects of mathematics.

This chapter examines the structure and recommendations of the NNS with respect to the teaching of geometry at primary school, as exemplified in the NNS' own published materials. It looks at ways in which these recommendations might be best taken forward and whether there are important aspects of geometry that the NNS has omitted or to which it has paid too little attention. Given that children experience life on a solid planet in a 3D world and that much of this experience is sensed through visual stimuli, the chapter concludes by suggesting what it might mean to give geometry appropriate consideration at the primary level.

Geometry in primary school mathematics

Geometry, says the renowned UK mathematician Sir Michael Atiyah (2001: 50), is one of the two pillars of mathematics (the other being algebra). Understanding and making sense of the world, claims Atiyah, is a very important part of what it means to be human. Sir Michael writes:

> spatial intuition or spatial perception is an enormously powerful tool and that is why geometry is actually such a powerful part of mathematics – not only for things that are obviously geometrical, but even for things that are not. We try to put them into geometrical form because that enables us to use our intuition. Our intuition is our most powerful tool . . .

The focus for this chapter is the development of spatial reasoning at the primary level. Work on measures, while often beginning with a spatial context, just as often very rapidly leaves this behind and is probably experienced by children as yet another way of doing calculations. By concentrating on *geometry*, the focus is on the development and application of *spatial concepts* through which children learn to represent and make sense of the world: 'Geometry is grasping space ... that space in which the child lives, breathes and moves. The space that the child must learn to know, explore, conquer, in order to live, breathe and move better in it' (Freudenthal 1973: 403).

Within the mathematics National Curriculum (for England), geometry is found as part of the attainment target currently entitled 'shape, space and measures'. This specification lists the content for this part of mathematics under the following headings:

- using and applying shape, space and measures;
- understanding properties of shape;
- understanding properties of position and movement;
- understanding measures.

The next section examines how this curriculum specification is implemented within the NNS.

Geometry in the NNS

In the introduction to the main NNS document, the *Framework for Teaching Mathematics from Reception to Year 6* (DfEE 1999b: 4), the following definition of numeracy is offered:

> Numeracy is a proficiency which involves confidence and competence with numbers and measures. It requires an understanding of the number system, a repertoire of computational skills and an inclination and ability to solve number problems in a variety of contexts. Numeracy also demands practical understanding of the ways in which information is gathered by counting and measuring, and is presented in graphs, diagrams, charts and tables.

Disappointingly, perhaps, there is little sign of geometry in this definition. Nevertheless, the *Framework* does identify teaching objectives designed to cover all the requirements of the National Curriculum for mathematics, including geometry. Some of these objectives are identified as *key* objectives, ones that are 'more critical than others' (DfEE 1999b: 3). Based on these Key Objectives, Table 1.1 shows the geometrical priorities as set out in the *Framework*.

As is made clear in the NNS training materials, the priority at Key Stage 1 is to develop pupils' facility with the language associated with shape and space through practical exploration. At Key Stage 2, the training materials highlight the following three aspects of shape and space (DfEE 1999c: Ch. 7):

- 2D and 3D shapes and their properties;
- position and direction;
- transformations.

In terms of the progression of geometrical ideas, there is nothing in the NNS materials equivalent to the advice on number and algebra (for instance, there is nothing comparable to the sections on 'The approach to calculation' and 'Laying the foundation for algebra' in the *Framework* document). Nevertheless, it is possible to glean a reasonably clear model from a close study of the *Framework* (and its associated specification of suggested mathematical vocabulary). For example, the *Framework* suggests that children should be taught to identify and name certain geometric shapes, ranging from cube, pyramid, sphere, cone, circle, triangle, square and rectangle in Reception through to dodecahedron, rhombus, kite, parallelogram and trapezium in Year 6. A progression can also be traced in the topological and rectilinear properties that children are taught to identify and use in order to classify shapes. These range from descriptive terms in Reception (flat, curved, straight, hollow, solid, corner, face, side, edge, end) through to congruent, concentric and intersecting (in Years 5 and 6), and from language to describe position and pattern

Table 1.1 The geometrical priorities in the NNS

Year	Key objectives	Additional objectives given in the yearly teaching programme
R	Position Geometrical language	Symmetrical patterns
1	Geometrical language	Properties of solids and flat shapes 2D representation Turning, position, direction
2	Sorting/classifying Position, direction, movement	Line symmetry Visualizing objects Recognizing turns
3	Line symmetry	Classifying and describing 2D and 3D shapes Compass directions and turns Straight line as two right angles
4	Classifying Symmetry properties	Describing and visualizing 2D and 3D shapes Nets of solids Whole turn as 360°
5	Parallel/perpendicular lines Properties of plane shapes	Classifying triangles Visualizing 3D shapes Nets of a cube Reflective symmetry Translation
6	Position	Describing and visualizing 3D shapes Reflection, rotation Sum of the angles of a triangle

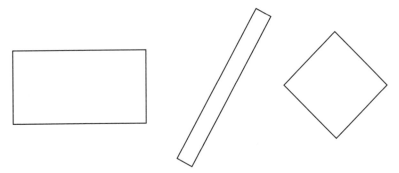

Figure 1.3 Examples of rectangles in different orientations

(e.g. on, in, symmetrical pattern, repeating pattern) in Reception through to more technical terms such as axis of symmetry, reflective symmetry, parallel, perpendicular, rotation, acute, obtuse and reflex in Year 6.

As the RS/JMC report indicates, this is a reasonably good geometry curriculum. The question to address now is how this curriculum is experienced by primary school pupils.

Children's experience of geometry in the NNS

According to the Office for Standards in Education (Ofsted 2002), the NNS had a positive impact on the standards attained in mathematics and on the quality of teaching in primary schools. For example, government pupil achievement targets were almost being reached and there were, says Ofsted, discernible increases in pupils' enjoyment of, and confidence and involvement in, mathematics lessons. In terms of pupil experience of geometry, an analysis of specially commissioned tests taken by pupils at a national sample of 300 schools (reported in Ofsted 2002: 7–8) indicated that among the topics with which pupils made the greatest amount of progress between 2001 and 2002 were 'recognition of squares and triangles' (Year 3) and 'finding the perimeter of a shape' (Year 4). Geometric topics with which pupils were still having the greatest difficulty were 'identification of parallel and perpendicular lines' and 'finding the coordinates of a missing vertex of a rectangle' (both Year 5 topics). At the same time, and as a result of the 2001 Key Stage 2 national tests taken by all 11-year-old pupils, the Qualifications and Curriculum Authority (QCA) recommended that teachers should give children opportunities to increase their familiarity with angle facts and with using precise geometrical terms for shapes, and associating these terms with their related properties (QCA 2002). The QCA also recommended that children needed more practice at working with shapes in less familiar orientations, as illustrated by the range of orientations given in Figure 1.3, and experience of, for instance, reflecting shapes in lines that are not solely parallel or perpendicular to a vertical mirror line.

While neither Ofsted nor the QCA appeared to comment on the balance of mathematics in the NNS, some mathematics teachers had the opportunity to do so in a survey of the perceived impact of the NNS at Key Stage 3 (Barnes *et al.* 2003: 38). While many secondary school teachers, the survey found, took the view that 'the constant practice of number work is necessary and beneficial', many others argued that equally significant aspects of the mathematics curriculum were being sidelined through the emphasis on number. The report noted that 'the profile and teaching of shape and space, and the proficiency of pupils in this area on entry to Year 7, were raised [by Key Stage 3 teachers] as particular concerns'.

Indicators of the profile of geometry within the NNS can be gleaned through examining the relative number of *key* teaching objectives devoted to geometry and by noting the number of hours allocated to geometry in the suggested Yearly Teaching Programme. For example, in the *Framework* only around 10 per cent of the Key Objectives are devoted to geometrical/spatial thinking and reasoning. As a result, between four and eight times as much number/calculation work (depending on the age of the pupils) is recommended as compared with geometrical/spatial work. In terms of the percentage of mathematics teaching time that should be devoted to geometry, the RS/JMC report (2001: 13) recommends that for secondary age pupils, 'geometry should occupy 25%–30% of the teaching time, and hence a similar proportion of the assessment weighting'. Even being generous with what can be counted as geometrical in the NNS *Framework*, the amount of geometry suggested at the primary level falls very much short of this, being about 12 per cent of the teaching time across the whole of the primary years, and in Year 2 falling to just 7 per cent (just at the time pupils take their first national tests).

This lack of priority for geometry within the NNS is also evidenced in the structure of the three-part daily mathematics lesson. The first part of the suggested lesson structure is entitled 'Oral work and mental *calculation*' (emphasis added) (DfEE 1999b: 13), with each of the examples of an oral and mental starter given within Section 1 being based either on recall of number facts or of number calculations. The implication of this concentration on calculation is that mental geometry is neither feasible nor, indeed, desirable while, given the importance of spatial and visual thinking, just the opposite is the case – see Figure 1.4 for a suggestion of a useful mental geometry activity. The emphasis in the NNS on oral and mental *calculation* is further highlighted within the objectives given in the Yearly Teaching Programmes (DfEE 1999b: Section 3). Strategies for the development of rapid recall of number facts and mental calculation are clearly identified in discrete sections. Mental geometry is not given this status. Despite the modification of 'oral and mental *calculation*' to 'oral and mental *starter*' in some of the NNS training material, within the NNS documentation as a whole almost the only guidance on geometry is given within the supplementary training document *Shape and Space Activities*, yet even here it is revealing that a number of the suggested pupil activities are, in fact, number and/or algebra activities simply contextualized within geometry.

A particularly influential way in which pupils experience the curriculum is through the commercial mathematics scheme, or set of textbooks, used in

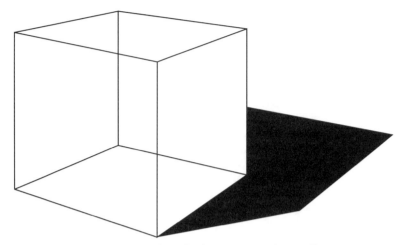

Figure 1.4 Mental geometry: what shadows can a cube cast?

their classrooms. A small-scale survey of such schemes carried out in preparation for this chapter suggests that the majority of those used within schools in England reflect the priorities of the NNS in giving far greater prominence to work on number as compared to work on geometry. For instance, many commercially produced schemes have multiple books devoted to developing number, compared with maybe only one containing the whole of geometry and measures (and frequently data handling too).

Overall, all the above evidence suggests that the advice to pupils should be 'do not be ill at primary school or you might easily miss whole sections of the geometry curriculum'! While this lack of emphasis on geometry at the primary level is replicated in many countries, it is important to re-examine the treatment of geometry, beginning with what can be gleaned from the research that has been carried out.

Evidence from research

There is a considerable amount of research on the teaching and learning of geometry. It is neither feasible nor sensible to attempt to summarize it all. Rather, major themes are identified below with a view to examining the aspects of geometry that the NNS has omitted or to which it has paid little attention (for details of references to this research, see Appendix 14 of the RS/JMC report 2001).

Piaget argued that the progressive organization of geometric ideas in children follows a definite order and this order is more experiential (and possibly more mathematically logical) than it is a reflection of the historical development of geometry. For example, although topology is a recently developed area of mathematics, Piagetian research suggests that, for learners, topological relations, such as connectedness, enclosure and continuity, are formed first. After this come the ideas of rectilinearity (such as the outline of objects) associated with projective geometry. Finally, the child is ready to acquire Euclidean notions of angularity, parallelism and distance. At best, this suggested learning sequence has received mixed support from research. The available evidence indicates that all types of geometric ideas appear to develop over time, becoming increasingly integrated and synthesized as children progress.

Another learning sequence, suggested by van Hiele (1986), puts identifying shapes and figures according to their concrete examples at the first ('visual') level for learners. At the second ('descriptive') level, learners identify shapes according to their properties (e.g. that a rhombus is a figure with four equal sides). At the third ('abstract') level, students can identify relationships between classes of figures (e.g. that a square is a special form of rectangle) and can discover properties of classes of figures by simple logical deduction. At the fourth ('formal') level, students can produce a short sequence of statements to logically justify a conclusion and can understand that deduction is the method of establishing geometric truth. Available research, while generally supportive of this model, has identified various problems with the specification of the levels. Particular problems include the labelling of the lowest level as 'visual', when visualization is demanded at all the levels, and the fact that learners appear to show signs of thinking from more than one level in the same or different tasks, in different contexts.

Neither the Piagetian nor the van Hiele models are strongly evident in the *Framework*. This is especially true of the Piagetian model as the *Framework*, reflecting the National Curriculum, makes no mention of topology or of projective geometry even though such ideas can be accessible at the primary level.[1] In terms of the van Hiele model, the *Framework* could be said to include the progression from description to classification but the heavy emphasis on descriptive language, at the expense of *geometrical* problem solving, which is given relatively little attention in the NNS, is likely to mean that children's progression will be somewhat limited.

Overall, research on the teaching and learning of geometry indicates that physical experience, especially the physical manipulation of shapes, is important at all ages, that a wide variety of geometrical experiences are necessary in order for pupils to gain a firm understanding of geometrical relationships and that computer packages such as *Logo* and dynamic geometry software, while not being a panacea, have much to offer. While all these things are present in the NNS to some degree, the lack of time apportioned to geometry is likely to mean that none of them are fully realized. Given the importance of geometry within mathematics, the next section offers some idea of what it might mean to give proper space to geometry within the primary mathematics curriculum.

Making space for geometry in the NNS

When describing what they see as the impoverished nature of school geometry at the primary level in the USA, Battista and Clements (1988: 11) note that the poor performance of primary age pupils in geometry 'is due, in part, to the current elementary school geometry curriculum, which focuses on recognizing and naming geometric shapes and learning to write the proper symbolism for simple geometric concepts'. To remedy this situation they argue that geometry at the primary level should be 'the study of objects, motions, and relationships in a spatial environment'. This means that pupils' first experiences with geometry should emphasize the informal study of physical shapes and their properties and have as their primary goal the development of students' intuition and knowledge about their spatial environment. Subsequent experiences should involve analysing and abstracting geometric concepts and relationships in increasingly formal settings.

While the NNS could be said to attempt to provide children with an appropriate grounding in geometrical ideas, it is limited by the amount of curricular time it allocates to geometry. As a result, opportunities are missed which could mean that children do not make the kind of progress envisaged. For example, the NNS could be seen to provide a strengthening of the treatment of transformation geometry as, by the end of their primary schooling, children should be confident with rotations, reflections and translations. Yet the link between symmetry and the various transformations is not always made explicit. In the *Framework*, for instance, rotation appears to be considered solely as a transformation and the opportunity is missed to extend this to include rotational symmetry, even though the latter is specified in the statutory National Curriculum.

Other ways in which opportunities are missed occur when so few of the *Framework*'s 'supplements of examples' encompass geometrical problem solving (most of the examples use terms like 'recognize', 'identify', 'describe') and when connections are not made between geometrical ideas. For example, the *Framework* appears to make no mention of tessellations, yet this area of geometry can provide an intuitive visual foundation for a variety of geometric content that can be treated more formally in a deductive manner at a later stage.

Studying tessellations, as Figure 1.5 illustrates, can be a springboard into the angle properties of regular and irregular polygons and because each tile has to be identical and can be made to fit onto any other tile exactly (by means of translations, rotations or reflections), pupils can be introduced, intuitively, to the concept of *congruency*. Pupils can also be encouraged to look for larger figures with the same shape, thus intuitively introducing them to the concept of *similarity*. Of course, the *Framework*, in its supplement of examples, does provide illustrations of how, for instance, as an outcome of 'recognizing translations', pupils might 'make patterns by repeatedly translating a shape' (DfEE 1999b: 106). Yet not only does the *Framework* fail to mention that the outcome of repeatedly translating a shape can be a tessellation, it also signally fails to develop the example so that it becomes possible to make the sorts of links

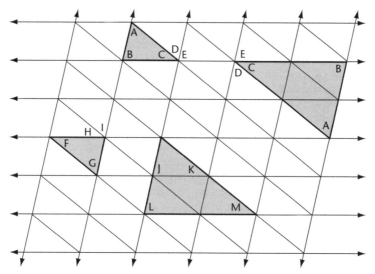

Figure 1.5 Analysing a tessellation

Make a building out of ten cubes by looking at the three pictures of it below.

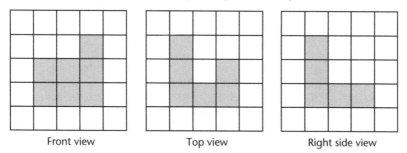

Front view   Top view   Right side view

Figure 1.6 An example of a 3D problem

between geometrical ideas, such as those indicated above, that are essential if pupils are going to progress.

Other geometrical topics where omissions are likely to limit pupil development include the limited treatment of 3D geometry, where the emphasis appears to be on recognizing and describing rather than on solving problems like the example in Figure 1.6, and where some topics, such as initial ideas about planes of symmetry, and about polyhedra, could have been included. Further examples of omissions are the lack of some experience of early topology and the failure to include suitable applications of geometry (such as in various mechanisms).

Conclusion

No doubt the development of the NNS was heavily influenced by the work of the Numeracy Task Force (established by the UK government in May 1997), with its explicit focus on the teaching of number skills. Yet in comparing the statutory requirements for geometry, as laid out in the National Curriculum for mathematics, with the suggested time allocations recommended within the NNS *Framework*, it is clear that it is extremely difficult to adequately address all the geometry requirements within the time allowed (146 hours of geometry across the whole of the primary years, out of 1200 hours of mathematics altogether). Given the vitally important role of geometry, and the emerging concerns voiced by Key Stage 3 teachers about the lack of geometrical skills of incoming secondary pupils (Barnes *et al.* 2003), it would be sensible to research the impact of the allocation of time given to geometry within the NNS to ensure that it is not failing to enable children to develop clear and lasting geometrical knowledge, skills and understanding. In addition, it would also be helpful if further studies of the development of spatial thinking and geometrical visualizing were carried out with a view to making the specification of mental geometry in the NNS documentation far more explicit, probably in ways similar to the prominence given to oral and mental calculation. On the available evidence it is likely that, until spatial and visual thinking is given greater status within the mental and oral segment of the daily mathematics lesson, and until more curriculum space is devoted to geometry, children may well continue to have insufficient opportunity to develop the fundamental visualization and spatial reasoning skills that are so important in an increasingly visual world.

The success of any revised NNS *Framework* that gives greater prominence to geometry would inevitably depend, to a large extent, on the expertise of the teachers who teach it and the teaching methods that they use. In respect of the latter, the RS/JMC report (2001: 11) affirms that 'in many respects, we need to develop a completely new pedagogy in geometry', something on which teachers and researchers can collaborate in devising and evaluating. In respect of the former, ongoing research is suggesting that geometry is the area of mathematics in which prospective primary teachers have the most to learn (Jones *et al.* 2002). The urgent need for professional development opportunities for teachers in the area of geometry is stressed by the RS/JMC report and supported by the recommendation from the Advisory Committee on Mathematics Education (2002: 2) that 'the Government should initiate urgently the process of developing and funding a long-term programme of CPD [continuing professional development] for teachers of mathematics that can meet their needs at various stages of their careers'. Such an initiative is needed to help ensure that any improvement in the treatment of geometry in primary mathematics is a success.

Note

1 The mental geometry activity suggested in Figure 1.4, for example, can be used to introduce, at the intuitive level, ideas of affine geometry (where parallelism is preserved) and projective geometry (where parallelism is not preserved), in that if the cube is held so that one face is parallel to a screen, the transformation from shape to screen (in the form of the shadow) is an affine transformation, while if a face is not held parallel, the transformation is projective.

References

Advisory Committee on Mathematics Education (2002) *Continuing Professional Development for Teachers of Mathematics*. London: ACME.

Atiyah, M. (2001) Mathematics in the 20th century: geometry versus algebra, *Mathematics Today*, 37(2): 46–53.

Barnes, A., Venkatakrishnan, H. and Brown, M. (2003) *Strategy or Straitjacket? Teachers' Views on the English and Mathematics Strands of the Key Stage 3 National Strategy*. London: Association of Teachers and Lecturers.

Battista, M.T. and Clements, D.H. (1988) A case for a Logo-based elementary school geometry curriculum, *Arithmetic Teacher*, 36(3): 11–17.

DfEE (Department for Education and Employment) (1999a) *Mathematics: The National Curriculum for England*. London: DfEE.

DfEE (Department for Education and Employment) (1999b) *Framework for Teaching Mathematics from Reception to Year 6*. London: DfEE.

DfEE (Department for Education and Employment) (1999c) *Professional Development Materials 3 and 4: Guide for your Professional Development, Book 3: Raising Standards in Mathematics at Key Stage 2*. London: DfEE.

Fielker, D. (1986) An analysis of geometry teaching in the United Kingdom, in R. Morris (ed.) *Studies in Mathematics Education, Volume 5: Geometry in Schools*. Paris: UNESCO.

Freudenthal, H. (1973) *Mathematics as an Educational Task*. Dordrecht: Reidel.

Jones, K., Mooney, C. and Harries, T. (2002) Trainee primary teachers' knowledge of geometry for teaching, *Proceedings of the British Society for Research into Learning Mathematics*, 22(1&2): 95–100.

Ofsted (Office for Standards in Education) (2002) *The National Numeracy Strategy: The First Three Years 1999–2002*. London: Ofsted.

QCA (Qualifications and Curriculum Authority) (2002) *Mathematics National Curriculum Tests: Standards at Key Stage 2: English, Mathematics and Science*. London: QCA.

RS/JMC (Royal Society and Joint Mathematical Council) (2001) *Teaching and Learning Geometry 11–19*. London: Royal Society/Joint Mathematical Council.

van Hiele, P. M. (1986) *Structure and Insight: A Theory of Mathematics Education*. Orlando, FL: Academic Press.

Deconstructing the National Numeracy Strategy's approach to calculation

Ian Thompson

Introduction

The aim of this chapter is to take a close and detailed look at the recommended progression from mental to written calculation for the four basic operations as specified in a range of publications produced by the National Numeracy Strategy (NNS). Given that mental calculation is listed as one of the four key principles underpinning the NNS (DfEE 1999a: 11), it could be argued that this emphasis on mental calculation and progression to written work is one of the cornerstones of the NNS. After a brief overview of the Strategy's approach to calculation this chapter will include a discussion of each of the four basic operations. Issues will be raised, questions asked and suggestions made in the hope of providing items for discussion should the 'learning trajectory' of this important topic be reconsidered by some future project, be it government, local education authority (LEA) or locally sponsored.

The structured approach to calculation in the NNS is set out clearly in the *Five-day Course: Notes for Course Tutors* (DfEE 1999b: 35):

- mental counting and counting objects;
- early stages of mental calculation and learning number facts (with recording);
- working with larger numbers and informal jottings;
- non-standard expanded written methods, beginning in Year 3;
- standard written methods, beginning in Year 4;
- use of calculators, beginning in Year 5.

This particular approach has the appearance of following a perfectly logical sequence: counting, mental calculation, jottings, expanded written, compact written, calculators. It also shows excellent chronological progression through the school years. However, the devil is in the detail. And this chapter is about examining this detail.

Progression in addition and subtraction

Mental

In Key Stage 1, mental work builds on the counting skills acquired in Reception and develops them into a range of mental calculation strategies for adding and subtracting single-digit numbers. Included in these strategies are:

- counting on and counting back;
- using doubles to find near doubles;
- using fives (partition into 5 and a bit);
- adding or subtracting 10;
- bridging up or down through 10;
- adding or subtracting 9 by working with 10 and compensating;
- counting up (for difference problems).

For older children the six main strategies for adding or subtracting two-digit numbers mentally are:

- find a difference by counting up through the next multiple of 10, 100 or 1000;
- count on or back in repeated steps of 1, 10, 100 or 1000;
- partition into hundreds, tens and ones;
- identify near doubles, using known doubles;
- add or subtract the nearest multiple of 10, 100 or 1000 and adjust;
- use the relationship between addition and subtraction.

Interestingly, the only strategy to achieve 'Key Objective' status is 'Add and subtract mentally a near multiple of 10 to or from a two-digit number': a strategy which the NNS itself classifies as a 'special case' method rather than as a 'general' strategy. 'Bridging', the most important and generalizable strategy of all the basic procedures is accorded the same status as 'using fives'. Also, unlike the list of strategies for single-digit calculations there is no real progression in the two-digit calculation list: 'near doubles' and 'the relationship between addition and subtraction' are really special case methods.

Focusing more closely on just one of these strategies, *'partition into hundreds, tens and ones'*, we find that the two examples given to illustrate this method are:

$24 + 58 = 82$ because it is $20 + 50 = 70$ and $4 + 8 = 12$, making $70 + 12 = 82$; and $98 - 43 = 98 - 40 - 3$ which is $58 - 3 = 55$.

One problem with these particular examples, given that there are no explanatory notes in the *Framework*, is that two important basic mental two-digit calculation strategies have been linked together under the same heading. The underpinning logic of these two procedures is very different, and much has been written about these differences (Beishuizen 2001). One such difference is that with the partitioning strategy (illustrated in the addition example above) both of the numbers are split into multiples of ten and the remaining ones before the calculation is effected. In the subtraction example (a *sequencing* rather than *partitioning* example) one of the numbers remains 'non-partitioned' during the calculation while chunks of the other number are added to or subtracted from it. No mention whatsoever is made of the 'mixed method' strategy that Thompson and Smith (1999) found was the most common choice among 144 Year 4 and 5 children.[1]

Another important implication of this difference is that sequencing methods lend themselves naturally to representation on an empty number line (ENL), whereas partitioning methods do not (see Rousham, Chapter 3). Children whose natural inclination is towards one method could well experience difficulty if teachers concentrate their teaching on the other. Those who use the more common strategy of partitioning both numbers are also likely to struggle when asked to demonstrate their method to the rest of the class on such a line.

Written

As *jottings*, in the form of the ENL, are covered in Chapter 3 this section will consider the NNS' approach to written calculation. It is here that a substantial shift in philosophy can be observed. In what might be considered its main in-service training pack, *Developing Mathematics in Years 4, 5 and 6: The Five-day Course* (DfEE 2001: 74), we are informed that: 'The aim for written calculations is different from the aim for mental calculations – with mental work, the aim is to teach children a repertoire of strategies from which to select, whereas with written calculations the ultimate aim is proficiency in a compact method for each operation'.[2] The obvious question to ask is, 'Why should the aim for written calculation be any different?' The NNS would appear to be providing conflicting messages about mathematics. We appear to be saying to children, 'When calculating mentally you can use whatever method you like, but when doing written calculations you should use just one method, which I will teach you'. This is likely to result in children having difficulty in deciding when it is acceptable to use one's own methods.

In Years 4, 5, and 6 (DfEE 2001: 76) the advice for progression towards a compact written method is:

- establish mental methods, based on a good understanding of place value;
- present calculations in horizontal format;
- show children how to set out calculations vertically, initially using expanded layouts that record their mental methods;
- as children become more confident, refine the written record into a more compact method;
- extend to larger numbers and to decimals.

Certain aspects of this list will be considered in the following sections.

A teaching progression for written addition

The recommended sequence begins with a two-digit mental calculation recorded horizontally:

$$47 + 76 = (40 + 70) + (7 + 6)^3$$

In the second stage this jotting of a mental calculation is set out vertically:

```
  47
 +76
 ───
 110
  13
 ───
 123
```

and is then followed by the same calculation with the least significant digits added first:

```
  47
 +76
 ───
  13
 110
 ───
 123
```

In the next two stages larger numbers are presented, and then the major step of introducing carrying takes place:

```
  47
 +76
 ───
 123
  1
```

Teachers are exhorted to ensure that they refer to the actual value of the digits when demonstrating this calculation: they should say '*40 plus 70 equals 110*'. This would appear to be quite feasible when adding two-digit numbers (which the children are actually expected to be able to do in their heads), but it is much more cumbersome with the addition of three-digit numbers. The following example involves 'two carries', and comes from Stage 4 of the recommended progression (although the example is actually best done by compensation, i.e. add 500 and subtract 7). The progression is from:

```
 368
+493
────
 700
 150
  11
────
 861
```

to

```
 368
+493
────
  11
 150
 700
────
 861
```

which, in turn develops into

```
  368
 +493
 ────
  861
  1 1
```

Trying to follow the NNS advice to refer to the actual value of the digits (DfEE 2001: 35) makes it much more difficult with numbers of this size. After saying '*8 plus 3 equals 11, put down the 1 and carry the 10*' we write 1 (rather than 10) under the 6 and the 9. The next stage is to say '*90 plus 60 equals 150, plus 10 more*' (there could be a potential minor problem at this point as we have written a 1 – albeit in the tens column). However, assuming that we perform the correct calculation and get 160, the problem is where do I write what? The official answer is '*put the 60 as a 6 next to the 1 in our answer*' (or '*in the tens column*'); '*ignore the zero and put the 100 as a 1 under the 4 and the 3. . .*' No doubt the reader finds this procedure somewhat confusing. This is because in Thompson's terms (see Thompson, Chapter 15) we are having to shift backwards and forwards between 'quantity value' and the more sophisticated 'column value'.

We are told (DFEE 2001: 75) that the NNS now 'structures the introduction of written methods, building on secure mental methods which lead to the introduction of compact written methods'. The example discussed above suggests that for the operation of addition, mental methods might not necessarily lead naturally to compact written methods.

Information is also provided (DfEE 2001: 79) for teachers of children with special educational needs:

> children with special learning difficulties find it difficult to 'unlearn'. Those who have been taught a mental strategy of 'adding the most significant digit first' may need to continue using this strategy in written methods of calculation. For example:

```
  234
 +788
 ────
  900
  110
   12
 ────
 1022
```

The obvious question to ask here is 'Why not recommend this as the main written addition algorithm for all primary children?' It complements mental methods perfectly, moving from left to right and involving work with quantities. Other addition algorithms can be found in the *Framework* (DfEE 1999a: 48).[4]

A teaching progression for written subtraction

The original and the revised version of the *Five-day Course* (DfEE 1999b: 49, 2000: 49) focus solely on progression towards the standard compact decomposition algorithm. This is introduced via the 'expanded method', initially using an example that requires no 'exchanging' or 'borrowing'.[5] We are taken through a progressive sequence from 563 – 241 as

$$
\begin{array}{l}
500 + 60 + 3 \\
\underline{-200 + 40 + 1} \\
300 + 20 + 2 \text{ leading to}
\end{array}
\qquad
\begin{array}{l}
563 \\
\underline{-241} \\
322
\end{array}
$$

moving on to 563 – 278 as

$$
\begin{array}{l}
500 + 60 + 3 \\
\underline{-200 + 70 + 8}
\end{array}
\quad \text{or} \quad
\begin{array}{l}
400 + 150 + 13 \\
\underline{-200 + \ 70 + \ 8} \\
200 + 80 + 5
\end{array}
\quad \text{or} \quad
\begin{array}{l}
\overset{\displaystyle 150}{\overset{\displaystyle 400 \quad\, 50 \quad 13}{500 + 60 + 3}} \\
\underline{-200 + 70 + 8} \\
200 + 80 + 5
\end{array}
\quad \text{leading to} \quad
\begin{array}{l}
\overset{4 \ 15 \ 13}{563} \\
\underline{-287} \\
285
\end{array}
$$

Now this seems a perfectly logical development. However, we know from research and a wealth of shared teaching experience that children have great difficulty with decomposition. Hart (1989) found that children struggled to make the anticipated connections between the manipulation of practical apparatus and their pencil and paper calculations.

American research (Ross 1989) suggests that children have much more difficulty with non-canonical partitions (73 = 60 + 13) than they do with canonical partitions (73 = 70 + 3). Unfortunately, most books tend to gloss over this difficulty, making the assumption that because children appear very competent at the latter (particularly given its great emphasis in the *Framework*), the move to those partitions needed for decomposition will be smooth. Unfortunately, this is not the case, and could well be one of the reasons why many children have great difficulty with this concept. Given that a clear aim of the NNS is to develop written procedures that build on children's mental strategies, it is important to point out that in the extensive literature on children's idiosyncratic mental calculation strategies there is, to my knowledge, no example of any child inventing decomposition. This would appear to provide important evidence that might help explain why children find decomposition difficult.

The third version of the *Five-day Course* (DfEE 2001) adds a section on progression towards an alternative method for subtraction: complementary addition. Links are made to equivalent calculations on an ENL, and reference is also made to the fact that the number of steps can be reduced as the children's mental strategies improve. The following two examples illustrate this point:

$$
\begin{array}{rl}
326 & \\
\underline{-178} & \\
2 & (\rightarrow 180) \\
20 & (\rightarrow 200) \\
100 & (\rightarrow 300) \\
20 & (\rightarrow 320) \\
\underline{6} & (\rightarrow 326) \\
148 &
\end{array}
$$

can develop into

326
−178
 22 (→ 200)
126 (→ 326)
148

Despite the inclusion of alternative written algorithms for subtraction[6] it is difficult not to conclude from reading its teacher and its consultant training materials that 'decomposition' is the favoured strategy of the NNS, and that inevitably this is the algorithm that the vast majority of teachers will attempt to teach their children.

Progression in multiplication and division

Mental

Expectations for mental multiplication and division begin with counting in multiples, progressing from twos, fives and tens in Year 2 to sevens, eights and nines in Year 4. These counting skills are gradually converted into table fact knowledge, with the expectation that most Year 5 children will know the multiplication facts up to 10×10, and most Year 6 children will know the associated division facts. In parallel with the development of table facts, children should develop a range of strategies (some more sophisticated than others) to help them calculate unknown products and quotients. These include being aware that:

- if they know that four sevens are 28, then eight sevens will be twice as many (56);
- they can find eight sevens by doubling 7 three times (14, 28, 56);
- if they know that six sixes are 36, then they know that seven sixes are six more (42);
- they can find $36 \div 4$ (a quarter of 36) by halving and then halving again (9);
- if $12 \div 3$ is 4, then $24 \div 3$ is twice as many (8);
- if $12 \div 3$ is 4, then $24 \div 6$ will be the same, as will $48 \div 12$ (4);
- knowing how to multiply by 10 allows them to multiply easily by 20, 30, 40 . . .;
- knowing how to divide by 10 allows them to divide easily by 20, 30, 40 . . .;
- they can find 14×4 by halving 14 and doubling 4, provided that they know 7×8 is 56;
- to multiply by 25 they can multiply by 100 and then divide by 4;
- they can find 14×12 by multiplying 14 by 3, then by 2, and then by 2 again because 12 is $3 \times 2 \times 2$ (168);
- they can find 19 sevens by finding 20 sevens and then subtracting one seven (133);
- they can find 15 thirteens by adding 10 thirteens to 5 (half of 10) thirteens (195).

	10	3	
10	100	30	
5	50	15	= 195

Figure 2.1 Using the grid method to multiply 13 by 15

	20	3	
7	140	21	= 161

Figure 2.2 Finding 23 × 7 by the grid method

A teaching progression for written multiplication

For multiplication the recommended informal written strategy is the *grid method*: a written version of the final example described above. This uses the *distributive law* to find 15 thirteens by adding 10 thirteens to 5 thirteens: more formally $13 \times 15 = (13 \times 10) + (13 \times 5)$. Using the recommended layout for the grid (or area) method this calculation would look like that shown in Figure 2.1.

The progression from the grid method is best illustrated by an example involving a single-digit multiplier. Using this method 23×7 would be set out as shown in Figure 2.2. This would later be written vertically as:

        23
       ×7
       ───
       140 (20 × 7)
        21 (3 × 7)
       ───
       161

and finally as

        23
       ×7
       ───
       161
        2

As was argued in the case of addition, there is an issue concerning the language to be used. In order to operate with quantities rather than digits, as recommended by the NNS, a child would have to say (or think) *'seven threes are 21, put down the 1 and carry the 20 as a 2 in the tens column. Seven twenties are 140 plus the 20 is 160 which gives 161 with the one that is already there'*. This seems quite a reasonable explanation for the multiplication of a two-digit by a one-digit number, but it is much more difficult to work with the actual value of the digits when two- and three-digit numbers are involved.[7]

A teaching progression for written division

The build-up to written division in the *Framework* is a fairly gradual one (although not gradual enough for Anghileri and Beishuizen 1998). It progresses through the following stages:

- the development of an understanding of the operation, the associated vocabulary and its relationship to subtraction and multiplication;
- an understanding of the idea of a remainder; the use of closely related known facts, partitioning and the distributive law;
- the development of a range of mental division strategies;
- work on repeated subtraction that culminates in the *chunking* algorithm (illustrated in Figure 2.3).

In a section entitled '*B: long division HTU ÷ TU*', the *Framework* (DfEE 1999a: 68–9), shows two calculations adjacent to each other (see Figures 2.3 and 2.4), with the implication that the first leads naturally to the second. The two look very similar, and in fact the only visible difference between the two layouts is the missing zero on the second line of the second example (see Figure 2.4).

The language and thinking associated with the *chunking* method runs something like: '*I need to find out how many thirty-sixes there are in 972. I know that there are 10 of them in 360 and so there are 20 of them in 720. If I take this from 972 I get 252. Five thirty-sixes are 180 (half of 360), and 180 is 72 less than 252, so 7 thirty-sixes must be 252. The answer is therefore 20 and 7 which is 27*'. However, the procedure shown in Figure 2.4 demands a very different way of thinking and reasoning: one that utilizes a different vocabulary. The following is one of several possible ways of talking the procedure through: '*36 into 900 doesn't go. (No. I cannot say that, as it does go! Try again.) 972 contains 97 tens, so that's two lots of 36 tens with 25 tens left over. Write a 2 above the line in the tens column. If we change the remaining 25 tens to 250 ones and add the 2, then we have 252. By trial and improvement we find that 36 into 252 is 7. Write the 7 in the ones column. So the answer is 27*'. As you would probably agree, this is not too easy to follow!

The point being made is that there is not a particularly smooth transition from the language and reasoning associated with chunking to the language of the standard algorithm. The strength of the chunking algorithm lies in its transparency and its great potential for differentiation: it allows for a range of

```
36 ) 972
    -720      20 × 36
     252
    -252       7 × 36
       0
  Answer: 27
```

Figure 2.3 Calculating 972 ÷ 36 by chunking

```
        27
  36 ) 972
      -72
       252
      -252
         0
    Answer: 27
```

Figure 2.4 Calculating 972 ÷ 36 by standard algorithm

levels of sophistication in children's confidence and understanding, in that the less confident can remove small chunks; the more confident can take away larger chunks; and the most confident can subtract the maximum-sized chunks. The question that needs to be asked is: 'Is it worth the effort and the potential risk of confusion involved in teaching the procedure in Figure 2.4 – the standard algorithm for division – for the sake of a layout which, in this particular case, has one zero fewer than the chunking method, and which few teachers understand?'

Conclusion

Throughout the range of NNS publications, Qualifications and Curriculum Authority (QCA) documents and Her Majesty's Inspectorate of Schools (HMI) reports that discuss calculation there is a strong message that work on mental strategies leads naturally to written methods using expanded notation, and that these in turn lead inexorably to standard (or is it *compact*?) algorithms. In fact, an Office for Standards in Education (Ofsted) report on the teaching of calculation in primary schools (Ofsted 2002) states the following: 'However, at Key Stage 2 they [teachers] often overlook the importance of linking pupils' mental strategies to the introduction of expanded and compact written methods'. My argument is that this progression is not as natural as it first appears to be, and that more thought needs to be given to, and more research carried out concerning, the links between strategies, both mental/mental and mental/written. Another important aspect of the argument is that often what appears to be logically or mathematically sound is not necessarily always pedagogically sound. This situation obtains with reference to the final step from informal to compact methods suggested in the *Framework* for each of the four arithmetic operations. In each case this step involves a major shift in the way the digits in a number are interpreted: a shift from treating them as quantities to treating them as digits in columns (see Thompson, Chapter 15).

The overall aim in this chapter has been to raise issues and ask questions about the NNS' approach to calculation, in the hope that there will be opportunities in the future to engage in an open discussion of this approach.

Notes

1 Using the 'mixed method' strategy 37 + 26 would be calculated as follows: '*30 and 20 is 50, 50 add 7 is 57, and 57 add 6 makes 63*'. With nearly 35 per cent of children using this strategy it was the most popular strategy for the addition of pairs of two-digit numbers.

2 The phrase '*a compact method for each operation*' was introduced as a replacement for '*a common standard method*' which had appeared in an earlier version of this course (DfEE 1999b: 44). This indicates a slight change in the Strategy's philosophy towards standard algorithms. Other instances of this attitude change can be seen in an important key statement in the *Three-day*

Course: Course Tutor's Pack (DfEE 1999c: 68): 'The aim is that, for each operation, all children by the age of 11, can carry out a standard written method'. In the *Five-day Course: Notes for Course Tutors* (DfEE 1999b: 44) this became: 'For each of the four operations, as many children as possible can, by the age of 11, carry out a standard written method' and finally in *Developing Mathematics in Years 4, 5 and 6: The Five-day Course – Notes for Tutors* (DfEE 2001: 74) we read: 'For each of the four operations, as many children as possible can, by the age of 11, carry out a compact written method'. It is interesting to note that '*all*' has become '*as many as possible*', and '*a standard written method*' has, more gradually, become a '*compact written method*'. This is an improvement: the word '*compact*' is relative, allowing for a range of interpretations, whereas '*standard*' is not, despite the information given in the following debatable statement: 'There is no "correct" standard method for any particular operation – for any operation there are a number of different "standard" written methods which work' (DfEE 1999c: 68). The words may very well have changed from 'standard' to 'compact', but unfortunately the examples given in the *Framework* remain the same: the informal methods always culminate in what are recognized as being the standard algorithms for these operations in England.

3 This notation is in itself confusing, as are other similar examples in the *Framework*. Is it a mathematical explanation of the underlying procedure involved in *partitioning* – i.e. the brackets show us that the 40 and the 70 are added separately, as are the 7 and the 6, and then the subtotals 110 and 13 are added together, or is it anticipated that children will record in this way? Setting out the calculation in this manner gives it the flavour of a 'statement of intent', indicating what is going to happen next. However, when children are normally asked to explain their methods they nearly always write down the successive steps in the process using words like: '*I added 40 and 70 and that was 110 . . . 7 and 6 is 13, and 110 and 13 is 123*', or, with some guidance, '*40 + 70 = 110, 7 + 6 = 13, 110 + 13 = 123*'.

4 Two different procedures are included in the category 'Informal written methods': adding the most significant digit first and compensation (add too much, take off). The latter is a written version of the mental compensation strategy discussed above. The example given for Year 4 children is:

$$
\begin{array}{ll}
754 & \\
+86 & \\
\hline
854 & (754 + 100) \\
-14 & (86 - 100) \\
\hline
840 &
\end{array}
$$

It is difficult to believe that children will be able to understand the 'explanations' in parentheses, particularly (86 – 100), given that this level of understanding of negative numbers is beyond that expected of a Year 4 child. However, the main problem with this strategy can be clearly seen in the following example:

```
 716
 +67
 816   (716 + 100)
 −33   (67 − 100)
 ???
```

In this case we have ended up with a calculation that is obviously much harder than the original. The reader might like to investigate in what circumstances this situation will obtain.

5 'Borrowing' is a word that makes many British mathematics educators cringe when it is used in this context. The word 'exchanging' is considered to be more accurate when talking about decomposition. This language has developed from a popular approach to teaching the subtraction algorithm using base 10 materials, where we 'exchange a ten rod for ten unit cubes'. I find it interesting that in all the mathematics education books from the USA that I have ever read, 'borrowing' is the standard word used to describe this operation when using decomposition for subtraction.

6 An alternative strategy using negative numbers can be found in the third professional development guide (DfEE 1999d: 36):

```
 842
−276
 600
 −30
  −4
 566
```

This self-study unit provides no explanation as to how or why the algorithm works; no advice on the appropriate language to use when demonstrating it; no suggestions as to essential prerequisite skills and strategies; and no hints as to potential misunderstandings or misconceptions. The 'self-studier' is simply asked to try a couple of examples like the one illustrated, and is quickly guided to the next activity with the words 'Eventually, children should move on to more compact standard methods'.

7 The reader might like to work through the long multiplication example given in the *Framework* for Year 6, thinking how they would retain the actual meaning of the digits as they calculate each line of the answer:

```
  352
  ×27
 7040   (352 × 20)
 2464   (352 × 7)
 9504
   1
```

References

Anghileri, J. and Beishuizen, M. (1998) Counting, chunking and the division algorithm, *Mathematics in School*, 27(1): 2–4.

Beishuizen, M. (2001) Different approaches to mastering mental calculation strategies, in J. Anghileri (ed.) *Principles and Practice in Arithmetic Teaching*. Buckingham: Open University Press.

DfEE (Department for Education and Employment) (1999a) *Framework for Teaching Mathematics from Reception to Year 6*. London: DfEE.

DfEE (Department for Education and Employment) (1999b) *Five-day Course: Notes for Course Tutors*. London: DfEE.

DfEE (Department for Education and Employment) (1999c) *Three-day Course: Course tutor's pack*. London: DfEE.

DfEE (Department for Education and Employment) (1999d) *Professional Development Materials 3 and 4: Guide for your Professional Development, Book 3: Raising Standards in Mathematics at Key Stage 2*. London: DfEE.

DfEE (Department for Education and Employment) (2000) *Five-day Course: Notes for Course Tutors – Revised Edition*. London: DfEE.

DfEE (Department for Education and Employment) (2001) *Developing Mathematics in Years 4, 5 and 6: The Five-day Course – Notes for Tutors*. London: DfEE.

Hart, K.M. (1989) Place value: subtraction, in D. Johnson (ed.) *Children's Mathematical Frameworks 8–13*. London: NFER-Nelson.

Ofsted (Office for Standards in Education) (2002) *Teaching of Calculation in Primary Schools* (HMI 461) http://www.ofsted.gov.uk/publications/index.cfm?fuseaction=pubs.summary&id=2313.

Ross, S. (1989) Parts, wholes and place value: a developmental view, *Arithmetic Teacher*, 36(6): 47–51.

Thompson, I. and Smith, F. (1999) *Mental Calculation Strategies for the Addition and Subtraction of 2-digit Numbers* (Report for the Nuffield Foundation). Newcastle upon Tyne: Department of Education, University of Newcastle upon Tyne.

The Empty Number Line: a model in search of a learning trajectory?

Laurie Rousham

Background and introduction

The empty number line (ENL) is a relatively new model to support children in developing mental strategies for addition and subtraction, and it was developed in Holland in the early 1990s. Use of the ENL and the teaching programme associated with it has been a success story. The Dutch, somewhat to their own surprise, emerged as the most successful European country in the Third International Mathematics and Science Survey (Keys *et al.* 1996): a study of children's performance in mathematics. If we look at the results of their 9-year-olds in mental arithmetic the ENL appears to be a superior model (particularly for weaker children) than the 100 square for numbers up to 100 that had previously been in use. This is very interesting from an English view-point, since awareness of the ENL in this country dates only from about 1997: shortly before the National Numeracy Project (NNP) was starting to develop into the National Numeracy Strategy (NNS). This gave primacy at last in English schools to mental methods over written, but featured heavy use of the 100 square, a model which the Dutch had replaced with the ENL because their weaker children had found it too difficult (Beishuizen 1997).

Of course it is true that a few examples of ENL use were included in the final draft of the *Framework for Teaching Mathematics from Reception to Year 6* (DfEE 1999), in associated publications such as *Teaching Mental Calculation Strategies* (QCA 1999) and particularly in early NNS videos – hence the strong current interest among English teachers in the ENL – but there had not been time for the implications behind its use to be fully assimilated, nor for the all-important Teaching and Learning Trajectory (the teaching programme that was developed in Holland to accompany it) to be studied (Freudenthal Institute 2001). As a result, the *Framework* does not incorporate many important aspects of ENL usage, nor a coherent account of how to put all the elements together in a clear and unified teaching strategy, particularly for subtraction. The Netherlands, in common with other Continental European nations, has a longer tradition of teaching mental methods first and so has much more experience of them. In important respects their approach conflicts with the Piagetian, place value oriented English tradition of primary school arithmetic which of course, prior to the NNS, was aimed mainly at achieving competence in *written* methods for the four rules of number. It is not surprising that teachers in England find it difficult to combine an ENL approach with following the *Framework*, since that document contains some elements of the old English tradition, much new practice aimed at establishing mental methods, plus what appear to be a few elements of the Dutch approach grafted on at the last moment.

How the ENL works in Holland

I shall begin by describing and commenting on experience of observing ENL use, over the course of several years, in a number of Dutch schools and classrooms (*Groep 4* in the Dutch nomenclature, Year 3 in our own). In a sense this is starting in the wrong place because it is the end-point of a process, rather than the beginning; but when we look closely at what those Dutch children who are fluent and flexible mental calculators actually do, issues such as preparatory work stand out in an obvious way.

In Year 3 a Dutch lesson might begin with an oral and mental starter, such as promoting recall of number facts important for mental methods, like instant recall of the number pairs that make 10. The teacher goes on to give a context for the problems to be solved that day – for example, considering the ages of members of an imaginary family (see Figure 3.1). Realistic Mathematics Education (RME), the tradition in Holland within which the ENL was developed, tries always to introduce a context like this for a set of calculations. The context (in this case the family) does not have to be 'real' in the sense of a real family – just so long as it is real in the children's imaginations. Starting off with Figure 3.1 allows the teacher to pose a whole series of addition, subtraction and difference questions during the rest of the lesson, as well as for the children to make up their own. In one lesson I observed, the teacher asked, 'How much older is Grandma than Luke?' This translates into symbolic terms as $91 - 37$ and can be viewed either as a 'take-away' or a 'difference' type of subtraction. A number of children put up their hands and one was asked by the teacher to come out to the board with her solution. Utilizing one of several pre-drawn empty lines on the board, her calculation, beginning with the 91 and ending by circling the correct answer of 54 is shown in Figure 3.2.

The teacher talked through her solution method with the class, saying 'Marijke starts with 91, then she subtracts 10, and another 10, and another . . . then a 1. So, how much altogether?' (The class respond that she has taken away 31 at this point) 'So, good. What has she left to subtract? Yes, 6 to make 37. Good, Marijke. You have used the N10 method. Could you have done it any other way?', to which Marijke responded: 'Oh yes, you could have done A10' (these labels will be explained shortly), and when the teacher indicated

Figure 3.1 A context for solving problems

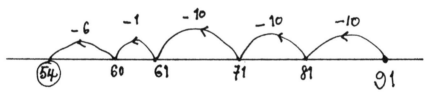

Figure 3.2 Using N10 to calculate 91 – 37.

that she should do so, Marijke recommenced the calculation on the line above
the one she had used previously (see Figure 3.3).

Again the teacher ran through Marijke's steps with the other children:
'She takes 1 to get to the tens number, good. Oh, she has taken away the 30
in one go this time, well done Marijke! And so she gets to 60. Why does
she take away 6 now? Yes, and how did she know it would be 54? Yes,
Ton? Because 6 and 4 are "hearts in love" [we would say pairs that make 10]
good, good. And now N10C?' she asked. 'Could we have used N10C here?' As
Marijke looked uncertain, the teacher asked if anyone could help her out,
choosing another child who came forward, pulled the board down lower

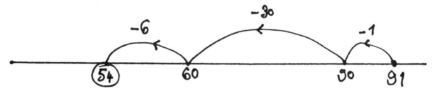

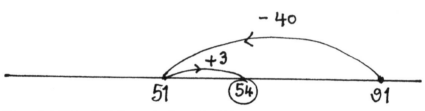

Figure 3.3 Using A10 to calculate 91 – 37.

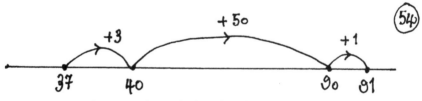

Figure 3.4 Using N10C to calculate 91 – 37.

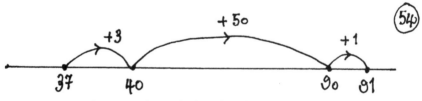

Figure 3.5 Using 'count on' to calculate 91 – 37.

on its runners, and used a third line to lay out a third solution method (see Figure 3.4).

At this point another child who had been waving her hand for some time called out 'There is another way' and, invited out to the front and this time starting with 37 wrote the calculation shown in Figure 3.5.

Commentary

We can examine some of the things that were going on in the lesson section described. At no point was anyone vitally interested in the 'answer' of 54, apart from the circle drawn round it by most children to indicate that it was the solution. Instead, the teacher kept the focus upon the *methods* used by each child to get to it. So far, we might say, this is entirely consistent with NNS practice: encouraging a variety of mental strategies. However, look a little closer and there are important differences, born of the much greater experience of teaching mental methods on the other side of the North Sea. The Dutch teacher is *not* just drawing out as many different methods as she possibly can, a situation that currently happens regularly in English classrooms.

In the plenary following a lesson involving subtractions like the one above (in England this would generally happen at Year 4 rather than Year 3 with numbers like 91 – 37) I watched a teacher putting up an example and asking children how to solve it. 'Good, Jenny, did anyone do it another way? Good, Grant, can we do it any other way?' and so on and on, ending with the comment: 'What a lovely lot of different methods!' The crucial difference between these superficially similar interactions is that the Dutch teacher is deliberately drawing upon a limited number (four or five) of previously taught strategies which are well-known to *all* the children, and to each of which a 'label' has been given (N10, A10, etc.) so that both teacher and children have a shorthand way of referring to them without having to explain the whole process. (The four methods above were exemplified for the Dutch children on small printed sheets on each table. Also on each table were some pages with ENLs pre-printed on them. As the lesson progressed some children used these to record what Marijke and the others were demonstrating on the board, creating greater involvement, while others used them to try out another method.) In the English classroom by comparison, Grant's method may be known only by Grant, Jenny's by Jenny and probably one or two others whose preferred method it happens to be.

One consequence of this is that English teachers can feel overwhelmed by the apparently endless diversity of minor variations which children are able to come up with, and there is often no real discussion of which method is the best *in a specific situation* – i.e. for 91 – 37. Another consequence is that some teachers have come to see diversity as an aim in itself, feeling that so long as their class comes up with a variety of strategies they have done their job. Dutch teachers would not think so. One more consequence, incidentally, is that the Dutch children are far more attentive while one of their number is operating at the board: they all know that Marijke has used N10 and is now attempting A10 and what those methods are – so they are more inclined to take part than the English children who, not unnaturally, tend to lose interest when the problem has been solved several times and the teacher prompts for yet another way.

The 'labels'

These arose in Holland as an administrative device aimed at classifying methods for teachers, but some schools quickly began to share them with children, although not all do. This is what they mean:

N10

Marijke begins with a counting-back (taking away) method: jumping backwards on the number line. This is seen as the basic method for both addition and subtraction in Holland and is codenamed N10. The '10' refers to jumping in whole tens. So N10 means take the whole number (i.e. don't partition it) and start your tens jumping: forwards on the line if you are adding, backwards if you are subtracting. (This is why all these methods are called 'sequential'.) When teaching English children I have usually just called it 'N10' – explaining it as 'keep the first number whole, then jump in tens', although at other times I have invited them to think up their own labels.

A10

The next method Marijke uses can be translated as something like 'Add to the nearest 10'. In this method (a development of N10) the first step is not to start with tens-jumping but instead to add or subtract units to reach a multiple of 10. Notice how coming to rest on such a comfortable place allows her time to do the subtraction of 30 in one jump (see Figure 3.3). The user must remember, of course, how many units have already been used and how many more remain, carrying out this residual calculation at the end – but it will be easy since she will be resting on a multiple of 10. Dutch teachers put in lots of practice at the 'hearts in love' ('What is in love with 8? Yes, 2, because 8 and 2 together make 10'), almost always including them briefly in the starter activity. Pairs to 10, of course, is a Year 1 Key Objective here, but is often learned in isolation as if it were an end in itself. In lessons like the one described, Dutch children practise the bonds and go on immediately to see their usefulness (as when a child says '60 take away six . . . it must be 54 because 6 and 4 are hearts in love'), and so you do not see them counting on their fingers.

N10C

English Year 3 teachers will recognize this third method from the supplement of examples in the *Framework* (DfEE 1999: 45), which refers to it as 'compensation'. Compensation is in fact what the 'C' stands for, and the 'N' functions as before, reminding the children to keep the first number whole. (Just imagine how difficult subtractions like these become if the child begins by partitioning *both* numbers into tens and units).

Count-on

The final child's strategy should also be familiar. It is known as complementary addition, 'shopkeeper's arithmetic' or 'counting-on', and is illustrated on the same page of the *Framework* as compensation (N10C). This method, with recording carried out on an ENL, featured so heavily in NNS videos that some teachers at first thought that this was *'the* ENL method' instead of understanding, as they would have done from watching the Dutch lesson, that the ENL is just a blank canvas upon which *any* sequential strategy can be recorded and displayed.

We may note in passing that while the last two methods can be found in the *Framework*, what would puzzle Dutch educators is the lack of emphasis on one, basic, unifying method for addition and subtraction: the equivalent of N10. It can be argued that the *Framework* contains too many 'special case' methods (near-doubles and compensation, for example) which are presented to teachers as if they are equal to more basic and generally applicable methods. I would prefer these to be listed as 'sub-methods' or refinements of a basic one. And while some have names ('compensation', 'near-doubles') others do not. A little thought given to 'labelling' would be most helpful because it is the use of the labels as a tool by both teachers and children that encourages the children to function at a higher, metacognitive level. Crudely oversimplifying, when English children are faced with 91 − 37 they tend to dive straight into the calculation. Dutch children say, 'What would be best here? Hmm, perhaps N10C, as 37 is only 3 away from 40 . . . but maybe it would be easier to count up from 37'. They are not cleverer than English children but they have been taught and supported to operate in a 'cleverer' way. It has been shown that English children could do this too (Rousham 1997).

Pathological splitters

Ponder this question for a moment before you read the discussion below: why do English children, if you ask them to add a pair of two-digit numbers like 35 and 26, tend immediately to split both numbers ('30 and 20, that's 50, and 5 and 6 is 11, and so that makes . . .')?

The answer is, of course, that this is how they have been taught to do it. From an early age they have been encouraged to partition any two-digit number into its tens and units components, and this tradition is still alive and well within the *Framework*: arrow cards, place value charts, etc. If your instinctive response to the question was 'Well, why shouldn't they?' or 'What other way is there to do it?' you are, like 99 per cent of the rest of the English-speaking world, what I light-heartedly call a 'pathological splitter'. We do this because it is the way we were taught.

Dutch Year 3 children would not say '30 and 20 is 50' because N10 dictates that they keep that first number (35) whole, although you do need to split the second number. So they would say something like: '35 add 20 is 55, and another 6 makes . . .' So what? The pathological splitters still get the right answer. Yes, but only in addition. Addition is 'easier' than subtraction (defining 'easier' as meaning that you will get a higher success rate if you give ten two-digit additions to Year 3 or Year 4 children than if you give them ten subtractions). In this sense, subtraction is harder. The point is that this is not wholly to do with subtraction itself, and certainly not with the children, but with the way they are taught to do it.

Suppose that instead of 35 + 26 it was 35 – 26. Pathological splitters would say '30 take away 20 is 10, and 5 take away 6 is . . . er . . .'. Many will now go on to perform that 'false reversal' which says, '5 take away 6 you can't, so 6 take away 5 is 1 . . . so the answer is 11'. A Dutch colleague calls this 'the English mistake' and I call it that now too. Dutch children just do not make this mistake as routinely because they are not splitters: using N10 they keep the first number whole (just as they do for addition): '35 take away 20 is 15, and now 15 take away 6 is 9, so the answer is 9'.

Splitting is a legacy of that place value based, Piaget and Dienes tradition which assumes that learners will soon be doing column additions and subtractions. We do not need it any more. The Dutch do not teach place value overtly but their Year 3 children, as well as being able to do 91 – 37 four or more different ways, can all split the second number into 30 and 7. Much of the effort and time we expend doing exercises on what we term 'place value' (see Thompson, Chapter 15) might be better utilized working with real problems using a sequential model like the ENL.

In Holland, the existence of a basic method which works for both addition and subtraction is of great advantage to teachers. Our tradition of early teaching of splitting in the guise of 'place value' endows both us and the children with the handicap of thoroughly learning a method which works for addition but not for subtraction. What is even more confusing is that splitting *does* occasionally work for subtraction. If the problem had been 36 – 25, splitting would have done no damage. A result of this is that a child can be using exactly the same method for all calculations but, puzzlingly, sometimes they come out right while at other times they come out wrong! Maths needs to make sense. When it stops making sense, learners tend to give up on it, reacting with dislike: a quite natural and intelligent response. It is our job to make sense of it and see that it makes sense for them. In this respect, a slight reorganization of our major teaching tool (the *Framework*) would be inestimably helpful to both teachers and learners.

Think back for a moment to Marijke. She operates confidently, gets the right answer in two different ways when asked, and does not need to resort to counting on her fingers. She is a Year 3 child. Holland, which like us has government-set targets for the end of primary school with intermediate attainment targets on the way to them, is largely succeeding in getting all children to our Year 4 Key Objective a *year earlier*. At the moment, many English children fail with subtractions (not additions) like 91 – 37, even by the end of Year 4. The ENL was developed in Holland as a model to support children's mental calculation in addition and subtraction with numbers up to 100 by Adrian Treffers of the Freudenthal Institute at the University of Utrecht, in the early 1990s. There is not room here to examine RME as developed by Hans Freudenthal and others, and the history of ENL, but good British accounts of its development and use can be found in Anghileri (2001) and Thompson (1999).

Implications for learning and teaching

The Dutch did not simply invent ENL and start using it in a haphazard way. It grew out of a perceived need to serve their overall aim of proficiency in mental addition and subtraction to 100. Although the Dutch government publishes expected standards for the end of the primary school, RME already had a clear idea of its goal: flexible, mental methods for addition and subtraction up to 100 that could be successfully applied by children, with understanding, in a range of simple contexts. By 'flexible' they mean that the child should know a range of methods and, from them, choose the one most suited to the numbers in the problem. Our corresponding goal is that Year 4 Key Objective which says that children should be able to 'Use known number facts and place value to add or subtract mentally, including any pair of two-digit whole numbers'. I would prefer the words 'use known number facts and place value' to be removed, but in any case I would argue that this is the single most 'key' Key Objective in the *Framework*. Children who can do it go into Years 5 and 6 with confidence and high self-esteem. Conversely, those who do not have effective mental methods for subtraction know it, are already worried, and are certain to struggle with understanding written ones.

Dutch experience shows that children who have really secure mental methods cope easily with written methods (even standard ones like decomposition) at a later stage. In England, children who move up to the next class unable to accomplish subtractions like 91 – 54 in their head are in a dangerous position. The units of work on mental addition and subtraction which are such a feature of the *Framework* at Year 3 and Year 4 are largely replaced in Year 5 and Year 6 by units on multiplication and division. There may be no more explicit whole-class teaching of subtraction (addition is not the problem) and teachers may tend to expect that it *ought* to have been achieved by Year 5. Unless the teacher identifies it as a whole-class problem, any more teaching input is likely to be ad hoc, to individuals as and when they show they are unable to perform subtractions. However, children are adept at concealing shortcomings like this in day-to-day work, and so many can avoid ever really getting the help they need.

The NNS, the Qualifications and Curriculum Authority (QCA) or someone else could helpfully publish for all teachers a slim volume solely on the teaching of mental strategies for subtraction which picks out the most important preliminary skills (all of which are already there) but which shows how they can all be linked up into a coherent theory of basic processes for addition and subtraction to 100, with agreed, Anglicized labels like N10 which could be understood nationwide, as in Holland. Such a booklet would amount to what the Dutch call a 'learning trajectory'; a suggested teaching programme with a clear end always in view. The existence of such trajectories, constantly subject to practitioner-theorist research and improvement, is another of the strengths of their system. Without an English equivalent, teachers have to construct their own, with the attendant danger that they may unconsciously be creating false trajectories. The transition from mental strategies to written ones is one of the areas of mathematics teaching that schools and teachers currently say they find most problematic (see Thompson, Chapter 2).

Most of the elements required are contained in the *Framework*, but for sub-traction they are not drawn together in a way that is clear enough for teachers to accomplish the Year 4 Key Objective with all children. Moreover, English texts which purport to interpret the *Framework* are weak in comparison with Dutch ones. Bierhoff's (1996) comparison of textbooks unfortunately did not include Holland, where the new generation of RME textbooks was introduced following prototypes developed by the Freudenthal Institute and the SLO (a government sponsored curriculum development body).

Thompson (2001: 71) asked: 'Is the time now ripe to address the issue of "official" approval of commercial mathematics schemes, or do the dis-advantages that might accrue from this outweigh any advantages?' This is not the place to discuss the shortcomings of English textbooks but we should note in passing that, perhaps because of the persistence of the tradition of written algorithms, many are so poorly designed that they actively inhibit the acquisition of powerful mental methods. They promote early development of weak methods for subtraction which are not robust enough to withstand later encounters with more difficult subtraction situations. Dutch RME texts do not structure in this way. They provide support for the crossing of tens boundaries from an early stage and present children with 'difficult' examples from the start: in this way children are not able to begin using a restricted strategy which will later break down.

In the meantime, since the NNS is non-statutory, it is open to schools to do what a few pioneers have done – invent their own labels or acronyms, starting preparatory work in Year 1 and Year 2 with physical materials like bead strings. Others, for example, have restructured the Year 3 and Year 4 programmes a little to give more time for mastery of mental addition, and, in particular, subtraction, by giving over some place value units to it. It is entirely possible for between 80 and 90 per cent of children to master mental subtrac-tion by the end of Year 4, but it needs a greater and more concentrated time allocation than it commonly gets. Here the Dutch are at an advantage: their mathematics curriculum is slimmer (there is not much data handling for example) and the sound establishment of mental methods is their principal aim.

Conclusions

Subtraction is the first really big hurdle in making sense of mathematics. Of course there are later hurdles to come: division, fractions, algebra and so on: and at each of these hurdles there will be some fallers, who are ever afterwards lost to mathematics, becoming part of that large majority of British adults who say 'Maths? I hated maths. I still hate maths'. There is no need for us to lose so many children at the first hurdle. The relationship between numerical representations and operational calculation is subtle, and crucial to the way both teachers and children operate in classrooms. It is very far from being of solely theoretical importance. It deserves very close attention whenever the *Framework* becomes due for revision.

References

Anghileri, J. (ed.) (2001) *Principles and Practice in Arithmetic Teaching*. Buckingham: Open University Press.

Bierhoff, H. (1996) *Laying the Foundations of Numeracy: A comparison of Primary Textbooks in Britain, Germany and Switzerland*. London: National Institute of Economic and Social Research.

Beishuizen, M. (1997) Two types of mental arithmetic and the empty numberline. Paper presented at the British Society for Research in the Learning of Mathematics (BSRLM) conference, Oxford University, 7 June.

DfEE (Department for Education and Employment) (1999) *Framework for Teaching Mathematics from Reception to Year 6*. London: DfEE.

Freudenthal Institute (2001) *Children Learn Mathematics: A Learning-Teaching Trajectory with Intermediate Attainment Targets for Calculation with Whole Numbers in Primary School*. Utrecht: FI, Utrecht University and SLO.

Keys, W., Harris, S. and Fernandes, C. (1996) *Third International Study, First National Report, Part 1*. Slough: National Foundation for Educational Research.

QCA (Qualifications and Curriculum Authority) (1999) *Teaching Mental Calculation Strategies: Guidance for Teachers at Key Stages 1 and 2*. London: QCA.

Rousham, L. (1997) Jumping on an Empty Number Line, *Primary Mathematics and Science Questions*, 2: 6–8.

Thompson, I. (1999) *Issues in Teaching Numeracy in Primary Schools*. Buckingham: Open University Press.

Thompson, I. (2001) Issues for classroom practice in England, in J. Anghileri (ed.) *Principles and Practice in Arithmetic Teaching*. Buckingham: Open University Press.

Section 2

PEDAGOGICAL ISSUES

In this section we move from subject content to a range of aspects of pedagogy: a shift from the 'what' to the 'how'. Chapter 4 is by Carol Aubrey, whose research interest is children's early mathematical development, from the preschool period into Reception and through Key Stage 1, in a national and European context. The author considers the challenges of teaching mathematics in the Foundation Stage, such as issues of prior knowledge, the acquisition of the sub-skills of counting, assessment, organizational strategies, transition and mixed-age classes. She argues that the challenge for teachers lies in providing learning opportunities and high expectations to meet the needs of diverse groups of children, while paying close attention to the balance of whole-class, group and individual teaching. She also argues that responding to diverse needs with an increase in whole-class, teacher-directed activity constitutes the main threat to effective nursery and Reception class practice.

Steve Higgins is involved in research that involves investigating the impact of a range of thinking skills approaches on teachers, pupils and classroom interaction. In Chapter 5 he focuses specifically on the importance of talk and discussion in mathematics learning. The chapter begins with a brief overview of the role of talk in mathematics learning, and then details are given of three research projects that have used a focus on talk and discussion in mathematics lessons to improve pupil attainment. These projects are: *'Discussing Mental Calculation Strategies'*; *'Improving Attainment in Mathematics through Talking and Thinking Together'*; and *'Odd One Out – A Thinking Skills Strategy'*. The chapter ends with some practical implications for talk in the mathematics lesson.

Mundher Adhami has been involved as a research worker on the Cognitive Acceleration in Mathematics Education (CAME) programme for several years. In Chapter 6 he discusses lesson objectives and lesson structure in an attempt to reformulate the notion of the three-part lesson and of lesson objectives. He considers the extent to which lesson type influences the structure of a lesson, and he then identifies different types of lesson structure. He offers us a detailed example of the flow of a mathematics thinking lesson complete with a perceptive analysis of the sequence of the ensuing discussion, and ends the chapter by discussing the concept of an 'optimal plan' for a lesson, linking it to the NNS' recommended three-part lesson structure.

The next two chapters focus on different aspects of problem solving. Mike Askew was deputy director of the five-year Leverhulme Numeracy Research Programme that looked at teaching, learning and progression from Reception to Year 7. In Chapter 7 he concentrates particularly on what his classroom observations have led him to believe about word problems. He questions the advice often given to children to identify the significant words in a problem, and uses specific examples to illustrate the extent to which there can be a lack of match between the physical world and the mathematical world. The chapter finishes with some ideas for a possible way forward.

Lesley Jones' area of research is children's reasoning skills, and in Chapter 8 she considers the extent to which primary schools might include a broad interpretation of problem solving as part of the mathematics curriculum, while addressing some of the anxieties teachers may have about doing this. She defines a problem as 'an activity where the route to its solution is not immediately evident' and develops a model to represent the degree of openness and complexity within problems. She provides some recommended sources of problems, and suggests a range of activities and problems that teachers might like to use with their children.

'When we were very young': the foundations for mathematics

Carol Aubrey

Background

When the National Numeracy Strategy (NNS) *Framework for Teaching Mathematics* (DfEE 1999a) was introduced it ensured that the programme for Reception classes took account of the new Early Learning Goals (ELGs) in mathematical development that most children of 3 to 5 years should achieve by the end of the Foundation Stage (QCA/DfEE 2000). The intention was to provide a bridge from the ELGs to the National Curriculum.

The key objectives in the NNS for the Reception year are in line with these goals. By the end of the Foundation Stage, most children will be able to:

- say and use number names in order in familiar contexts;
- count reliably up to ten everyday objects;
- recognize numerals 1 to 9;
- use language such as 'more' or 'less', 'greater' or 'smaller', 'heavier' or 'lighter' to compare two numbers or quantities;
- in practical activities and discussion begin to use the vocabulary involved in adding and subtracting;
- find one more or one less than a number 1 to 10;
- begin to relate addition to combining two groups of objects and subtraction to 'taking away';
- talk about, recognize and recreate simple patterns;
- use language such as 'circle' or 'bigger' to describe the shape and size of solids and flat shapes;
- use everyday words to describe position;
- use developing mathematical ideas and methods to solve practical problems.

Mathematics in Reception classes

Guidance on the Organisation of the Daily Mathematics Lesson in Reception Classes (DfEE 2000a) reminds head teachers and teachers working with children in Reception classes that although the Foundation Stage prepares children for the beginning of Key Stage 1, it is also a distinct phase of education and one in which play is vital. Thus, a wide range of activities is acknowledged to support the teaching and learning of mathematics, including:

- observation of number and pattern in the environment and daily routines;
- board games;
- large and small construction;
- stories, songs, rhymes and finger games;
- sand and water;
- two- and three-dimensional work with a range of materials;
- imaginative play;
- cooking and shopping;
- outdoor play and 'playground' games.

It is noted that mathematics lessons will often include or be based upon well-planned opportunities for children's play and that planning and organizing such a range of activities is important for the promotion of social skills as well as the development of independence and the ability to concentrate and persevere. Such opportunities can include listening in small and large group settings; finding and using the equipment that they need; taking turns; and playing games – for example, becoming familiar with the repetitive structures of throwing dice and collecting objects.

Indeed, it is precisely through such activities that the daily mathematics lesson in Reception classes can be planned, so that the whole-class activity will almost always include some counting while the main mathematics topic or numerical concepts may be taught to the whole class, in group activities, usually supported by the adult, whether carried out simultaneously or in turn during the day. The plenary with the whole class, after the group activities are completed, then allows for follow-up discussion of the mathematical activities and key teaching points to be emphasized. The intention is that during their time in Reception classes, children should gradually become able to cope with the style of whole-class work and independent activities that they will encounter in Year 1.

As the self-study pack (DfEE 1999b: 107) indicates, children acquire the foundation for later numerical competence and confidence in Reception classes and it is crucial that number work at this stage is varied and comprehensive and takes full account of the ELGs. Three aspects identified are:

- drawing on children's previous experience in the environment at home or in preschool contexts where they will have already encountered counting and the language of measure;
- counting and the structure of the number system, provided through models such as the number track and grid in board games;

- recognizing numbers as sets of objects through practical activities and the manipulation of concrete materials, in order to understand cardinal numbers, where numbers can represent groups of objects or the frequency of events.

The strong emphasis placed on counting in as many different contexts as possible – knowing the number names, putting numbers in order, counting for a purpose as well as adding and subtracting by counting on and back – reflects the recognition in the *Framework* that counting is very complex. By contrast, there is little emphasis on reading and recording, apart from recognizing and tracing the first few numerals. In fact, children can be encouraged to record ideas using objects, pictures and their own symbols and tallies. Martin Hughes (1986) provided powerful evidence that a major cause of difficulty in school arithmetic related to its written form, in particular in the use of conventional signs: '+', '–', '='.

Mathematics in the nursery

If Reception teachers are being asked to draw upon children's prior experiences, just what are these? Just how should nursery staff introduce and teach different aspects of mathematics so that there is progression in both the mathematics covered and children's engagement with the subject? Again, turning to the self-study pack (DfEE 1999b: 116), three key principles of the mathematics curriculum in the nursery are:

- providing a wide experience of numbers, patterns, measurement and shapes in line with the Foundation Stage and the ELGs for mathematics;
- teaching mathematics and providing mathematical experiences so that children can work in small groups, as pairs or individuals and as a large group;
- enabling children to encounter mathematics in a variety of contexts, including free and structured play in child-led or adult-directed activities, in order to develop, rehearse and experiment with skills and ideas.

To ensure that children in the Foundation Stage have a balanced programme of mathematical experiences, staff will be called upon to deploy a range of organizational strategies to engage children in large and small groups, individual and pair activities, which may be adult-led for number songs and rhymes, child-led in the case of outdoor games, role play or small-world play, or adult-supported for sand and water play, bead threading or number puzzles and games. Moreover, activities which start as adult-initiated may later become adult-supported or child-led. Indeed, nursery staff require considerable skill in organization in order to develop the four strands to number work in the nursery:

- counting and manipulating sets of objects – for example, adding one more cake to a plate of cake so that there is one for every child or taking one sweet out of the bag so there is one fewer;

- numbers in everyday life – for example, *'I am 3 today'*, *'I live at number 8'* or *'What's the time, Mr Wolf?'*;
- chanting number rhymes and stories – for instance, *'Five little ducks went swimming one day'* or *'Ten fat tomatoes sizzling in the pan'*;
- patterns and structures – for instance, grids for *Snakes and Ladders*, number tracks, repeating patterns in bead threading, brick towers or sponge prints; partitioning sets of objects into subsets.

These strands also relate to measures, shape and space, and problem solving.

Just as Reception class work builds on nursery experience, each of these strands builds upon experiences children have had before entering nursery, as will be examined later in this chapter.

Challenges to teaching mathematics in the Foundation Stage

Prior knowledge

No matter what age or stage in the Foundation Stage we consider, children start in nursery or Reception class at different times of the year, with very different prior social, cultural and educare experiences and, inevitably, very different mathematical and numerical understandings. This means that teachers will need to adapt examples in the Stepping Stones of the Foundation Stage or the *Framework* to take account of what children already know, understand and can do. For some, this may be very little; for others, it may include instant recognition of small quantities or 'subitizing', recognizing some numerals, representing quantities in personal and idiosyncratic ways, as well as carrying out simple addition and subtraction in practical situations (Aubrey 1997).

Keeping records

When beginning to plan mathematics, teachers will need to consult with parents/carers about their child's progress, consider records passed on from other educare settings and draw on information gained from their own observations. The telephone survey *Implementing the Foundation Stage in Reception Classes* (Quick *et al.* 2002), for instance, showed Reception teachers to be relatively well-informed about their children before they began school. The majority always met with the child's parents, half always received written records from the nursery or other preschool providers and similar proportions met with the preschool staff concerned. However, while the majority of schools were keen to make parents aware of the Foundation Stage and the six areas of learning, more rated parents' understanding as moderate (56 per cent), low or very low (25 per cent) than high or very high (16 per cent).

Provided class teachers and classroom assistants work together closely on the Key Objectives, assistants will have an important role to play in whole-class sessions and in group work. They may monitor particular children's responses in class sessions; sit near and help individuals or groups to make contributions;

observe and talk to particular children to inform future planning; ask questions to stimulate thinking; reinforce mathematical vocabulary; or, more generally, support, discuss and help children get on with one another.

Sub-skills in counting

The *Framework*, which intended that all special educational needs (SEN) children in ordinary classes should be included in the NNS, suggested that adaptations be made to tasks and timing, such as tracking back to earlier stages where necessary, inserting extra small steps to simplify content, providing consolidation work and emphasizing oral and mental activity. In this respect, learning the sub-skills of counting is one area where substantial support may be needed. A five-day course developing teachers' own mathematics (DfEE 2000b) identified the many skills involved in learning to count objects:

- Know the number names in order.
- Synchronize saying words and pointing (young children find it difficult to coordinate saying number words with pointing and may need to move objects as they count).
- Keep track of objects counted (children may need prompting to rearrange objects in lines to simplify the process).
- Recognize that the number associated with the last object touched is the total number of objects and, when counting, distinguish the number of objects counted (cardinal numbers) from the order (ordinal numbers).
- Recognize small numbers of objects without counting them. (It is likely that this skill predates the development of counting. Some children will need a lot of practice in mapping number words onto very small groups of objects – one to three, then one to five or six. Dot patterns on dice, dominoes and playing cards are especially helpful.)
- Count objects of very different sizes (this can be very hard for young children, as is counting things which cannot be touched, seen or moved; in other words, things that are fixed, moving or hidden).
- Know when to stop counting out a number of objects from a larger set (this shows cardinality is understood).
- Recognize that if a group of objects already counted is rearranged, the total number stays the same (this indicates the child can conserve number).
- Make a reasonable estimate of a number without counting.

Just as understanding of our ten-base system takes a considerable amount of time to establish, counting principles are also established slowly over time and provide the basis for adding and subtracting. Section 4 of the *Framework* provides a supplement of examples with lots of ideas for counting and recognizing numbers, adding and subtracting.

Assessment

Most of the 752 Reception class teachers in the telephone survey (Quick *et al.* 2002) reported using a range of observation techniques and types of evidence to monitor and assess the progress of children. At least four out of every five used each of the following: general observations; their own baseline assessments; annotated examples of work; records from the nursery or preschool provider; and asking children's own views. As the skills in counting described above indicate, however, the effectiveness of the observation used and the evidence collected depends largely upon the teacher's understanding of the underlying sub-skills involved.

Organizational strategies

In terms of organization, the majority of the Reception class teachers in the telephone survey implemented the NNS flexibly in terms one and two but used the daily mathematics lesson in term three. The majority struck a balance between structuring teaching by Foundation Stage area of learning or integrating learning across the curriculum throughout the year. In terms of grouping strategy, there was an increasing trend towards grouping by ability by term three (nearly half of those questioned). Around two thirds of both head teachers and Reception class teachers felt that implementing the NNS with a more flexible approach for Reception-aged children had not been a problem. Less than 10 per cent felt that it had been a big problem.

Transition

In terms of the transition of children to Key Stage 1, 72 per cent of the 799 head teachers surveyed felt that this had not been a problem since the introduction of the Foundation Stage. Just 7 per cent felt that it had been a big problem in their school and where problems had been encountered these were generally related to concerns about children's adjustment to a formal teaching style and their having the skills required for progression to Key Stage 1. Three quarters (77 per cent) of Reception class teachers always discussed each child's progress with their future Year 1 teacher before the children moved on. While these observations related to *all six* areas of learning, they are pertinent to the mathematical area of learning to which this chapter is devoted.

Mixed-age classes

Of more concern in the survey were mixed-age classes, with 57 per cent of head teachers and 60 per cent of Reception class teachers with Reception-aged children in mixed-age classes reporting difficulties in teaching from both the *Curriculum Guidance for the Foundation Stage* (QCA/DfEE 2000) and the Key Stage 1 Programmes of Study in the same classroom. Concerns were raised about the increased planning required, and ensuring that work was tailored to both age groups. The different teaching styles of the two phases in a single classroom was also regarded as problematic, with Reception-aged children spending less time sitting at tables and making more noise than Year 1 children.

Overview and personal reflections on NNS in nursery and Reception classes

The strengths

The key objectives, the supplement of examples in the *Framework* and the guidance provided for mathematics in Reception classes and nurseries in terms of learning and teaching styles advocated, as well as organization proposed, are compatible with current notions of what young children's mathematical knowledge is and how it is acquired. It is a view which holds that children's mathematical knowledge is grounded in their activities and interactions with adults and that they learn mathematical structure within their social and material world. Children will have already formed a view of mathematics when they enter nursery or Reception and will bring into the classroom a mathematical understanding based on their everyday life (Aubrey 2001). Two aspects of this are particularly important: children's prior knowledge and the pedagogic role of the adult.

Children's prior knowledge

To understand this, it is essential to go right back to the start:

- Even infants, it is thought, may have a preverbal predisposition to represent and reason numerically about small quantities.
- In the language acquisition period, this knowledge is mapped onto counting skills in the context of nursery rhymes, stories and songs, the recitation of number strings (such as '*count them . . . one two, three, four*'), and the repetition and clarification of cardinality (to determine amount) with simple counts ('*one, your turn, two, three, your turn, four . . .*').
- Links between these numerical abilities and the development of verbal counting over the preschool period and beyond lead to the establishment of 'how to count' principles. These include the one-to-one correspondence principle, the stable order of counting principle and the cardinality principle attached to the last number in a count, which quantifies the whole set (discussed above).
- Calculation strategies emerge gradually from children's experience of counting or otherwise determining amounts, and their growing skill at 'abbreviated counting' in which they recognize structured amounts of differing sizes, with ordered and unordered, visible and partly visible sets of objects.

This process takes place in real-world contexts and standard procedures evolve gradually from children's own informal ones as they explore number relations, properties and notations under the guidance of the teacher, who builds interactively upon their existing ideas.

The role of adults

Studies of early caregiver-child interactions in the home have shown that the relationship between parental strategies and the child's advancement (for instance in number and counting) is by no means entirely clear, and it is thought that not all parental strategies are equally effective. This is a point to be borne in mind when considering the guidance on mathematical activities in the Foundation Stage (DfES 2002a). Walkerdine (1988) classified mother-child exchanges as *instrumental* when the main focus of the task is its practical accomplishment and in which number or mathematical language is an incidental feature; and *pedagogical* where number, counting or size comparison, for instance, would be the explicit focus of a purposeful activity – i.e. the teaching or practice of mathematical or numerical skills. Furthermore, such practice could be distinguished by the particular role adopted by the mother, as playful but equal partner and helpmate for the child. The adult, as equal participant, recognizing the pedagogical purpose of the activity, joined in *and* extended the child's knowledge.

The challenge

The challenge for teachers, it seems, lies in knowing how to plan and structure the curriculum to take account of and extend this rich knowledge by close attention to the balance of whole-class, group and individual teaching, as well as child-initiated, adult-directed or adult-supported activity. Planning, monitoring and assessment in mixed-age classes poses a particular challenge, though this appears to be less problematic when there are adequate levels of qualified support staff. Whether or not classes are mixed-age, however, the challenge is to provide learning opportunities and high expectations to meet the needs of diverse groups of children in order to ensure that most Reception-aged children achieve the ELGs and, at the same time, the older or more mature children are extended beyond, to Key Stage 1. To ensure that *all* children make the best possible progress, a wide range of teaching strategies will be required to motivate, support and extend appropriately.

The threats

Responding to diverse needs with an increase in whole-class (large group), teacher-directed activity constitutes the main threat to effective nursery and Reception class practice. The DfES (2002a) guidance *Mathematical Activities for the Foundation Stage* sadly falls into this trap. The aim of the two booklets (for nursery and for Reception class children) and video provided is to help Foundation Stage practitioners plan mathematical activities that are linked to the Stepping Stones identified in the *Curriculum Guidance for the Foundation Stage* (QCA/DfEE 2000), progressing towards the ELGs. The activities are organized for three specific teaching and learning contexts:

- large group (which might be the whole group in a nursery or Reception class);

- small group (of similar-aged children from a range of Foundation Stage settings);
- planned play and cooking activities (which might take place in any preschool setting).

The lack of mathematical discussion, exploration or sustained, child-initiated play and the emphasis on artificial activities dominated by teacher talk is a concern.

On the positive side, the activities *do* make use of children's props and toys, their jingles and rhymes. There is an argumentative puppet who makes deliberate mistakes, hidden number problems which involve partly visible snakes on a clothes hanger and number washing lines with missing numerals. There is counting and comparison of toy cars, plastic animals and pizza toppings. There are sets of children's clothes to pack in a suitcase to sort and objects buried in the sandpit. Some activities do involve instant recognition of small configurations such as currants on shortcake and there is some use of actions and sounds.

On the negative side, many activities focus on numbers 1 to 5 but surprisingly few on very small quantities numbers 0 to 3. In fact, no mention at all is made of 0. Little attention is given to counting backwards and 'skip counting' does not appear. Early introduction to numerals and representations of quantities on fingers is strongly emphasized. Some reference is made to counting, comparing and recounting sets of objects but the general expectation is that children will 'count on'. This takes little account of children's early attempts to count both sets separately *before* counting on, or the time taken to establish the later and more efficient strategy of counting on from the larger number.

Conventional number sentences are introduced with no indication that children's own informal representation of problem situations have been exploited. They are asked to 'guess' amounts of between 10 and 20, as well as between 50 and 100, though children's difficulties with estimation have been documented since the first version of the National Curriculum mathematics document was published.

Well-trained and experienced practitioners may select judiciously from these activities and deploy as appropriate. There is a real danger in their literal and inappropriate use by less experienced and less informed staff who insufficiently understand the complexity of children's early learning. The structure and approach is in some contrast to the new Foundation Stage Profile which carries *no* set assessment activities or tasks, is based entirely on ongoing observations and leads to a profile being completed for each child at the end of the Foundation Stage. Now that the Foundation Stage is bedding down, it is unfortunate that head teachers and teachers may feel, once again, that they are receiving unclear guidance and 'mixed messages'.

Implications for teaching and learning

For Reception classes

The vast majority of head teachers and Reception class teachers do view the Foundation Stage as 'a good thing' according to the telephone survey. Few (less than 10 per cent of either group) have regarded implementing the NNS with a flexible approach as a big problem. Mixed-age classes have proved more challenging but for Reception children the elements of the NNS can take place at different parts of the day (DfES 2002b). This means that Reception class teachers may decide to teach both groups together:

- for part of the lesson (the oral and mental starter, for instance);
- for some topics (counting);
- towards the end of the year (in the summer term).

They can be flexible about decisions regarding direct teaching, group activity (whether independent pupil activity, structured play or choice) and plenary, and about how classroom assistants are deployed.

Using the knowledge and experience children already have allows them to contribute to the teaching/learning process and teachers to develop formal mathematical knowledge from children's informal strategies. A particular challenge here is for those children who have *not* had rich prior experience and for whom no such assumptions can be made.

In the nursery

Understanding how children learn mathematics and knowing how to link this to mathematical properties and relationships, using an increasing variety of mathematical language, is central to effective nursery practice. This means providing a practical learning environment with stimulating, varied and challenging activities which are relevant to children's lives.

Observing and recording children's responses in free and structured play can be used to inform future planning. Posing questions and sharing explanations can be used effectively in order to clarify and extend their ideas. Regular exchange of information between parents and carers concerning children's mathematical experiences and progress keeps both parties in the picture.

Everyday mathematics will be constructed through children's own investigations in the social and cultural environment when they are given some responsibility in the choice and direction of their activities. Fostering a positive disposition to learning is more likely to occur where there is an opportunity for ideas to be tried out, mistakes to be made and time set aside to review and refine. At the same time, continuous evaluation of the way we, as adults and the main resource, use our own mathematical skills in organizing and planning the day will be central to this process.

Conclusions

Such evidence as we have of the incidence of mathematical and numerical activity in informal settings suggests that relative to literacy-based experience this is low. A recent examination of a subset of Gordon Wells' data on early mother-child conversations (Aubrey *et al.* 2000) indicated that just 2.1 per cent of samples contained reference to mathematics. Similarly, in Scottish nurseries, Munn and Schaffer (1993) noted the scarcity of numerical experiences for 2- and 3-year-olds, which occupied just 5 per cent of the time. Indeed, studies of early caregiver/child interactions have suggested that in the third year adults are found to *diminish* their input just as children, in turn, increase their own output. This finding argues all the more strongly for appropriate and thoughtful planning throughout the Foundation Stage to ensure that this area of learning gains the attention it deserves.

References

Aubrey, C. (1997) *Mathematics Teaching in the Early Years: An Investigation of Teachers' Subject Knowledge*. London: Falmer Press.

Aubrey, C. (2001) Early mathematics, in T. David (ed.) *Promoting Evidence-based Practice in Early Childhood Education Research and its Implication*, pp. 183–208. Greenwich: JAI/Elsevier.

Aubrey, C., Godfrey, R. and Godfrey, J. (2000) Children's early numeracy experiences in the home, *Primary Practice*, 26: 36–42.

DfEE (Department for Education and Employment) (1999a) *Framework for Teaching Mathematics from Reception to Year 6*. London: DfEE.

DfEE (Department for Education and Employment) (1999b) Mathematics in Reception, in *Self-Study Pack*, pp. 93–132. London: DfEE.

DfEE (Department for Education and Employment) (2000a) *Guidance on the Organisation of the Daily Mathematics Lesson in Reception Classes*. London: DfEE.

DfEE (Department for Education and Employment) (2000b) Teaching mathematics in Reception, in *Five-day Course*, pp.118–30. London: DfEE.

DfES (Department for Education and Skills) (2002a) *Mathematical Activities for the Foundation Stage*. London: DfES.

DfES (Department for Education and Skills) (2002b) *Organising the Daily Mathematics Lesson in Mixed Reception/Year 1 Classes*. London: DfES.

Hughes, M. (1986) *Children and Number: Difficulties in Learning Mathematics*. Oxford: Blackwell.

Munn, P. and Schaffer, R. (1993) Literacy and numeracy events in social interactive contexts, *International Journal of Early Years Education*, 10(2): 217–52.

QCA/DfEE (Qualifications and Curriculum Authority/Department for Education and Employment) (2000) *Curriculum Guidance for the Foundation Stage*. London: DfEE.

Quick, S., Lambley, C., Newcombe, E. and Aubrey, C. (2002) *Implementing the Foundation Stage in Reception Classes*. London: DfES.

Walkerdine, V. (1988) *The Mastery of Reason: Cognitive Development and the Production of Rationality*. London: Routledge.

Parlez-vous mathematics?

Steve Higgins

Introduction

'Bitzer,' said Thomas Gradgrind. 'Your definition of a horse.'

'Quadruped. Graminivorous. Forty teeth, namely, twenty four grinders, four eye-teeth, and twelve incisive. Sheds coat in the spring; in marshy countries sheds hoof too. Hoofs hard, but requiring to be shod with iron. Age known by marks in mouth.' Thus (and much more) Bitzer.

'Now girl number twenty,' said Mr Gradgrind. 'You know what a horse is.'

Charles Dickens, Hard Times, 1854

I was recently struck by the similarity of this exchange with an observation of a Year 6 class where the pupils were revising the required 2D shapes for this age group. They displayed adeptness at spelling 'parallelogram' and in reciting a definition ('two pairs of opposite sides that are parallel') but struggled with the idea that a square could be a parallelogram. The aim of this chapter is to try to explain why this happens and to highlight the importance of talk and discussion in mathematics teaching. It begins with an overview of the role of talk in mathematics learning. Then, three research projects are summarized which have used talk and discussion to improve children's learning of mathematics. A final section considers some of the implications for teaching.

Mathematical talk and mathematical thinking

Hughes (1986) used the Peanuts cartoon reprinted in Figure 5.1 to illustrate the challenge of making mathematics meaningful to young learners. The issue it so neatly highlights is that pupils develop their own ways of coping with the demands of the mathematics classroom, often with considerable success, but that this may still leave them feeling like a foreigner when 'mathematics is

Figure 5.1 Maths is like learning a foreign language, Marcie . . .

being spoken'. Shuard and Rothery (1984) identified different types of mathematical words used in schools:

- technical vocabulary (words which are primarily mathematical like 'polygon' or 'divisor');
- lexical vocabulary (words which have a similar meaning in mathematics as in everyday English such as 'multiple' or 'remainder');
- everyday vocabulary (where words might have an overlapping meaning but have a particular sense in a mathematical context such as 'point' or 'difference').

It could be argued that almost all of the language used in mathematics lessons in primary schools has a particular sense or meaning which is determined by the context in which it is used. Sometimes this even varies between mathematics lessons, such as talking about 'difference' or a (decimal) 'point' in number and 'difference' between polygons or a 'point' in shape and space. One way of understanding mathematics teaching in primary schools is therefore to focus on such language and to use this perspective about talk and interaction to help tackle some of the challenging issues relating to improving attainment.

I'd like to use the analogy that 'maths is like learning a foreign language' (see Figure 5.1) to reflect on a number of current issues in mathematics teaching. I believe that the analogy is helpful because it can help us to recognize that many failures of performance in mathematics are due to failures of communication and subsequent (or consequent) failures of understanding. To pursue the analogy further, there are a number of helpful parallels with language learning. One of these is exemplified by what you might describe as the 'repeat after me' approach. Pupils are given a definition or phrase which they repeat. At this point in their learning there is little meaning in such rehearsal or repetition. This is not unlike some of the advice in the National Numeracy Strategy (NNS) *Framework for Teaching Mathematics from Reception to Year 6* (DfEE 1999a) and the associated *Mathematical Vocabulary* booklet (DfEE 1999b) (and is reminiscent of Mr Gradgrind's pedagogy cited at the beginning of the chapter), where pupils are told what to do and say in order to start using new vocabulary.

Another parallel is with what you might describe as 'phrase book' foreign language learning. Having bought a phrase book before going on holiday you ask a native speaker how to get to the shops. You don't follow exactly what is said in reply, but a few key words and gestures are enough to get you walking in the right direction. To an observer you might appear to have had a conversation. Similarly, in learning mathematics at school, pupils pick up from the teacher's instructions some of what they are supposed to learn, but their focus is more often on what they have to *do* or to *produce* (particularly in terms of written output). This can lead to children being able to perform aspects of mathematics satisfactorily (such as the standard vertical two-digit subtraction algorithm) but being unable to give an estimate or to explain how or why the algorithm works. This is the difference between learning the vocabulary of a language and being able to use that vocabulary to communicate and understand.

There is now considerable evidence about the nature of classroom talk (see e.g. Edwards and Westgate 1994) with clear implications for establishing distinct patterns for particular objectives. Wood and Wood's (1988) research demonstrated that, particularly for primary pupils, direct questions can be inhibiting, as children try to guess what the teacher wants as the reply, rather than make sense of the question. The dominant pattern of whole-class talk takes the form of a direct question from the teacher followed by a brief answer from a pupil, with a short evaluative follow-up statement from the teacher. This pattern can be effective, particularly when the objectives are to check for knowledge or information. However, if the objectives of a lesson are to promote pupil discussion and allow them to show or develop their thinking and reasoning, research suggests that direct questioning by the teacher can be counter-productive. This is particularly crucial in mathematics where the value of pupil talk is recognized as essential for developing understanding and making connections between mathematical ideas and mathematical skills and procedures (Raiker 2002).

Much of what happens in lessons is not explicit and children interpret what is expected by these unwritten rules and unspoken instructions. These linguistic or 'meta-discursive' rules (Kieran *et al.* 2003) regulate how mathematics classrooms operate and profoundly influence both teachers and pupils. An example might be the way in which children interpret word problems in mathematics lessons. They know that such problems are used so that they can practise number operations and so pay little attention to whether or not the answer makes sense in the context of the problem.

Three perspectives on changing talk in classrooms

In this section I describe three research projects that I have been involved with which used a focus on talk and discussion in mathematics lessons to improve pupils' attainment. In each project there was a practical emphasis on developing understanding through talking about mathematics which was used to try to improve the teaching and learning of mathematics. In the first project a group of schools looked at mental calculations and teachers listened to pupils' explanations of how they solved particular problems. In the second project pupils were taught to talk and listen to each other in order to improve their mathematical thinking, and in the final project a group of teachers investigated a simple game, 'Odd One Out', to see what they could learn about children's use of mathematical vocabulary and how this could help them understand their mathematical thinking.

Project 1: Discussing mental calculation strategies

In three mathematics lessons each week the teachers extended the length of the oral/mental starter by five minutes. The additional time was used to allow pupils to articulate and discuss the strategy or strategies that they used to solve a mental calculation. For example, when asked to calculate 23 + 23, a range of strategies was proposed by pupils in one class: 'I know the answer . . . double 23 is 46'; or '20 + 20 = 40, 3 + 3 = 6, 40 + 6 makes 46'; and '23 + 20 = 43, add 3 makes 46'. All of the pupils were able to describe to some extent how they had carried out a calculation, even in Reception classes.

The teachers interviewed some of the pupils to record and classify their strategies (following Thompson 1999). The explanations were recorded on assessment sheets, which were discussed by teachers at professional development meetings involving teachers from all of the schools. One major benefit of the project was that teachers were able to spend some time with individual pupils discussing mental calculation strategies and recording the pupils' responses. This kind of formative assessment is a powerful approach to raising standards (Black and Wiliam 1998). Some examples of exchanges between teachers and pupils follow.

Reception
Teacher: What comes before 6 when you are counting?
Pupil: 5. I counted backwards from 6.
Teacher: How do you know?
Pupil: Dad showed me how.
(Strategy: counting back)

Year 2
Teacher: 6 + 5?
Pupil: Eleven. 5 add 5 add one more.
(Strategy: using near-doubles)

Year 4
Teacher: 560 + 575?
Pupil: Double 500 is 1000, split 75 into 40 + 35, add 60 and 40 is 100. Then add 35 is 135. 1000 and 135 is 1135.
(Strategy: doubles, partitioning, complements)

The close focus on pupils' responses was an important part of the development work in that it highlighted the range of strategies that were and were not being used by pupils. It therefore gave the teachers an opportunity to extend the use of different strategies in subsequent lessons.

All of the pupils were usually able to describe how they had worked out mental calculations (though sometimes the teachers suspected that they were inventing or 'romancing' a plausible account). Analysis showed that across the four schools they used a range of vocabulary to describe strategies.

Sometimes they were able to articulate the type of strategy such as 'I counted on' or 'I used doubles' rather than a simple description or repetition of the actual calculation method: 'I went 7, 8, 9'. Quite often they were able to provide a name or descriptive word for the strategy they used. Surprisingly the younger pupils (in Reception and Year 1) showed the greatest frequency of using descriptive strategies in this way, often indicating that they had 'counted on', 'counted back' or 'counted in tens'. Older pupils (in Years 3 and 4) reported that they had 'used doubles' or 'split' two- and three-digit numbers or that they had used 'rounding'.

The greater use of strategy terminology by younger pupils may well reflect the level of modelling provided by the teacher. This interpretation is supported by evidence that the use of some terms, such as 'splitting', was only found in one particular class where the teacher acknowledged that this was the term that she used to describe partitioning numbers into more convenient chunks to calculate with.

The implication of this research is that teachers of older children may assume greater understanding on the part of their pupils and therefore spend less time making strategies explicit as a result. The identification of strategies and terminology within the NNS *Framework* gives the basis for a shared vocabulary, though the terminology for strategies is at times rather general, such as with 'compensation' and 'partition and recombine'. It may also be the case that the teachers involved were less familiar with both the terminology and the range of possible two-digit strategies (Thompson 1999). This finding certainly suggests that there is a need for teachers of older children to spend more time modelling strategies and identifying an appropriate vocabulary to describe them. It may also indicate that many pupils find using such mathematical vocabulary challenging and need more time and discussion to reinforce their understanding.

Evidence of impact

The pupils' standardized test scores in mathematics in the classes studied increased by an average of six points (from 107 to 113) over the five months between testing. As there were no formal control classes it is not possible to attribute this gain to the project alone, indeed some gain would be expected from the implementation of the NNS, though other schools' results in the area (three schools) were more modest (an average gain of just over two points on standardized tests in a comparable period).

A focus on mathematical talk and discussion did provide an effective focus for professional development which produced a measurable improvement in pupils' attainment. In terms of the metaphor of 'talk as a foreign language' the pupils developed confidence in expressing themselves when speaking mathematically to explain their mental calculations. The teachers also had the chance to hear them 'put it in their own words' and when this was done in a whole-class session, other children heard different ways of working things out that they could try for themselves. An emphasis on making strategies for counting and mental calculation explicit to pupils is therefore beneficial as a teaching strategy for teachers. The evidence from this project indicated that discussing strategies particularly benefited lower attaining pupils who made greater relative improvement. This may be because the emphasis on identifying, naming and modelling strategies made the process of mental calculation more explicit and therefore easier to learn.

Project 2: Improving attainment in mathematics through talking and thinking together

A project funded by the Nuffield Foundation and undertaken by a team of researchers led by Professor Neil Mercer at the Open University has also shown that a focus on talk can improve mathematical learning (Mercer *et al*. 2002). Using an experimental teaching programme, 'Thinking Together', children in Year 5 were taught to follow agreed 'ground rules' for talk as they undertook collaborative tasks where they discussed what to do and checked that each member of the group was happy before proceeding. Some of these activities used computer software (see Higgins, Chapter 14), others were paper based (see Adhami, Chapter 6 on the importance of embedding talk in an effective pedagogy of mathematics).

The challenge in mathematics was to identify questions and activities where the pupils might benefit from discussion before identifying a solution. These needed to be either open-ended activities where there was more than one possible solution or where a strategy could be successful. Alternatively the level of challenge had to mean that an individual could not easily see a solution, but by working collaboratively it was possible to come up with an answer. One example of this was a 3 × 3 magic square where the pupils had to find a solution where each row, column and diagonal added up to the same total. Another was a classification task where the children identified similarities and differences in sets of numbers and shapes.

Overall, the results showed that the children in the seven target classes gained significantly better scores in mathematics than those in the control classes. The impact of the intervention was equivalent to moving a class from fiftieth position in a league table of 100 schools into the top 30 (an effect size of .59). The findings from this project indicate that patterns of interaction and pupils' use of language changed after the introduction of the 'Thinking Together' lessons, and that there was improvement in their reasoning skills and science attainment as well as in mathematics.

Why should such an intervention which promoted collaborative discussion help children's individual scores on National Curriculum test questions? One explanation is that the children learned to be successful by talking with their peers and tentatively trying out new solutions as they articulated their thinking. Working as a group or working with a more successful peer 'scaffolded' their learning successfully so that they were then able to undertake more challenging tasks by themselves.

An extract from one of the transcripts of a lesson illustrates some aspects of this. The children are sorting numbers according to whether or not they are multiples of 4.

Gurjit:	Shall I start? Is 18 a multiple of 4?
Mehnaz:	4, 8, 12.
Sam:	Ss . . .
Gurjit:	Yes it is – 4 times 4.
Sam and	
Mehnaz:	No, no, no, no, no.

Gurjit:	16.
Sam:	No, no, no, no.
	[Gurjit put it in the 'no' box].
Mehnaz:	No, it's 16.
Gurjit:	Is 15?
Sam:	No.
Mehnaz:	No *[Gurjit puts it in the 'no' box].*
Gurjit:	Is 9?
Sam:	No.
Mehnaz:	No.
Gurjit:	Why do you think that?
Sam:	Um . . .
Sam and	
Mehnaz:	Because . . .
Sam:	Because it goes 4, 8 then 12 so it misses 9 out.
Mehnaz:	'Cos if you do 4 times 5 it isn't . . .
Gurjit:	And – and only – and only the even numbers end in 0, 2, 4, 6, 8.
Sam:	Yeah. And 4 is even. 8? Yes *[Gurjit drops it in the 'no' box].*
Gurjit and	
Mehnaz:	Yes.
Sam:	4, 8. Twenty-five?
Mehnaz:	No.
Sam:	It would be 4. 4, 8 . . .
Mehnaz:	No, no, no there's no 25 – no. 20 . . . 5 or 25?
Sam:	No, no, no, no.
Gurjit:	It would be 20 if it was in there.
Sam:	Yeah, 24 *[Gurjit puts it in the 'no' box].*
Gurjit:	12 is one?
Mehnaz:	Yes *[Gurjit puts it in the 'yes' box].*
Sam:	Yes, 4, 8, 12 – 3 times 4. Five?
Mehnaz	
and Gurjit:	No *[Gurjit puts it in the 'no' box].*
Sam:	100? [Pause]
Mehnaz:	I don't think so.
Sam:	Yes it is, isn't it?
Gurjit:	Yes it is innit, because all the times tables, the answers in the four times tables are even, innit!
Sam:	That's right, yeah! Sure?
Gurjit:	*[To Mehnaz]* Are you confused?
Mehnaz:	Yes, a little bit.
Gurjit:	OK, I'll explain it to her. I'll try to explain it. Look, if, if 4 is an even number and 100 is an even number and answers in the four times table are always even – you understand now?
Mehnaz:	Yes, I do know they're even.

This extract exemplifies some of the key principles of effective collaborative talk that 'Thinking Together' tries to promote. The children check with each other before completing the activity on screen by dragging the numbers to the correct boxes. For example, Gurjit asks the other two to explain 'Why do you think that?' and the others explain their reasoning using terms like 'because', 'then' and 'so'. In the final part of the transcript Gurjit undertakes to explain to Mehnaz his general rule though she seems a little unconvinced by his faulty reasoning. In other examples of talk you can identify where the children correct each other (or themselves) and how their confidence in sorting and classifying the numbers increases during an activity with the support of the other children in the group. As the pupils are given the opportunity to talk to each other, supported by the agreed 'ground rules', they seem to build on what each pupil knows and is confident with so that their overall confidence increases.

In terms of the analogy of mathematics as a foreign language the children have to make up short mathematical conversations in small groups. The agreed ground rules help to structure these exchanges, but the joint activity or purpose of the task ensures that they really have to listen to each other and work out if they agree and if not, why not. This means that they have to work quite hard at understanding each other and not just recite or exchange phrases from the tourist phrase book!

Project 3: 'Odd One Out': A thinking skills strategy

Five teachers from two first schools in Northumberland investigated a thinking skills strategy called 'Odd One Out' (Higgins 2001) as the focus for a Thinking Skills Research Scholarship funded by the National Union of Teachers (NUT). In this thinking skills strategy, pupils are presented with three numbers such as 9, 10 and 5 and asked to identify an 'odd one out' and to give a reason (see Figure 5.2). In this example the odd one out could be 10 because it is even or

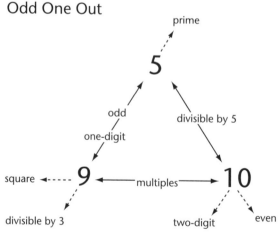

Figure 5.2 Which is the odd one out?

two-digit, or 9 because it is a multiple of 3 or a square number, or 5 because it is a prime number. Identifying an odd one out in this way helps pupils to identify and articulate mathematical properties of numbers and have an enjoyable and unthreatening context in which to do so. The other two numbers not identified also share mathematic properties such as odd, or single-digit, or multiples, which provides a challenging extension to the activity. The game-like nature of the activity helps pupils to feel confident to have a go. At the same time the teacher gets helpful feedback about the kind of language that pupils are using, and this provides information on the way that they are seeing numbers and recognizing their properties. The teachers in the project discovered that pupils had a 'default' vocabulary: some pupils 'defaulted' to vocabulary they were confident with such as 'it's in the pattern of threes' rather than 'it's a multiple of 3' which was the language they had covered and been encouraged to use in lessons.

This finding was explored further by looking at the reasons pupils gave for numbers being the odd one out and comparing these reasons with their scores on a standardized test of mathematical ability. What emerged from this analysis was that higher attaining pupils were more adept at picking up and using more recently introduced vocabulary. Pupils who did not score so well on the attainment tests either were not confident to use the vocabulary or preferred to give reasons that they felt secure with, such as odd and even numbers, or visual features such as the number of digits. The teachers concluded that it was important to include thinking activities such as the Odd One Out strategy for the following reasons:

- it provided them with important formative feedback about how confident pupils were at using mathematical vocabulary they had recently taught;
- pupils enjoyed the activities and all members of the class were able to participate;
- the 'game' was an effective context to enable pupils to use their knowledge of the properties of numbers and shapes.

In each of these projects the main focus was to develop mathematical thinking through talking about mathematics. The projects drew on research about the importance of talk in mathematics lessons and investigated ways to put these findings into practice to help children's learning. The projects provide persuasive evidence that articulation and discussion are helpful in mathematics to develop understanding. The evidence from these projects suggests that such talk is helpful at two levels. The pupils need to be able to describe what they are doing to avoid learning purely procedural skills based on an algorithm they will probably forget. The teacher also benefits from this articulation and discussion by identifying skills and understandings that are secure and areas of uncertainty or misconception that need to be addressed. In particular this seems to help those who have not been as successful in mathematics previously. This may be due to the increased time spent on explanation and modelling, or because the pupils begin to see that they can be successful by applying strategies rather than having to know or recall number facts.

Some practical implications for talk in mathematics lessons

Whole-class question and answer sessions are not enough to develop mathematical understanding. In this situation it is hard to do anything other than hold 'vocabulary tests' with short exchanges. Teachers therefore need to use a range of approaches and activities to ensure that children are not simply reciting or 'parroting' mathematical vocabulary.

Collaborative discussion by pupils in small groups can improve their attainment in mathematics. One way of thinking about this is to encourage productive mathematical conversations where the children have to discuss puzzles and problems and explain what they think to each other. Using whole-class games can also increase the range of talk that children use and teachers will benefit from the informal feedback that this type of activity offers about the 'default' language that children are using.

The broader implications are that when new mathematical terminology is introduced to a class the children will benefit from a range of activities where they need to use the vocabulary and terminology. Thinking about mathematics as a foreign language may help to understand the nature of this challenge. Part of the problem is that it is a foreign language where lots of the words are spelled and pronounced the same as words in everyday English, but these words have subtly or completely different meanings!

References

Black, P. and Wiliam, D. (1998) *Inside the Black Box: Raising Standards through Classroom Assessment*. London: King's College.

DfEE (Department for Education and Employment) (1999a) *Framework for Teaching Mathematics from Reception to Year 6*. London: DfEE.

DfEE (Department for Education and Employment) (1999b) *Mathematical Vocabulary*. London: DfEE.

Edwards, A.D. and Westgate, D.P.G. (1994) *Investigating Classroom Talk*. London: Falmer.

Higgins, S. (2001) *Thinking Through Primary Teaching*. Cambridge: Chris Kington Publishing.

Hughes, M. (1986) *Children and Number: Difficulties in Learning Mathematics*. Oxford: Basil Blackwell.

Kieran, C., Forman, E. and Sfard, A. (2003) *Learning Discourse: Discursive Approaches to Research in Mathematics Education*. Dordrech: Kluwer.

Mercer, N., Wegerif, R., Dawes, L., Sams, C. and Higgins, S. (2002) *Language, Thinking and ICT in the Primary Curriculum: Final Project Report to the Nuffield Foundation*. Milton Keynes: Open University.

Raiker, A. (2002) Spoken language and mathematics, *Cambridge Journal of Education*, 32(1): 45–60.

Shuard, H. and Rothery, A. (1984) *Children Reading Mathematics*. London: John Murray.

Thompson, I. (1999) Mental calculation strategies for addition and subtraction, *Mathematics in School*, 28(5): 2–4 and 29(1): 24–6.

Wood, D. and Wood, H. (1988) Questioning versus student initiative, in J.T. Dillon (ed.) *Questioning and Discussion: A Multidisciplinary Study*, pp. 280–305. Norwood, NJ: Ablex.

From lesson objectives to lesson agenda: flexibility in whole-class lesson structure

Mundher Adhami

Refining whole-class teaching pedagogy has become a key strand of the work of mathematics educators in England. Throughout the government series of initiatives, teachers and consultants have been sifting through official guidelines and distinguishing the valuable and empowering from the ritual. This chapter offers a perspective for this refinement process, developed through the continuing research across key stages on developing general powers of thinking in children through their mathematics lessons.[1] The chapter focuses on the two issues of lesson objectives and lesson structure.

Intentions and their tensions

Having a clear objective for a lesson is not a bureaucratic requirement. It clarifies for the teacher the lesson's focus and general flow. It also places the lesson in the wider mathematical curriculum for the class to be balanced over time. Without lesson objectives we are in the practice of 'take your folder and carry on', or the unthinking 'open at page 43 and start on question 1'. Pedagogically, a lesson objective favours structured whole-class teaching over the haphazard 'lonely learning' approach of individualized schemes. The intention is also to distinguish interactive teaching from drill-and-practice.

What *is* bureaucratic, however, is focusing on surface aspects of the lesson objectives rather than their underlying value. Teachers complain that some inspectors and advisers seem to pay attention less to the quality of interactions in the classroom than to rituals of writing the lesson objective on the board and sharing it with the class at the start and end of a lesson. Observations at times seem to teachers narrowly focused on pupils achieving or not achieving the objectives. Teachers point out, rightly, that not all objectives are able to be shared with pupils, and that in any case it is not realistic to expect all pupils to achieve an objective within a single lesson unless it is of a trivial kind.

A similar line of argument applies to the three-part lesson structure. It does offer a useful start for teachers in planning whole-class mathematics activity. Again, however, it can be interpreted in a ritual sense, so that largely unrelated classroom episodes at the start and end of the lesson are seen as the norm. Rather than being good practice, this of course undermines the idea of a lesson structure itself. It must be said that this was not the intention of the National Numeracy Strategy (NNS). In fact, the *Framework for teaching mathematics from Reception to Year 6* explicitly states that 'The outline structure of a typical lesson should not be seen as a mechanistic recipe to be followed. You should use your professional judgement to determine the activities, timing and organisation of each part of the lesson to suit its objectives'.[2]

But all documents are interpreted in the light of the use made of them by people with authority, and the focus of their use in in-service education and training (INSET) sessions and classroom observations.[3] The tension is evident between sections of text in the official guidance on the need for flexibility and the exercising of professional judgement on the one hand, and the manner in which the training is conducted, on the other: a clear case of conflict between medium and message. It is to the credit of many consultants that they have often managed more open and responsive sessions with teachers than the official guidance suggests. Their argument, and mine, is that active and responsive teaching can only be promoted through teachers experiencing active, responsive tutoring in INSET. But let us stay with classroom practice and official guidance as given.

There is a strong argument for reformulating both the notion of the lesson objectives and the notion of a three-part lesson, so as to avoid reducing all lessons to the same narrowly focused drill-and-practice type of lesson the *Framework* decries. These are the easiest lessons for which to write and share objectives, and where a three-part lesson is visible to all, including those outside observers of lessons less able to evaluate the quality of interactions in a class. These lessons are also, of course, the ultimate turn-offs for the youngsters.

Each of the main different types of lesson needed for a balanced mathematical diet for youngsters (e.g. instruction and practice, investigation and problem solving, and thinking challenge lessons) needs a different type of lesson objective and a different structure. This chapter discusses thinking challenge lessons based on an example, but suggests that some of the issues apply to other lessons. Discussion focuses on the quality of interactions within a progressive rise in thinking challenges, including from 'closed' to 'open' mathematics (see Jones, Chapter 8). A framework is proposed for analysing a lesson in terms of the richness of cognitive agenda, as opposed to a single objective; the richness of responsive questioning in different parts of the lesson, as opposed to ritual question and answer scenes; and the promotion of positive attitudes to the subject.

How the type of lesson influences its structure

We classify lessons to serve a purpose. When we discuss class organization we talk of whole-class, small-group and individualized work, even though more often than not there is some combination of these types of organization in any one lesson. Similarly we talk about practical, oral/aural and written-work based lessons (alternatively apparatus-based, discussion-based and paper-based lessons) to describe the nature of work on the activity. The two classifications cross each other, and both refer to outward characteristics of lessons. There are other distinctions – for example, between transmission (or closed) lessons versus investigative (or open) lessons, which are based on more fundamental aspects of teaching, but which are still related to the visible nature of activity.

Looking at aspects of teaching separately from curriculum coverage over time and from the teacher-class relationship is problematic. Indeed we should not expect that any one type of classroom organization or activity is necessarily better than others. Whole-class lessons or practical work can be organized badly or well, discussion can be banal or even confusing without the teacher's conceptual clarity, while insights can be promoted in lively ways suited to the particular class.[4] Hence the key feature is the *quality of teaching*.

This elusive feature seems to require another kind of distinction between lessons, this time in terms of matching the subject matter of activity to attainment, or ability range in the classroom, however that is defined.[5] These distinctions then determine the type of learning expected from the lesson. These lessons might take a range of different forms.

- *Revision and practice lessons*, where the subject matter is deemed well within the mastery level of most pupils in the class, having been largely covered earlier. Knowledge is just in need of refreshing and skills need to be applied in standard manageable contexts. The demands of the tasks are within or below the ability profile of the class. Pedagogically – i.e. in terms of teaching skills – revision and practice can be standardized and reliant on the textbook rather than the teacher. A good teacher, conducting such lessons (e.g. in preparation for public exams) can reduce students' boredom and antipathy with techniques for motivation and concentration. But the teaching materials, including revision books and programmed learning software, have the greatest weight, while interactive pedagogy is secondary.
- *Instruction lessons on new topics*, where fresh knowledge is introduced or skills applied in new contexts. The assumption is that the level of the new knowledge is matched to the range of ability or attainment in the class. Surprisingly we can include in this category both instruction and open-ended investigation or problem solving lessons. Students either assimilate knowledge given in their own ways and at their own levels, or follow their own different lines of inquiry, working also at their own level. Pedagogically, teaching a new topic or skill, at levels appropriate to a particular class, requires subject proficiency by the teacher and 'connectionist teaching' if it is to lead to understanding rather than memorizing of

procedures. Connectionist teaching is understood mainly as connecting concepts across topic areas, as in the oft-mentioned example of percentages, fractions and decimals. So, here the teacher's role crucially includes subject knowledge at levels above that of the class, and is at least as important as the teaching materials. The appropriate curriculum this time must be in the teacher's head, and connected. Interactive pedagogy is a bonus but again it is secondary. An interesting transmission of correct knowledge is preferable to confusing explorations, however lively or enjoyable they may be. But of no less importance is connecting the formal mathematics of the syllabus with the informal knowledge of the pupils, including handling misconceptions. That is the constructivist teaching in the sense of pupils building up their knowledge. For this aspect of pedagogy, the skills of listening to children and engagement with their ideas are needed.

- *Challenge and reflection lessons*, where the subject matter lies beyond that which the students can easily process, so that they need actively to explore new territory to construct or gain understanding. The aim is to develop not only the concepts, but the thinking power itself, and to develop 'learning to learn' skills that allow for further autonomous development by the student. The pedagogy in challenge lessons aims to build capacity and processing power in the students rather than transmit specific knowledge. The teaching materials are subsidiary to the interactive and responsive skills of the teacher. Crucially, deficiencies in subject knowledge by good teachers can be compensated for by a genuine open approach and a focus on construction of higher-order concepts through interactions in the classroom. Teachers would quickly build up their mathematics through practice: something that is unlikely in instruction teaching except as memorized procedures, or where an investigative approach is used in an 'anything goes' way. To be effective, challenge lessons require a new set of teaching skills, currently labelled 'cognitive intervention', to distinguish them from the more common type of interventions such as correcting errors, helping with solutions or just 'telling'.

We can usefully construct a 'semi-hierarchy' of the three types of teaching in terms of the learning outcomes of lessons (see Figure 6.1). Some revision and practice work is a prerequisite for instructions in new topics, and both are

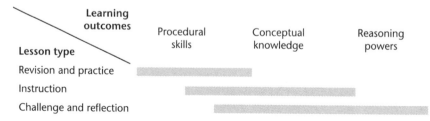

Figure 6.1 'Semi hierarchy' of learning outcomes dominant in the three types of lesson

prerequisites for a challenge and reflection lesson. In a challenge lesson, the agenda shifts gradually from concepts that are relatively well-known, or easily remembered, to those that follow from these, then on to areas not yet fathomed. The pupils are led to explore and make sense beyond their current powers of reasoning, so as to build up those powers in their own terms, and are only then perhaps offered some formalization, if at all. Taking the inverse direction in this hierarchy, the challenge lessons aim to raise the students' general reasoning capacity to process information, which makes assimilations and anchoring of concepts in their minds easier, therefore reducing the need for constant revision and memory.

How does all of this work out in practice? We first look at an example, then analyse it to see how general the features are.

Example of the flow of a thinking lesson[6]

The following is based on typical interactions in a 'Thinking Maths' lesson planned for the lower secondary and upper primary classroom. Included are some typical answers to key questions; examples of the teacher's further questioning; and some comments on the agenda at each step. In this scenario, pupils' responses to each key question or a set of related questions are collected after two to five minutes. Pupils' responses to the teacher's follow-up questioning, however, could be expected immediately. In both cases the teacher writes on the board some of the key words and phrases that the pupils use.

Engagement question: What do you think a 'digit' is?

Typical outcome and questioning flow

Pupils (Ps):   A number; digital camera; digital radio; digital TV; small number; fingers.

Teacher (T):   So many ideas you have! So what is the difference between a number and a digit? Is 376 a digit?

Ps: A digit is one number; a digit is a single number; 376 is a three-digit number.

T: So what else can we call a digit? And how many different digits are there?

Ps: Figure; numeral, 1 to 9, no! You also have 0.

Commentary

This short 'oral starter' allows near-full engagement in the class since everyone working from National Curriculum Level 2 upwards has something relevant to say. It builds on intuitive knowledge, links with natural language and mobilizes fragmentary prior knowledge. The teacher maintains motivation by accepting all answers and gently steering talk towards a mathematical step.

Question 1

In these simple sums, the star (*) stands for a single digit. It could be different or the same. I am really not interested in the answer, because that is easy, but in the way you get it.

1a $12 + * = 19$
1b $*** + 150 = 257$
1c $* + 8 = * 4$

Typical outcome and questioning flow for 1a

Three typical responses from pupils, P1–3, are listed then each is examined separately.

P1:   Just count on till you reach 19.
T: And what possible mistake is common when we count on?
Ps: You shouldn't count the 12; just keep track of the numbers after the 12.
P2:   You need 7 to go with 2 to make the 9.
T: How can we work on digits separately from each other? What could we call the 2 and the 1?
Ps: The ones and the tens; depends on where the digit is.
P3:   Take away 12 from 19.
T: Why does that work? What can we call this method?
Ps: If you take away one of the numbers from the total you get the other; you are doing the opposite; you reverse; doing the inverse operation, going backwards.
T: [Summarizing] So in this first easy sum you either used counting on, or the place or position of the digit, or the inverse or opposite. A simple question, but look how much thinking you can do!

Typical responses and questioning for 1b

Ps: Just take the 150 away; you need 100 to make the two hundreds, and then a 7; you can count on if you want; too long; boring; count on 100 then 7 more.
T: Can you recognize the same methods you used for the first sum? Can you describe them for me? [Rhetorical/consolidation questions]

Typical responses and questioning for 1c

Ps: That was hard; you can have anything; no, you cannot have more than 9 for the first star, but 9 and 8 does not make something with 4; I tried 5 first then went up to 6; the star on the right can only be 1.
T: Why is that?
Ps: Because you cannot have two single digits adding to 20-something.

T: And why is that?
P: The most two digits add up to is 18; 9 and 9.

Commentary

The teacher extracts key ideas on the methods used, including trial and improvement, and puts those on the board as reminders of methods. The class has now been mobilized to tackle harder questions.

Question 2

What do you notice about these calculations? Explain why this happens.

2a   * + 8 = 2 *
2b   2 * + 4 = 1 *

Then find out how many solutions are there to this calculation.

2c   33 + * = 4 *

Typical outcome and questioning flow

Ps: Something wrong; wrong sums; you can't have that; trick question.
T: Why is that?
Ps: Two single digits cannot add to 20 anything; the most the first star can be is 9, and that adds up to 17; the least the right-hand can be is 20 and there is no single digit to add to 8 to make 20-something.

Commentary

For both 2a and 2b pupils move from puzzlement to offering composite statements. They also realize that there is more than one solution for 2c, and that the range of solutions relies on the 'largest or smallest digit you can have'. The notions of the maximum and minimum are now made explicit as constraints in a chain of reasoning to prove or disprove mathematical ideas accessible to most of the class. Enough vocabulary has been practised and the class is now mobilized at about National Curriculum Level 4, to tackle further challenges. But even pupils who are working below Level 4 would by now have some insights, however hazy, of the constraints and at least a view of mathematics as something knowable through arguments about what is possible and not possible.

Question 3

Find the missing digits: explain how you solved the problem.

3a   3 * 6 + 5 * = 383
3b   8 * 3 − 7 * = 815
3c   8 * × *6 = 2158

Typical outcome and questioning flow

Each possible method requires a sequence of steps that have been used singly or in pairs before. For 3a, for example:

Ps: You need something to add to 6 to give you 13, so that must be 7. Then you take away 57 from the 383.

Or:

Ps: Take 5 away from 8, leaving 3, but really must be 2, because you need a 3, which means 13, which means you need 7 units.

Or:

Ps: Easier to put them underneath each other, so you can see the carry over.

Commentary

Exploring questions with three-digit numbers in both addition and sub-traction leads to composing a long chain of reasoning. While the teacher need not demand accurate formulations, the pupils will appreciate the powers involved in working out such sums, and how place value, decomposition and inverse are put together. Question 3c relies heavily on a sense of the size of numbers, rounding down and up to the nearest 10, and coordinating that with the unit numerals in the outcome of multiplication of units. This is best worked on with a calculator.

Question 4

In these questions the digits must be different. Find the largest total possible for a sum. Explain why it is the largest. Find the smallest total possible and explain.

4a $* * + * * =$
4b $* * \times * * =$
4c   Working in pairs, devise one or more similar questions, First try them on each other to make sure they are solvable. Then explain what makes them have a solution or not.

Commentary

These are questions for further consolidation, and in the case of 4c an extension at Levels 5 and 6. They address subtleties of the use of place value, within various constraints.

Agenda and structure of the example lesson

It is evident that the activity has a series of objectives, rising in steps of thinking demand. The best description of the objectives may be 'to explore how inverse arithmetic operations combine with place value and sense of number size, and how that is linked to what is possible and impossible'. You cannot share such an objective with the class at the outset. You could however talk about it in informal ways at the end of the lesson. It seems best in this case to talk about an 'agenda' rather than about objectives. This is not pedantic, but allows for the multiplicity of responses in the exploration of 'big ideas' in mathematics at different levels. Crucially, 'agenda' indicates issues to handle, whether arriving at a conclusion or not, rather than points to be reached by all.

The lesson has a structure of rising thinking demand in three or four episodes or cycles, each with an introduction, independent pair/group work and plenary phase. Each episode deals with a few questions at a time, first to build up confidence in ways of formulating ideas, then successively to integrate these ideas. The activity flow could be seen as an example of the use of 'mini-plenaries' currently promoted by innovative mathematics teachers. There is much flexibility in mini-plenaries. In response to some rich discussion and engagement that indicate that the class is groping for higher-order ideas, the teacher would decide to prolong an episode beyond what is originally planned, or even make a diversion. Alternatively if the class shows ready mastery of the concepts, then the episodes are shortened. Hence the same activity could take 30 minutes in one class, an hour or two in another.

In most Cognitive Acceleration in Mathematics Education (CAME) lessons there are at least two cycles, the earlier of which is relatively 'closed', in the sense that the teacher aims for agreement in the class, while the later can be left open, with the hope that the pupils will still be mentally engaged with the issues after the lesson. In the example of the missing digits activity, the lesson may end with no agreement on the best methods for solving Questions 3 and 4. For the higher attainers it may end with them still thinking about the conditions necessary for a number sentence of this type to have a solution.

Familiar curriculum is covered here without the need for memorizing procedures. Indeed the pedagogy encourages the sharing of informal descriptions. The teacher could suggest to pupils who come up initially with recently-taught formal phrases that they try to explain using natural language: 'Suppose you have not been taught this, how would you have described it or worked it out?' or 'How would you describe this to someone much younger than you?' The flow of activity shows the hierarchical nature of the three types of lessons discussed earlier. There is indirect 'revision and practice', more meaningful for not being routine. There is acquisition of new knowledge, skills and understanding through exploration of methods. Then there is stimulating thought beyond pupils' current capacity. Pupils struggle to link a few concepts, equivalent in their minds to struggling to coordinate several muscles in complex physical exercise.

Why can we not have all our lessons like this? One answer is that pupils' entitlement to full curriculum coverage requires as many direct revision and practice and normal instruction lessons as challenge and reflection lessons. Another answer is that devising good challenge lessons requires more time than is currently available for curriculum development, with efforts based on thoughtful and theoretical considerations on the one hand, and on cycles of classroom trials and refinement on the other. (Principles of the design of thinking lessons are addressed in the latter stages in teachers' professional development programmes in Cognitive Acceleration through Science Education – CASE – and CAME.)

The main feature of a cognitive acceleration lesson is that it provides multiple possibilities for rich classroom interactions at a range of levels in the same context or activity. However, any one actual lesson in the classroom would allow only some of these possibilities to be exploited, since the teacher would act flexibly in response to what the pupils in that particular class actually offered within the time constraints. A tension arises therefore between what is given in written guidance for a lesson, or covered in a teachers' session on it, and the actual conduct in any particular class. Hence it seems best to view the exemplar lessons as 'optimally planned' in the sense of showing the full potential of the lesson when conducted without time constraints in a fully mixed-ability class.

An 'optimal plan' for a lesson?

Perhaps this is worth examining further. An 'optimal plan' for a whole-class lesson is suggested as:

- a scenario of an exploratory route from the lowest to the highest concepts in the given context;
- feasible in a class that includes the full range of attainment levels in the age group and sufficient time available.

Only part of that route is attainable in any one actual lesson with an actual class, given the constraints of time and the ability profile. But a lesson can be judged as more or less successful by the match the teacher can make between parts of the optimal plan and the actual 'offers' of ideas in the class in real time.

An optimal plan could be understood as aiming to maximize benefit in three broad dimensions identifiable in any one lesson, simply labelled here as the 'task', the 'talk' and the 'attitude':

- The 'task' dimension refers to the range and quality of pupils' thinking encouraged by the task. This is the cognitive dimension based on classical psychological theory. In whole-class teaching, this dimension covers cognitive engagement by pupils, appropriateness of the task across levels and significance of the mathematics concepts. The 'missing digits' activity engages pupils of all abilities from the outset, partly because it allows them to play 'detective' using unthreatening number clues. This engagement is maintained in subsequent planned scenes so that there are challenges appropriate for the full range of working levels in the class. At the same time the concepts handled – i.e. of coordinating place value with inverse operations and with number sense – are of major significance in curriculum terms.
- The 'talk' dimension refers to the social processes in the lessons. This is the dimension of pupil-pupil interactions, teacher-pupil interactions, and

the use of board and paper records in natural and technical language and representations. Pupils' responses to each key question are only expected after they confer in pairs and pairs of pairs to formulate ideas. The teacher responds with follow-up questioning based on their responses, guided by the overall plan of the lesson and the various routes possible towards higher-order thinking. The interactions would naturally involve scenes such as pupils using paper, the teacher highlighting on the board parts of the elements of the task, pupils coming up to the board, gesticulating and the use of natural or technical language (see Higgins, Chapter 5).

- *The 'attitude'* dimension refers to the culture of learning, covering beliefs and values in mathematics, in learning, and in collaborative work. This is derivative or a natural outcome over time from the cognitive and social dimensions. Accepting and engaging with all answers alone changes pupils' culture of learning. However, pupils' values and beliefs can be explicitly promoted by the teacher. Such interjections in the account above as 'So many ideas you have', 'I am not really interested in the answer' and 'Look how much thinking you can do even on a simple question' help to reinforce a new outlook in pupils and give them confidence that their thinking processes are worthwhile to build upon.

Using these aspects of the quality of teaching, a lesson can be judged fruitful either because it contributes well in them all, or because it compensates for weakness in one by a greater strength in the others. Of course there are issues like difficult behaviour, or extremes of ability in a class, which are outside the 'optimal lesson plan' and need a different kind of response, or, if anticipated, prior arrangements. In practice any lesson with five to ten minutes of lively participation, insights and creativity by pupils is memorable and effective. But the adage that 'creativity is 90 per cent perspiration and 10 per cent inspiration' applies here. In order to create this effective scene, much ground-work is needed, with the teacher groping for different handles on different pupils and orchestrating discussion leading to creativity and insight.

Conclusion

A flexible use of the three-part lesson structure enables many lessons:

- to have a lesson agenda that can be covered or explored at various levels of attainment, rather than single or multiple objectives to be achieved;
- to have more than one cycle of the three parts, linked in a hierarchy that ensures initial engagement and then maintains that engagement through appropriate challenges across the ability range in the class;
- to combine the curriculum agenda with explicit attention to classroom interactions, responsive teacher's questioning and developing pupils' positive attitude to mathematics, learning and collaborative work.

This flexibility cannot be assimilated by teachers except through cycles of collaborative practice and reflection over a period of time. In this they need tutors who themselves work with the teachers in ways analogous to the ways the teachers are asked to work with the pupils.

Notes

1 The Cognitive Acceleration in Mathematics Education (CAME) series of research projects started in Key Stage 3 in 1993, extended to Key Stage 2 in 1997, then to Key Stage 1 in 2001. It is a combination of two strands of applicable research that have origins in the Concepts in Secondary Mathematics and Science (CSMS) 1974–9 research. The strand working in school science continued with the application of Piagetian and Vygotskyan psychologies in tandem in classroom practice, the other empirically charted the details of pupils' misconceptions and progression in school mathematics and analysed pupils' responses to open tasks. For the main work of CAME see Adhami, M., Johnson, D. and Shayer, M. (1998) *Thinking Maths: Accelerated Learning in Mathematics* (Oxford: Heinemann). A readable book by Adey, P. and Shayer, M. on the theory of cognitive acceleration is *Really Raising Standards* (Routledge 1994).
2 DfEE (Department for Education and Employment) (1999) *Framework for Teaching Mathematics from Reception to Year 6* (London: DfEE, p. 15).
3 The 'Lesson objectives' have probably acquired extra weight because they are listed, following the key word 'Directing', as the first of the eight bullets under 'The focus on direct teaching' (page 11 of the NNS *Framework*). They are also much more concrete and visible than others like 'Questioning and discussing' and 'Evaluating pupils' responses'. The appeal to professionalism in deciding the structure of a lesson takes a much smaller space in the document than the long and separate lists of bullet points under the headings of the three parts (*Framework*, pp. 13–15). The tension between content and form is clear in the guidance to colleagues conducting INSET (e.g. the NNS *Guide for your Professional Development, Book 1: The Daily Mathematics Lesson*, DfEE 1999). It almost looks as if expert reform-minded educationists have written the text, but some executive or political adviser put it in a mould that undercuts its value. Clear statements on flexibility and professional judgement (e.g. pp. 16–24) are to be delivered to teachers in strict timed order. Not only are the intended audience of teachers treated as trainees in a purely technical course, but the tutors themselves are told in prominent coloured boxes they should spend 7 minutes on this point an 3 minutes on that. They are also told that the key issues to be discussed for 5 minutes at the end of a 20-minute slot are the five bullet points on OHT 1.4, not, as expected in any responsive educational setting, what the particular audience raises, in their own words. So ironically the teachers are given lectures that they should not give lectures to children.
4 Margaret Brown (2002) has written 'Researching primary numeracy', in A.D. Cockburn and E. Nardi (eds) *Proceedings of the 26th Annual Conference of the International Group for the Psychology of Mathematics Education*, pp. 1–30

(Norwich: University of East Anglia), on the assigning to observed lessons of scores that were based on characteristics of effective teaching. A possible but low correlation with average gains was found in the given methodology of observation, ranking and tests. The research confirms that the effect of teaching factors on pupils' gains is relatively small when many classes of the same age are compared, although it is more salient for a particular class across the years.

5 Reed Gamble, an educational consultant in Yorkshire working on CASE has developed a similar typology.

6 The activity chosen as an example has a focus nearer to the mathematics school curriculum than to more general reasoning typical of most other thinking lessons. The thinking demand level of coordinating aspects of the number system and operations, with attention to both possible outcomes and constraints, would not exceed the 'concrete generalization' level in Piagetian terms (or 'relational level' in terms of Biggs and Collis and their 'SOLO taxonomy) (see Biggs, J.B. and Collis, K.F. *Evaluating the Quality of Learning: The SOLO Taxonomy*, New York: Academic Press 1982). This corresponds roughly to the National Curriculum Levels 5 and 6 boundary. Hence the activity is suggested for both secondary and primary classes and can be fruitfully repeated in the same class with modified questions. The thinking demand level would rise if principles of designing workable questions are explored by the students, or if principles of the base-10 number system itself are investigated (e.g., through comparison with binary, hexadecimal, or base-5 systems). For a report on primary CAME see the author's chapter in Shayer, M. and Adey, P. (eds) *Learning Intelligence* (Open University Press 2002).

7

Word problems: Cinderellas or wicked witches?

Mike Askew

'You've forgotten to underline the date.' There is not much that I can remember of my primary mathematics lessons (actually, I am old enough for them to have been arithmetic lessons) other than doing curve stitching with a student teacher (what was that about?) and the importance of underlining the date. I never came to understand why the latter was so important, but it stuck with me.

Going into numeracy lessons these days I see a lot of underlining going on: not just of the date, but of 'key words' in word problems. Keys that will unlock the casket and reveal the mathematical operation needed to solve the problem? The only trouble is, evidence suggests that children are not getting much better at solving word problems. There must be a lot of wrong keys and rusty locks out there.

Other than issuing children with sets of skeleton keys and oil cans, how can we help them get better at solving word problems? Some would argue that this is not the right question to be asking. Instead the question should be 'why expect them to solve word problems at all?' Word problems are something of the castor oil of the mathematics curriculum: fairly unpleasant but possibly good for you. But just as some nutritionists argue that a balanced diet means you do not need food supplements, so some educationists would argue that word problems are an unnecessary supplement to a balanced mathematics curriculum (and actually have the opposite effect to that of castor oil).

Teachers seem not to like word problems. Many have asked me why these are used to 'trick' children in assessments: 'they can do the calculation when it is presented to them in numbers, but why put it into a context when it simply confuses them?' Children at best tolerate doing word problems and some do become skilled at 'seeing through' the context and cutting to the chase of the calculation. This was beautifully illustrated by an anecdote told to me by a mathematics adviser.

A teacher had explained that she had been working with her class of 10-year-olds on the notion of redundant information in word problems. She had explained that not all problems needed to contain only the exact information and that additional information could be added, information that may not be necessary for solving the problem. She set the children off to write some word problems with redundant information but was surprised to find that many of the children were coming up with problems like:

> Three cars go on a trip. If there are four people in each car, how many people went on the trip?

Asked what was the redundant information in such a problem, the children replied 'Oh, all that stuff about cars and trips'.

Given the general unpopularity of word problems and the fact that they seem difficult to teach and learn, is it only test setters who care for these Cinderellas of the curriculum? In this chapter I want to argue that perhaps one difficulty is the popular perception of the purpose of word problems. If we were to change what we think word problems can offer to the curriculum, and change how we think about the way to approach them, then they might provide a vehicle for some rich classroom discussions; help children (and teachers) appreciate more fully what it means to think mathematically; and be allowed to go to the ball.

Vertical and horizontal mathematizing

Visiting a Year 3 class a couple of years ago, I joined a group of children who were struggling to solve this word problem:

> Mrs Chang bought some video tapes. She bought five tapes each costing the same amount. She spent £35. How much did each tape cost?

In the oral and mental starter part of this lesson, the children had been working on the five times table and had shown an impressive knowledge of this, dealing with calculations such as 35 divided by 5 with confidence. Yet this problem was stumping them. Each child in the group was approaching it using trial and improvement: guessing what the price of one tape might be (say, £6) and then using repeated addition to find the price of five. Depending on whether or not that total was greater or less than £35 they adjusted their estimate, recalculated and continued in this fashion until they 'hit' £35.

Taking individuals aside to talk about this problem, I presented them with a similar situation:

> Mr Chang bought some video tapes. He bought some tapes costing £7 each. He spent £42 pounds. How many tapes did he buy?

The children had no difficulties with this. Each of them counted on in sevens, putting out one finger for each count, until they reached 42 and saw that they had put out six fingers. Several spontaneously commented that this was a much easier problem than the other one.

Part of the reason why the Mr Chang problem is easier than the Mrs Chang problem may be the familiarity and 'realness' of the context. When we go shopping we usually know the price of each item; it is rare that we need to find the price of an individual item given a total price. But I want to suggest that the reason for the second problem being so much easier than the first goes beyond familiarity with the context. To explore this, I shall draw on the notions of 'vertical' and 'horizontal' mathematizing (Treffers 1991).

When acting in the world, some 'problems' are solved by direct action: I want a nail in the wall, I hammer it in. But problems in classrooms, and particularly word problems, usually require setting up some representation or model to 'act' upon, rather than act on the actual situation. The children discussed above did not go and get real video tapes to help them, they used their fingers to represent the tapes. Fingers are still part of the real world but not part of the world of video tapes. So in the course of setting up this representation, the children have engaged in the act of mathematizing the situation. And this is a horizontal mathematizing: a move from 'the perceived objects to the world of symbols' (Treffers 1991: 32). Even though fingers can still be perceived they have been used not as fingers *per se* but as a representation of something else. A model has been set up and horizontal mathematizing has taken place.

But setting up a model in this way is not the end of the story. The model itself may have to be adapted and changed: shifts may be made in the world of representations and symbols. Such shifts would involve vertical mathematizing.

Horizontal mathematizing

An analysis of the mathematical reasonings involved in the Mr and Mrs Chang problems illustrates the complementary processes of horizontal and vertical mathematizing. Through analysing in detail the processes involved in these two problems, I hope to show why solving either of them is a much more complicated process than it might first appear to be.

Taking Mr Chang's problem first, stripping the essence of the problem out of the context leads to 'reading' the problem as 'what do I have to multiply 7 by to get 42?' This can be expressed as an initial mathematical model:

$$7 \times \square = 42$$

This is the mathematical model that the children implicitly worked with when counting on in sevens to 42. And it is one that they found easy to work with. (Note that here, and in what follows, I am interpreting $7 \times \square$ as '7 multiplied by something' not '7 times something'. The children, in counting on in sevens with their fingers, were figuring out what to multiply seven by, or times it by.)

Turning to Mrs Chang, the essence of her problem is 'what number do I have to multiply by 5 to get 35?' Symbolically:

$$\square \times 5 = 35$$

This is more difficult to represent in the physical world – you have to guess at what goes in the box and hence the children's difficulty with this problem.

Vertical mathematizing

Although the children set up representations of the problem through horizontal mathematizing, none of them went on further to recast the model through vertical mathematizing (i.e. working with the symbols). Further analysis shows why this is a far from straightforward process.

In the Mr Chang problem, where an initial mathematical model of $7 \times \square = 42$ was set up, we can use the fact that division is the inverse of multiplication to set up the mathematically equivalent model $42 \div \square = 7$. Now this mathematical model is not the easiest to solve. As adults we 'know' that an equivalent equation is $42 \div 7 = \square$. But note that this is only equivalent mathematically. If we perform horizontal mathematizing in the reverse direction, from the mathematical world to the real world, $42 \div \square = 7$ and $42 \div 7 = \square$ do not lead to the same situation. 'What do we have to divide 42 by to get 7?' ($42 \div \square = 7$) is a question that arises from very different situations from those that give rise to 'what do we get when 42 is divided by 7?' ($42 \div 7 = \square$). Compare 'I want to put 42 apples equally into seven bags, how many do I have to put into each bag?' with 'I want to put 42 apples into bags, with seven in each bag'.

Strictly speaking, to get from $42 \div \square = 7$ to $42 \div 7 = \square$ there is an intermediate (and largely implicit) step in the vertical mathematizing process:

$7 \times \square = 42$
$\square \times 7 = 42$
$\square = 42 \div 7$

Since most adults just 'know' that seven sixes are 42 these vertical mathematizing shifts are usually not necessary (or at least not done consciously) and this level of analysis may have the feel of a sledgehammer to crack a nut. But both the need for and the power of this vertical mathematizing become clearer if we make the numbers less familiar. Suppose Mr Chang is a wholesaler who buys some stereos at £78 each and spends a total of £1404. Which would you solve

$78 \times \square = 1404$ or $1404 \div 78 = \square$?

The latter is more straightforward to calculate, but, as pointed out above, does not actually 'mirror' the action of the real-world situation. Mathematical equivalence does not correspond with real-world equivalence.

Perversely, the vertical mathematizing steps in the Mrs Chang problem are more straightforward. Because multiplication is commutative, $\square \times 5 = 35$ can be vertically mathematized in one step to:

$5 \times \square = 35$

But notice that the children did not do this. Instead they took guesses at what might go in the box (I am not suggesting of course that they were aware of doing this). Although they might 'know' that $\square \times 5 = 5 \times \square$, when it comes to 'uncoupling' from the real-world context and moving around the mathematical world instead, children find this difficult.

Other contexts

This lack of 'match' between the physical world and the mathematical world is not confined only to problems involving multiplication and division. Consider this pair of 'simpler' problems:

I have £203 in my wallet and spend £198. How much do I have left?
I have saved £5 towards a CD player costing £203. How much more do I have to save?

Most adults, and many children, would have little difficulty solving either of these problems. I would expect that many people would solve the first problem by counting up from 198 to 203 and the second by taking away 5 from 203. But look again at the relationship here between the situation in the problem and the method of solution. The first problem involves a 'take away' situation: 198 is removed from 203. The efficient method of solution treats the calculation 203 − 198 as though it were 'find the difference'. The reverse happens in the case of the second calculation. The 'situation' is 'find the difference': what is the difference between the amount that I have and the amount that I want? However, the effective mathematical solution method treats the numbers and the relationship between them as 'taking away': remove 5 from 203. Had I saved £198 then I am likely to find the difference by counting up. One aspect to explore with children is when a shift in strategy is sensible: if I had saved £89 would I count up or count back?

My point again here is that in both cases subtle but important vertical mathematizing shifts occur and that these are so subtle that experienced problem solvers are not likely to be aware of them happening. However, novice problem solvers may have difficulty in making such shifts.

I suggest that there are three steps going on here:

1 translating the 'problem' into a mathematical model;
2 dealing with the mathematical model;
3 reinterpreting the solution to the mathematical model in terms of the problem.

The difficulty for children is that dealing with Step 2 means 'uncoupling' the mathematics from the context of the problem. To illustrate this with the first 'spending' problem:

1 spending £198 out of £203 is equivalent to the mathematical model 203 − 198;
2 looking at the numbers involved here, a sensible 'reading' of 203 − 198 is 'find the difference' between the two numbers;
3 the difference between these two numbers is 5, so I must have £5 left.

Note that Steps 1 and 2 are quite independent. If I had £203 and spent £5 then I would probably calculate 203 − 5 by doing a 'take away' (i.e. counting back). Whether I spend £198 or £5, the real-world situation is the same: taking away. But this real-world situation does not in and of itself determine the best method of carrying out the mathematical calculation. That is determined by looking at the numbers, the calculation and the relationship between these.

Experienced problem solvers are probably not aware of these steps that they are going through, they just happen automatically. We need to help children 'unpack' what they are doing to help them understand the processes that they are going through.

From the mathematical world to the physical

There are times when the reverse process might be called into play – horizontal mathematizing (real world) to help better understand the mathematical world. In a (setted) class of low attaining 8-year-olds, the teacher posed two problems:

> I went out and bought some pencils and rulers. If I bought 20 pencils and 8 rulers how many items were in my carrier bag?

> On the way home the carrier split and some things fell out. If six things fell out, how many were left in the bag?

By and large the children managed to solve the first problem, but several seemed to be having difficulty with the second. One boy in particular looked most bemused, and when the teacher asked what the matter was, he replied 'Miss, did you drop pencils or rulers?' What a splendid opportunity that might have been for him to go off and explore the different combinations of pencils and rulers that might have been dropped and whether or not this made a difference to the final total. But of course this was not part of the objective for that day's lesson and he was told that it didn't matter: 'Just do 28 take away 6'.

Key words

One of the implications of the above analysis and the need to distinguish between vertical and horizontal mathematizing is that it calls into question the notion of word problems having the 'key' to the mathematics in the wording of the problem. The wording of the problem is going to reflect the 'action' of the real-world context. By equating this with the 'action' of the mathematical-world solution we may be restricting children's ability to do vertical mathematizing.

As an aside, I think that there are also difficulties with the way that we talk with children about problems. What does it really mean when we ask 'what is the problem (or word) telling you to do?' Problems cannot speak, we can only interpret them and bring meaning *to* them, not take meaning *from* them.

The current approach emphasizes the deductive and logical approach. Each problem is treated on its own – how can we figure out what this particular problem requires us to do? By working on problems one at a time and in isolation from each other they are treated as self-contained 'islands' where everything you need is there in that one situation. A teaching approach that could challenge this would be to present children with pairs of problems (much as I did above). By exploring why one or the other may be more easily solved, children's insights into the nature of problem solving could be deepened.

I suggest also that we might make more use of analogical thinking in problem solving. Rather than treat each problem afresh, the experienced problem solver has knowledge of a wealth of problems, some of which provide generic 'archetypes' that can be used to decide what category of problems a specific example fits into. For example, take problems involving division, where a decision has to be made about whether or not to round up the answer when there is a remainder. When I work with teachers on such problems more often than not people talk about them in term of likeness to an archetypal such problem. Popular archetypes include 'egg boxes' (you need to round up the number of boxes for eggs when there is a remainder) or 'buses' (rounding up the number of buses so that everyone can travel).

So, rather than looking for key words, a more productive question to ask might be 'is this problem like any other that you have ever done?' Children's initial responses to such a problem are likely to focus on the surface features of the context: it's about money or beetles. But over time they can be encouraged to think structurally about the situation.

Instead of working on sets of problems that are related through the fact that they share a context, children might be given sets of problems that are structurally similar, again encouraging analogical thinking. The work of the Cognitively Guided Instruction project (Carpenter *et al.* 1983) provides a detailed breakdown of such structuring. For example, simple addition problems can be broken down as:

- *change* – a given quantity is increased; or
- *combine* – two separate quantities are brought together.

Each of these can give rise to further categories of problems depending on the position of the 'unknown' in the 'story'. For example, within change problems we can have:

- *end unknown* – four frogs were down a well when three more jumped in;
- *change unknown* – in the morning there were four frogs in the well, by the afternoon there were seven;
- *start unknown* – three more frogs jumped in and then there were seven.

Introducing children to the language of 'change', 'combine' and so forth may help them to establish generic sets of problems, especially if these are accompanied by vivid context images that can form the basis of archetypal problems.

Conclusion

In his book, *The Real World and Mathematics* (1981: 8), Hugh Burkhardt proposes the following taxonomy of problems:

- *action problems*: problems, the solution to which may directly affect everyday life (how can I finish writing this chapter and go out to the cinema?);
- *believable problems*: problems which could be action problems (for oneself or others) but are not at the moment (how can this book get edited?);
- *curious problems*: problems that intrigue, either because the context is interesting or the analysis is (why do steel ball bearings sink but steel ships float?);
- *dubious problems*: existing only to provide dressed-up exercises (how many eggs in five egg boxes?);
- *educational problems*: essentially dubious but clearly or beautifully make an important point (what would 1p invested at 10 per cent compound interest in AD 1000 be worth now?).

As this list indicates, and as most people would agree, word problems as currently encountered are by and large dubious. But if the essence of mathematics is the setting up of and working with mathematical models, and if we treat word problems in such a way, then they might have a role to play in helping children better understand the processes of mathematizing. And with the increasing mathematizing of the world (from national test scores to pension prospects), informed and critical citizens need to be aware that mathematizing is not something that arises *from* the world, but something that is done *to* the world. In a small way, working on word problems might help begin to develop this awareness.

References

Burkhardt, H. (1981) *The Real World and Mathematics*. Glasgow: Blackie & Son.

Carpenter, T.P., Hiebert J. *et al.* (1983) The effect of instruction on children's solutions of addition and subtraction word problems, *Educational Studies in Mathematics*, 14: 55–72.

Treffers, A. (1991) Didactical background of a mathematics program for primary education, in L. Streefland (ed.) *Realistic Mathematics Education in Primary Schools*. Utrecht: Freudenthal Institute, Utrecht University.

The problem with problem solving

Lesley Jones

Introduction

The value of problem solving in mathematical education, as a way of using and applying mathematics, has been recognized for many years. The aim of this chapter is to consider the way in which primary schools can include a broad interpretation of problem solving as part of the mathematics curriculum.

The effect of the National Numeracy Strategy (NNS) on primary mathematics teaching in the UK was dramatic. Many teachers welcomed it for the structure and guidance it provided for the curriculum content. The *Framework for Teaching Mathematics from Reception to Year 6* (DfEE 1999a) provided detailed guidance about the planning and implementation of the curriculum in a way that was quite novel for UK teachers. Problem solving is identified as one of five strands in the *Framework*, and takes its place as the third of these five. However, when you look in detail at the subdivision of the strand into topics covered, the ambivalence of the NNS to this area of the curriculum is clear.

The *Framework* states that problem solving involves:

- making decisions: deciding which operation and method of calculation to use (mental, mental with jottings, pencil and paper, calculator);
- reasoning about numbers or shapes and making general statements about them;
- solving problems involving numbers in context: 'real life', money and measures.

The ambivalence is indicated by, on the one hand, placing problem solving as the third of three strands, thus giving it status and value in the curriculum, and by the inclusion of many investigative ideas in the supplement of examples. On the other hand, decision making is illustrated throughout with examples where the only decisions children are asked to make concern which operation and method of calculation to use. Problem solving is almost invariably reduced to the idea of 'word problems' which, in themselves, are thinly disguised calculations wrapped in words (see Askew, Chapter 7). The decision-making process seems to be operating within a very limited set of expectations. There is no suggestion here that children will be faced with problems in which they will need to decide how to tackle the problem, how to gather and organize the data and how to represent and communicate their findings.

The Key Objectives provide a very useful overview of the essential areas to be covered. For each year group, at least one of the Key Objectives relates to problem solving. Interestingly enough, this is usually the last in the list, perhaps because problem solving brings together all of the other knowledge and understanding. The choice of specific language used for the Key Objectives suggests that a limited view of problem solving has been taken:

- *Year 1:* use mental strategies to solve simple problems using counting, addition, subtraction, doubling and halving, explaining methods and reasoning orally.
- *Year 3:* choose and use appropriate operations (including multiplication and division) to solve word problems, explaining methods and reasoning.
- *Year 4:* choose and use appropriate number operations and ways of calculating (mental, mental with jottings, pencil and paper) to solve problems.
- *Year 5:* use all four operations to solve simple word problems involving numbers and quantities, including time, explaining methods and reasoning.

Thus the view of problem solving offered is one that involves choosing from a range of calculation strategies the most appropriate to apply to the problem presented. The context for this seems to be most frequently the 'simple word problems' (e.g. 'Mark got into the pool at 3.30 p.m. He swam for 40 minutes. What time did he get out?'). This view can be contrasted with the guidance in the National Curriculum (DfEE 1999b: 62) where it is suggested that children should be taught to approach problems in a variety of forms; develop flexible approaches to problems; and make decisions about which operations and problem solving strategies to use.

When reminded about these requirements in the National Curriculum, many teachers express anxiety about the amount of time they have available for teaching mathematics. Typical concerns are:

- 'How can we find time in an already crowded maths curriculum?'
- 'I am anxious that introducing reasoning to young children may detract from time spent acquiring basic number skills.'
- 'How can I fit problem solving in with everything else I have to do in the daily maths lesson?'

This chapter attempts to address some of these anxieties. It is unfortunate that a document that has provided so much support for teachers has also had the effect of narrowing the curriculum and squeezing out problem solving. This may not have been the intention of the NNS team, and there is plenty of evidence within the documentation that investigation is seen as a useful way for teachers to approach much of the content. However, the ambivalent approach to problem solving and the narrow interpretation of this to mean 'application of calculation methods' or 'solving word problems' has been widely interpreted to imply that solving 'real problems' no longer properly belongs in the mathematics curriculum. This concern seems to have been recognized in some later publications, such as the Five-day course materials and the support for more able pupils in Year 5. In the latter, the interpretation of problem solving is much wider than in earlier documentation, and teachers are encouraged to involve children in all stages of the problem solving process.

What is meant by problem solving and investigation?

The Cockcroft Report (DES 1982: 73) stated that 'The ability to solve problems is at the heart of mathematics'. Problems can appear in many forms, and may bring together different aspects of mathematics and other subject areas. A problem is an activity where the route to its solution is not immediately evident. There will usually be different ways to approach and solve the problem and the solution may involve areas other than mathematics. Investigations are usually more 'staged' and take less account of the world outside mathematics. They often arise from a particular finding in mathematics and involve the child (or adult) in exploring one or more aspects of that finding in the hope of making general statements. For example:

> Many of the whole numbers can be made from the sum of two prime numbers. Investigate which numbers cannot be made this way.

Problem solving and investigations are not entirely discrete, but the distinction helps to clarify the discussion in this chapter. It is also possible to distinguish 'puzzles' which are often 'closed' in the sense that there is just one solution. Many children (and adults) thoroughly enjoy puzzles and many arise within mathematics. Puzzles are one of the few popular forms of recreational mathematics and many daily papers and magazines include a section with mathematical and word problems.

Why is problem solving an important aspect of mathematics education?

Problem solving provides the opportunity to use and apply mathematical skills and knowledge. A mathematics curriculum without problem solving can be likened to a diet of PE in which children practise football or netball skills, but never get to play the game. It gives purpose and reason to mathematics and allows children themselves to see why and how mathematics is relevant to their lives.

When presented with a problem children need to exercise their ability to interpret the question, to decide on an approach, to apply their knowledge to the situation and use it to head towards a solution. Some children may prefer to work alone, but many will prefer to work in collaboration with others, requiring them to communicate their ideas and listen to others, to suggest strategies and take on board strategies suggested by others. They are very likely to need to make connections between different aspects of mathematics which they already know and they may well have to tackle or use aspects of mathematics which have not yet been studied. Working at this level offers the opportunity for using advanced cognitive skills such as 'synthesizing'. In fact, pupils solving problems have the opportunity to work at each of the levels of cognition identified by Bloom (1956) in his *Taxonomy of Educational Objectives*: knowledge, comprehension, application, analysis, synthesis and evaluation. This opportunity is not frequently available to children through a diet of mathematics where the emphasis is on knowledge and facts. It is important that all children are presented with ideas which challenge them at an appropriate level, and this is particularly true for the most able children.

What makes problem solving seem difficult to teach?

For many teachers, problem solving is an extremely challenging aspect of mathematics to teach. The NNS has encouraged and increased the amount of whole-class teaching. Teachers are more overtly 'in control' of the lesson, with the objectives and outcomes clearly identified. With problem solving and investigations, this type of control is not really possible. Where problems and questions are open-ended, children may choose different routes and emerge with different findings. Groups and pairs are likely to progress at different rates and it is unlikely that a problem solving session will fit neatly into the daily mathematics lesson. Many teachers are concerned about using an approach which may seem more 'ragged' and less controlled. They may doubt their ability to follow the children's reasoning, and may be concerned that children will not be able to reach a satisfactory conclusion in their investigation. It is interesting that many of these concerns could be paralleled in English or art lessons, yet teachers are usually quite happy to ask children to write a story, knowing that some will attack it with gusto and produce a minor work of art, while others will struggle, lacking some basic skills and possibly failing to complete the assignment.

It is always helpful for teachers to spend time exploring an investigation themselves, before working with pupils. If it is a 'rich' investigation it is unlikely that they will explore every avenue, but at least it gives an idea about interesting findings that are likely to emerge and it does help to match the investigation with the curriculum content that is planned. It will also help with following children's reasoning. Brown *et al.* (1998: 55) discuss the value of using the same problem over again and the way in which this can add insight into the children's approaches and help the teacher to 'listen better to the student's understandings of the problem'. They suggest that in using 'well rehearsed and frequently used' problems teachers use their skills most effectively.

Another concern is the requirement for written evidence. Children may spend a considerable time investigating or approaching a problem, but may have little to show for their efforts at the end. In these days of accountability, teachers feel it necessary to justify how their time has been spent and may prefer to have a neat exercise book to produce the written evidence. A 'writing frame' can be a helpful way of keeping a record of investigations attempted and some of the main findings (Rawson 1997). This might simply be a sheet where children fill in the starting point for the investigation and some of the findings which they found exciting and/or significant. Alternatively, it may be a set of headings that act as prompts for the children to write an account of their work.

As mentioned above, a major concern is the time factor. The introduction of the NNS has meant that mathematics is taught every day of the week and usually occupies at least an hour a day. The NNS guidance suggests a mental/oral starter, a main part of the lesson, then a plenary that brings together the main ideas. Some investigations or problems are suitable for exploration within such a time frame, but many are not. Some teachers may be uncomfortable about allowing topics to stray across two or more numeracy lessons, feeling that this endangers their long-term planning. However, since the introduction of the NNS it has been made clear that teachers have the flexibility to use the *Framework* as they see fit and to use their professional judgement in its implementation. The Five-day course refers to extended problems or investigations which might be spread over several lessons. The advice within the *Framework* document also suggests that time should be found in other subjects for pupils to develop and apply their mathematical skills. Some mathematical problems lend themselves well to cross-curricular work, involving such themes as packaging (design and technology), mapping and measuring (geography), explaining, enquiring and writing for different audiences (English) and data handling (science).

Teachers are also very concerned about the curriculum coverage, and feel that time set aside for problem solving will eat into the time they have available for teaching facts and skills. These fears indicate a very particular view of the way in which children acquire knowledge and one which is at odds with much cognitive research. Denvir and Brown (1986) produced some interesting findings when they tracked the knowledge that children acquired after a programme of teaching, showing that facts which had been taught and the knowledge which had been acquired had only a loose correlation. It is possible to target certain areas and attempt to improve children's understanding in them, but much of the time children acquire knowledge which is not high on the teacher's agenda, as they make their own connections and build their own schemata. Investigations and problems may well stray across specific subject content areas, but it is only through such work that application of mathematical skills can really take place.

Ways to introduce problem solving

Different ways of including problem solving and investigation in the mathematics curriculum will be considered in this section of the chapter. The ideal situation would be for teachers to adopt problem solving as a *teaching approach* that characterized their mathematics teaching every day. However, schools and teachers are different and some will feel able to adopt the approach more fully than others, given their local situation. Within the confines of the daily mathematics lesson investigations are easier to incorporate than problem solving. When completing their medium-term and short-term plans, teachers can identify investigations which fit in with each strand in the content areas planned. There are some suggestions within the *Framework*, but others can be collated and fitted into the appropriate place in the curriculum. It helps if teachers who jointly teach one year group plan together, as each will have his or her bank of familiar activities and these can be pooled.

When planning activities for the main part of the lesson, look at the possibility of 'opening up' questions. Rather than giving children a set of calculations to practise, give them a set of numbers and ask: 'How many calculations can you make using only these numbers?' In order to answer this, children have to use their reasoning skills to identify properties of the numbers and think about ways to combine them. There are some suggestions about using this approach in the NNS booklet *Mathematical Vocabulary* (DfEE 1999c).

'Following through' an activity can also help to extend the understanding of mathematics. For example, ask children to find a way to place the numbers 1 to 9 in a 3×3 square to produce a magic square, where all the rows, columns and diagonals add to the same total. Some children will complete this quickly. Follow it through by asking them:

- Can you see any patterns within the square?
- Where are the even numbers, where are the odds?
- What is the sum of two opposite corner numbers?
- Can you use your findings to suggest a different set of numbers that would make a magic square?
- How many of your findings apply to the new square?

Such investigation takes them into the structure of the problem and is likely to give them insight into different but related problems.

Introduce a 'problem of the week'. This might appear on a notice board in the classroom or corridor and ask for solutions to be added to the display or have a 'solution box' for children to post their solutions. It could be opened up to the whole school or kept within the class. You may decide to allow parental involvement, or to confine it to children only.

If your school has one day a week which is not dedicated to the daily mathematics lesson, this provides the ideal opportunity for a broader approach to problem solving, which can allow you to stray into other areas of the curriculum. A 'design and make' problem such as 'Design a box to carry a kitten to the PDSA' involves measuring and calculating, but might also involve using facts and opinions to argue a case, gathering evidence and presenting an argument. The children will have to consider the strength and suitability of different materials and finally find a way to design a box which is strong enough and suitable for its purpose. If it is possible to devote a whole day to the task, it can address many areas of the curriculum and involve the children in an interesting and meaningful project.

Differentiation in problem solving

One advantage of including problem solving in the mathematics curriculum is that it can provide an appropriate level of challenge for the most able children in a class. Children who have already developed a high level of knowledge and skills can use these and bring them together to tackle challenging problems. However, they will still have areas which need development. For instance, many able children find it difficult to record their work systematically and in a way which can be read and interpreted by others.

For some children it will be helpful to discuss ways of approaching the problem, to give them some ideas about the kinds of questions they need to ask and the type of approach which might lead to discoveries. A 'brainstorm' session where children each contribute their ideas can be useful, enabling the teacher to steer them into methods which are accessible and are likely to lead to success. It may also be useful to discuss the type of record keeping children can use, helping them to develop a systematic approach and keep track of their findings.

Children who struggle with mathematical ideas can be provided with a recording system, if appropriate, so that they can still engage with the mathematical problem, but are given the additional support of a structure within which to work. A 'writing frame' can help them to clarify the steps that are necessary in the problem solving process and find a way to approach the problem and identify the mathematics they need to use in its solution. Mathematics is a multi-faceted subject and different aspects appeal to different abilities. It is important to ensure that the problem 'diet' includes a range of different kinds of mathematics. Often, children who are generally seen as mathematical 'low attainers' show the greatest insight when faced with visual and spatial problems.

Another approach that can offer benefits to children of all abilities, but which is particularly supportive for the less able in a group, is to 'revisit' problems. By identifying a set of problems which are similar in their mathematical structure, but differ in their context, children can use the understanding gained previously to find solutions in the new context. One teacher-researcher who has used this system successfully is Vicki Zack (Zack and Graves 2001). Introducing similar problems, with a gap of about a month between, allowed children to gain confidence and competence in their approach. It can also be beneficial for children who have previously solved a problem as part of a group to work through it again individually, as this helps to embed into their own repertoire the systems and approaches used by the group.

Developing children's reasoning skills

Reasoning is a central skill in problem solving and children need to be given plenty of opportunity to develop their reasoning skills. It is also closely bound with communication skills. It is very difficult to assess children's reasoning ability if they are not able to communicate their ideas to others in some way. They need support and experience in order to develop their ability to communicate mathematical ideas and to verbalize their thinking. This is not always easy! Take a few minutes to investigate and explain one of the ideas set out below:

- The sum of two odd numbers is always even.
- The sum of three consecutive numbers is a multiple of 3.
- The product of three consecutive numbers is a multiple of 6.

When you have found a solution, try to justify your reasoning to a friend. Even when you have reasoned something out for yourself, explaining your reasoning and justifying your ideas can be very challenging.

However, children's ability to reason and justify their ideas can be developed. The NNS suggests that children are frequently asked to explain their reasoning. When there are opportunities to do so, take this a step further by asking children *why* something works. This is particularly valuable when dealing with general statements such as:

- Why have you put all those shapes together in one set?
- Tell me one way in which all these shapes are the same.
- Why do consecutive multiples of 3 switch from odd to even?
- Why are all multiples of 4 also multiples of 2?
- Why do multiples of 5 end in 5 or 0?
- What happens when we add two consecutive triangular numbers?

Encourage children to question each other about their reasoning and their hypotheses and to ask for clarification when they need it. This approach may take a while to establish, but it can help children not only to express themselves clearly, but to see the elements of mathematical argument that are necessary to provide justification for their findings. It should, ideally, be part of a whole-school policy, so that children develop and refine these skills over an extended period of time.

The questions listed below can help you to delve into children's thinking and help them to express their ideas. They could also prove to be a helpful *aide-mémoire* as a classroom poster so that children include them in their mathematical discussions as well.

Questions to prompt children to reason and justify their ideas
- Why do you think that happens?
- How do you know that?
- How can you be sure?
- Can you explain how that works?
- Can you explain it to a friend?

- Will it always work?
- Do you agree with him/her?
- How sure do you feel?
- Are you convinced?
- How can you convince her/me?

Problem types

Problems and investigations span a wide area and come in many different shapes and sizes. Figure 8.1 shows one way of considering problems, using two axes to represent the degree of openness and the complexity of the problem. It is interesting to note how many of the examples provided in the NNS fall into the category of 'closed' problems. This, of course, ties in with the aim of maintaining 'controlled, manageable differentiation' and keeping the class working together. Unfortunately, few closed problems provide an appropriate level of challenge for the more able children in a class and the opportunity genuinely to use and apply mathematical skills and knowledge is limited in such problems.

When planning to include problem solving in a teaching programme, teachers should try to include a variety of styles of problem. Different types of problem appeal to different children and teachers are often surprised by the level of children's involvement. Some show unexpected ability with problems involving 2D and 3D shape and space. Some prefer the safer environment of closed problems whereas others will rise to the challenge of open-ended or extended problems.

Sources of problems

There are many popular mathematics books on the market which are solely devoted to puzzles and problems, but other sources can be equally useful. Many of the primary mathematics schemes that have been written in the last 20 years contain ideas for investigations and problems. However, some of the most exciting and interesting ideas are those which arise from a personal interest of the teacher, or a question raised by children themselves. These may be concerned with improving the school environment:

- Redesign the classroom layout
- Establish efficient fire escape routes round the school
- Run a snack shop
- Share jobs fairly in the classroom
- Write to the council arguing for another lollipop person outside school

  Plan and run a school event
- Sports day
- A class visit
- Netball league fixtures

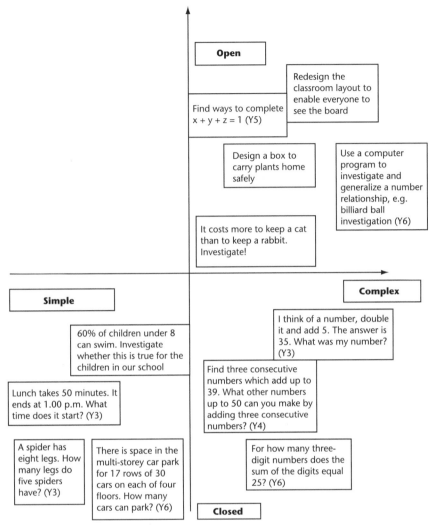

Figure 8.1 A classification of question types

- A fundraising event
- A maths trail

Design or make something
- An educational board game
- A chart for the weather
- A box to carry the hamster home
- A carton to contain four tennis balls

Use the news or data about current events to investigate
- Only 30 per cent of schoolchildren walk to school
- The average English family eats an acre of pizza a year
- 60 per cent of children under 8 can swim
- Children spend half their pocket money on sweets
- It costs more to keep a cat than a rabbit
- 10 per cent of 10-year-olds speak more than one language
- How long would it take to walk from Land's End to John O'Groats?

Develop ideas from children's literature
- *Jack and the Beanstalk:* scale problems, make a belt or hat for the giant
- *Tom Thumb:* design a house for Tom Thumb
- *Would you rather?* Would you rather have 100g in pennies or a 10cm stack of pennies?
- *Katie Morag Delivers the Mail:* problems with routes, weights of parcels, postage stamps
- *Bears Go Shopping:* packaging and stacking problems

Explore questions posed by children
- Who has the widest smile?
- Who can run fastest?
- Who lives furthest from school?
- How many words in a book?

Conclusion

The emphasis on National Curriculum test results and league tables pushed many teachers into a position where they felt their efforts should be concentrated on teaching 'mathematical facts' and knowledge of the curriculum content. Problem solving and investigation may have seemed like a luxury that they could not afford. Recognition of problem solving skills within the National Curriculum tests placed problem solving more clearly back on the agenda. Hopefully, teachers will continue to embrace the opportunity to broaden the mathematical experience of primary children through incorporating a wider view of problem solving in their classroom practice. Far from being a luxury we cannot afford, problem solving should gain its rightful place at the heart of the mathematical experience.

References

Bloom, B.S. (1956) *Taxonomy of Educational Objectives*. London: Longman.
Brown, L., Reid, D. and Zack, V. (1998) On Doing the Same Problem, *Mathematics Teaching*, 163: 50–5.
Denvir, B. and Brown, M. (1986) Understanding of number concepts in low attaining 7–9 year olds, *Educational Studies in Mathematics*, 17: 15–36 and 143–64.
DES (Department of Education and Science) (1982) *Mathematics Counts* (Cockcroft Report). London: HMSO.

DfEE (Department for Education and Employment) (1999a) *Framework for Teaching Mathematics from Reception to Year 6*. London: DfEE.

DfEE (Department for Education and Employment) (1999b) *The National Curriculum*. London: HMSO.

DfEE (Department for Education and Employment) (1999c) *Mathematical Vocabulary*. London: DfEE.

Rawson, B. (1997) Working with writing frames in mathematics, *Education*, 25(1): 49–54.

Zack, V. and Graves, B. (2001) Making mathematical meaning through dialogue: 'once you think of it the z minus three seems pretty weird', in C. Kieran, E. Forman and A. Sfard (eds) Bridging the individual and the social: discursive approaches to research in mathematics education, *Education Studies in Mathematics*, 46(1–3): 229–71.

Section 3

ASSESSMENT ISSUES

The two chapters in this section explore different, but related, approaches to assessment. Rosemary Hafeez worked in the Assessment Division at the Qualifications and Curriculum Authority (QCA) before becoming a mathematics inspector. In Chapter 9 she provides an overview of the approach to assessment found in a wide range of National Numeracy Strategy (NNS) materials, where the emphasis is on short-, medium- and long-term assessment, and compares this with specific recommendations made by a range of researchers. This leads, inevitably, to a comparison of the role and purposes of summative and formative assessment. The author argues that NNS materials do include advice on the latter, but that this has not been successfully communicated to schools, teachers, consultants or heads. She argues that many teachers see assessment as 'practising test-taking' and that too many children see it as something that 'labels them'. In the final section, ideas both from the NNS and research are drawn together into a nine-point list of suggestions for successful assessment to help improve teaching and learning.

Malcolm Swan has been involved in curriculum development for many years through his work at the Shell Centre and at the University of Nottingham. In Chapter 10 he considers an important aspect of formative assessment: the recognition of and ability to deal with children's misunderstandings and misconceptions in order to bring about learning. He shifts the focus away from the traditional view of teaching that sees misconceptions as things to be avoided or corrected through careful explanation, and argues that we should welcome misconceptions (which he calls 'alternative conceptions') as opportunities to engage children in learning through discussion. The author uses specific examples to explore the nature and causes of the mistakes that children make, and tries to show that many so-called misconceptions are actually unavoidable. He then describes the design principles of a teaching approach developed to generate the active learning of mathematics: an approach that involves the concept of 'cognitive conflict'. The chapter concludes with examples of two types of activity that have been found to generate this conflict and lead to purposeful discussion in the classroom.

Using assessment to improve teaching and learning

Rosemary Hafeez

This chapter will examine the recommendations of the National Numeracy Strategy (NNS) regarding assessment. These suggestions will then be developed further, in the light of recent research. The chapter will conclude with practical recommendations for teachers to improve teaching and learning.

Defining assessment

Assessment is the process that enables teachers to make judgements about what children know, understand and are able to do. This can be done by observation of children working on mathematical activities and by questioning them about their thinking as part of their normal daily routine. When this is used to inform future teaching it is called *formative assessment*. Assessment can also mean a test or a task, often at the end of a topic, term or year. When assessment happens after the teaching it is referred to as *summative assessment*: it summarizes learning.

Statutory assessment has been in place since shortly after the beginning of the National Curriculum. In the primary years, this takes place at the end of the Foundation Stage, at the end of Key Stage 1 and at the end of Key Stage 2. The outcome of statutory assessment for a child is either based on the Foundation Stage Profile or the award of a National Curriculum level. In addition to the end of stage assessments, teachers are able to use optional tests produced by the Qualifications and Curriculum Authority (QCA) to assess children in Years 3, 4 or 5.

The Numeracy Task Force

The Numeracy Task Force was set up to develop a national strategy for raising standards of attainment in mathematics. This followed concerns that children in England were not performing as well mathematically as their peers in other countries. The Task Force (DfEE 1998a) identified 11 factors that would ensure success in the teaching of numeracy. The sixth factor was assessment. The Task Force referred to a review of international research by Black and Wiliam (1998) regarding the effect of formative assessment on attainment, and their recommendations included the following points:

- teachers are clear about the progression of mathematical skills, knowledge and understanding;
- assessment is used to identify children's strengths and weaknesses;
- feedback is given to children about their strengths and weaknesses;
- children are involved in self-assessment and in setting their own targets;
- planning is based on information from assessment.

The *Final Report of the Numeracy Task Force* (DfEE 1998b: 59) contained the programme of training and support for schools just as the NNS was launched across the country. Chapter 3 of this report argued that: 'high quality formative assessment by teachers can make an important contribution to helping pupils improve their numeracy skills ... and ... in raising the standards of attainment overall'. It described how teachers should talk to children either individually or in small groups about their progress once a term. Summative assessment measures were recommended as a tracking mechanism.

The *Framework* for teaching mathematics

The *Framework for Teaching Mathematics from Reception to Year 6* (DfEE 1999a) was circulated as part of a three-day training programme run by local education authorities for each head teacher and their mathematics subject leader. Assessment, however, was not a focus of the training programme and was only referred to in passing. The main emphasis was on completing an audit of mathematics, the three-part daily mathematics lesson, the teaching of mental and written calculation strategies and planning how the *Framework* would be used.

The *Framework* (DfEE 1999a: 33) has a detailed section on assessment. It is described at three levels: short-, medium- and long-term. The purpose of short-term assessment is to:

- check that children have grasped the main teaching points in a particular lesson or unit of work, whether they have any misunderstandings that need to be put right and whether they are ready to move on to the next activity;
- check that children are remembering number facts and can use mental calculation strategies;
- give information which will help teachers adjust day-to-day lesson plans and brief any support staff or adult helpers about which children to assist and how to assist them.

The first two points are summative, the third is formative. The *Framework* also suggests that sometimes short-term assessment might take the form of a homework activity or a short test: 'tests of this kind should be followed immediately by marking and discussion with the whole class to give pupils feedback on their performance and what they need to do to improve' (p. 33).

The *Framework* describes medium-term assessment as mainly summative, assessing children's progress, their strengths and weaknesses, against Key Objectives in order to give parents feedback and to provide information for long-term assessment. The assessments should take place at the end of each half term, in the form of 'assess and review' days indicated in the medium-term plans. Teachers are again expected (p. 35) to: 'mark any written task that is part of medium-term assessment to give feedback to children on what they have achieved and how to improve . . . constructive written comments are more helpful than mere ticks and crosses, or scores "out of 10" '. Medium-term assessment should comprise feedback to children via a ten-minute target setting discussion focusing on the practical steps that they need to take to improve. The importance of informing parents about their child's targets is also mentioned.

Long-term assessment is described summatively as taking place towards the end of the school year, assessing progress against the Key Objectives for that year group, and against school and national targets. This is done through teacher assessment and the use of QCA tests, expressed as National Curriculum levels. Moderation of teacher assessments should involve all staff. The only reference to the use of long-term assessment formatively is that this provides information about children to be reported to their next teacher.

The mathematics audit

The booklet *Auditing Mathematics in Your School* (DfEE 1999b: 15) contains several sections. Neither the section on teaching nor the section on planning contains any reference to necessary adaptations based on assessment evidence. The section on assessment informs us that:

- Teachers use informal observations in class, quick-fire questions and some planned tasks to judge how children are getting on.
- Teachers' evaluations and assessments guide their planning and identify when pupils are ready to move on.
- Marking clearly shows what a child has to do to improve. Teachers identify misconceptions as opposed to careless slips when they mark. Comments help children to improve their work.
- Individual children have personal targets that are discussed regularly and updated.
- Teachers use the optional end-of-year tests for mathematics provided by the QCA. Test papers are analysed to see the kind of errors children are making.

- Records are manageable to maintain and easy for others to extract information from. There is a system of keeping more detailed records for children whose progress differs markedly from the norm.

These actions are almost all summative. The third action is formative but teacher-led.

The *Guide for your Professional Development, Book 2*

A pack of professional development materials, containing the booklet *Guide for your Professional Development, Book 2: Effective Teaching and the Approach to Calculation* (DfEE 1999c) was sent to each school to enable them to run an in-service education and training (INSET) day followed by staff meetings. The pack addressed 13 topics, one of which was assessment and record keeping. Short-term assessment was allocated 45 minutes of INSET time; medium- and long-term planning were allocated 30 minutes. The section on short-term assessment referred to the *Framework* and suggested that participants discuss how they monitored children's progress on a daily basis, related to five bullet points (p. 125):

- observe groups or individuals as they work on an activity or task, questioning them about the strategies they used;
- monitor individual children's performances as they respond when the teacher is working with the whole class;
- collect and evaluate carefully any written or recorded work done in class or at home;
- provide an occasional short informal test, either in written or oral form;
- analyse errors carefully, trying to determine if they are careless slips or basic misunderstandings.

These actions are all initially treated summatively. There is no suggestion that planning and teaching should be altered in the light of the assessment. However, the analysis of children's errors is then examined in more depth in the context of five children's work. Participants are then asked to use the assessment findings formatively to suggest teaching points. The section concludes (p.133) that 'The purpose of short-term assessment is to inform planning and teaching'.

The section on medium- and long-term planning ensures that teachers are familiar with the appropriate sections of the *Framework*. The activities in this section are based on assessment being done summatively at the end of a half term, a term or a year.

Assess and review lessons

Assess and review lessons are identified in the sample medium-term plans and they take place at the end of each half term. A pack, *Using Assess and*

Review Lessons (DfES 2001), includes 75 minutes of INSET time, probing questions for each Key Objective for each year group and nine sample lessons for Years 1, 3 and 5 with three video examples. The purpose of assess and review lessons is to give teachers a clear picture of which children have met or partially met the Key Objectives for their year. This then allows teachers to modify their teaching appropriately. The INSET time for a teacher to discuss how assessment impacts on planning and teaching is less than ten minutes.

Many other materials have been produced by the NNS, including 'Booster' lessons, 'Springboard' lessons, Transition and Unit plans. However, none of these add anything further regarding the importance of formative assessment. In addition to the publication of materials the NNS has funded training for head teachers, mathematics subject leaders and leading mathematics teachers. None of these training programmes has referred to the use of formative assessment explicitly.

Research on assessment

Inside the Black Box

Black and Wiliam (1998) undertook the most significant recent research on assessment, based on over 250 studies from around the world. The classroom is treated as a black box, the input is the teaching and the output is the attainment of the children. The research was based on these questions (p. 2):

1 Is there evidence that improving formative assessment raises standards?
2 Is there evidence that there is room for improvement?
3 Is there evidence about how to improve formative assessment?

There *is* evidence that improving formative assessment raises standards. Black and Wiliam found at least 20 studies which showed (p. 3) that 'strengthening the practice of formative assessment produced significant, and often substantial, learning gains'. In addition some of the studies showed that the less able children made more progress than the rest, thus reducing the overall attainment spread.

There is evidence of room for improvement. Reports including those from the Office for Standards in Education (Ofsted) highlighted a lack of good formative assessment. Classroom assessment practice encourages short-term learning for summative tests, where quantity and presentation are more highly regarded by teachers than understanding. Teachers were using assessment to complete summative records and not for analysing learning needs or adjusting future planning or teaching. These summative records are sometimes not even being used by the child's subsequent class teacher. Feedback to children often has a negative impact, reinforcing the notion that ability is innate rather than capable of being developed by effort.

A number of the studies researched by Black and Wiliam contained evidence about how to improve formative assessment. Recommendations included:

- Build children's self-esteem, giving them positive feedback about what they can currently do and what they need to do next to improve further, avoiding comparisons with other children. This requires a classroom culture where the teacher and all the children believe they can achieve.
- Involve children in self- or peer-assessment. They need to have a good understanding of their learning targets, what evidence of achieving those targets looks like and a clear picture of how to get there.
- Integrate opportunities for children to explain their thinking into all lessons. The atmosphere in the classroom should be conducive to innovation and appropriate time should be allowed to formulate thoughts, ideas and explanations.
- Use tests to identify individual strengths and weaknesses and give immediate feedback on how to improve, with structured time and support to develop children's learning further. Ideally the feedback should not contain marks or levels.

Black and Wiliam concluded that further work was necessary in a small number of schools in England to confirm the research findings. Alongside this it is vital that the good practice regarding formative assessment moves into policy; that standards are improved, not merely measured.

Assessment for learning

The Assessment Reform Group (1999) followed up the work of Black and Wiliam (1998) with some further advice about the urgent need to change policy. The current education climate focuses on comparisons of children, teachers and schools. Too many teachers see assessment (p. 5) as 'practising test-taking' and too many children see assessment (p. 5) as something that 'labels them'. Five key factors, stemming from the earlier work of Black and Wiliam (1998) are identified (pp. 4–5):

- the provision of effective feedback to pupils;
- the active involvement of pupils in their own learning;
- adjusting teaching to take account of the results of assessment;
- a recognition of the profound influence assessment has on motivation and self-esteem of pupils, both of which are crucial influences on learning;
- the need for pupils to be able to assess themselves and understand how to improve.

The pamphlet concludes with a range of proposals for the government, initial teacher training, continued professional development, inspectors, local education authorities and schools.

Unlocking formative assessment

Clarke (2001) builds on the work of the Assessment Reform Group (1999) with some practical examples. She focuses on the five key factors for successful learning:

- *Feedback*, oral or written, can come from the teacher, or from another child. It should relate directly to the learning objective and not administrative or presentation features. The feedback should identify how well the learning objective was met and what needs to be done next. Children need to understand their feedback and have time to put it into practice. If feedback is given orally during a lesson, development time is usually available. However if feedback is given in writing after the lesson, time needs to be built in to allow follow-up action. In a classroom with a supportive atmosphere and agreed ground rules, peers can give feedback.

- *Ensuring active involvement of children*, understanding the purpose of their learning and agreeing their own personal targets. It is important that they know when the learning has been successful and what the evidence might look like. They can play an active part in discussing this as part of the lesson starter. Agreed targets should be based on a list appropriate to the child's ability but not identifiably linked to a specific level.

- *Adjusting the planned teaching daily*, in the light of informal assessment of specific groups or children. Detailed notes need to be made at the end of a topic, indicating the starting point for different groups of children when the topic is returned to in the future.

- *Motivation and self-esteem* are crucial. It is vital that children understand that with time and effort they all have the ability to improve. Comparison with other children's performance can result in low self-esteem. Even for children who are successful, comparison with others can take the focus off their learning. Rewards including public celebrations take the focus off learning and replace it with an emphasis on doing better than others. It is important that teachers concentrate on the learning gains and that celebrations are done privately with the child.

- *Self-assessment* gives children ownership of their learning, something that they have control over and not something that is done to them. Teachers can help children structure self-assessment through the use of evaluative questions and modelled responses. Genuine evaluations by children that their work is too difficult or too easy provide valuable insights into their understanding, allowing learning to be improved by modifying future teaching.

Working Inside the Black Box

Following work in six schools in Medway and Oxfordshire, Black and Wiliam (2002) discussed further how formative assessment could be improved. The findings are reported under four headings:

- *Questioning*. Teachers need to ask questions requiring more thought and to allow appropriate time for children to consider and formulate their response. This can sometimes be done with a partner or a small group. All children are expected to contribute an answer even if it is incorrect. This allows teachers to get a clearer picture of the children's understanding in order to give immediate feedback.

- *Feedback through marking.* Comments should be given without grades; they should identify what the child has done well, what still needs to be improved and how that improvement can be made. Time must be allowed for children to follow up comments.
- *Peer-assessment and self-assessment.* Children need to understand what their learning goals mean and how they can reach them. Reference to the National Curriculum's level descriptions can be useful. When a supportive atmosphere has been established in the class, children are happy to ask each other for advice and to accept their suggestions for improvement. A traffic-light system of self-assessment can be used to pair children appropriately or to identify a group for focus teaching.
- *The formative use of summative tests.* Children can use test papers to identify questions that they are unsure of or those they are confident with. The traffic-light system and paired work can then follow. Children can also mark each other's test papers and then provide peer-tutoring.

Summary

Most of the NNS material gives too little emphasis to formative assessment. There is a lot of very useful information about formative assessment in the Numeracy Task Force publications (DfEE 1998a, 1998b), but this was not communicated well to schools or teachers. Most have long lost their copies of the two publications or if they do exist they are rarely referred to. The major emphasis is on summative assessment, driven by school targets for the percentage of children attaining Level 4 or above in the end of Key Stage 2 tests. The format of the QCA statutory or optional tests is not conducive to their use in identifying children's strengths and weaknesses on an individual, class or school level.

The suggestions in the *Framework* regarding immediate feedback following assessment tests or tasks are not explained explicitly in practical terms. It is noted that constructive comments are more useful than marks, however this is not emphasized strongly enough. Assessment is seen as a tracking mechanism against Key Objectives in order to report children's progress to their parents and their next teacher.

The *audit* booklet (DfEE 1999b) contains a useful checklist regarding assessment, with a good balance of formative as well as summative actions. However, this is teacher-led, with no input from the child. *Book 2* from the *Professional Development Materials 1 and 2* (DfEE 1999c) and *Using Assess and Review Lessons* (DfES 2001) place far too low a priority on formative assessment.

There is much more useful information regarding assessment from the research of Black and Wiliam (1998, 2002) and practical suggestions for implementation from Clarke (2001). The research shows clearly that the emphasis should be on formative assessment, in order to analyse learning and adjust teaching immediately, within the lesson if appropriate. There is also a strong need to involve children explicitly in agreeing and evaluating their learning, ensuring that feedback to them increases ownership and empowerment. Developing a supportive class environment is important, as is providing time to think and time to act on evaluation. It is more effective to teach less, but to teach it better.

Suggestions for successful teaching and learning

The suggestions from the NNS and research findings have been drawn together into nine points for successful assessment to improve teaching and learning.

1 *Class atmosphere.* Children need to know that you are working as a team of learners. You should explicitly refer to your own learning: 'I didn't realize that square numbers made squares until I was an adult! I arranged nine tiles in a square array. It is so helpful to use practical real-life things to help us understand maths'. They should feel able to challenge you and each other, in order to develop their own understanding. This can be encouraged by playing devil's advocate: '15 + 6 = 6 + 15 so 15 − 6 = 6 − 15!' If you have another adult working with you in the classroom, they can play the challenging or questioning role as a model for children. You could also use a puppet: 'What does factor mean, because I have forgotten!' Children also need to know that they can all improve and that ability is not innate. Careful use of flexible grouping for different aspects of mathematics is important as is the opportunity for open-ended whole-class activities.

2 *Subject knowledge.* You need a good understanding of the structure of learning mathematics, the hierarchy of skills, knowledge and concepts. The objectives from the *Framework* or the level descriptions from the National Curriculum are useful for this, when displayed as a chart. However it is important to remember that children do not always learn in a linear way and are often further ahead with one aspect of mathematics than another. These charts should be shared with children. They need to know where they are and what their next step is, however it is detrimental for them to see this as linked to year groups or levels, therefore these references must be removed. Teachers should keep information on the level that each child is working at for their own records.

3 *Joint decisions.* Make judgements jointly with children, involving them in agreeing what they know and are able to do, and what the evidence is. This should be done ideally at the beginning of every half term. The probing questions from the *Using Assess and Review Lessons* pack (DfES 2001) are useful for this. One or two new targets should be jointly agreed, discussing what the evidence will look like and how these targets can be reached. These targets can also be shared with parents.

4 *Focus on learning.* Discuss with children at the beginning of the lesson the purpose of the learning objective, how it relates to other aspects of mathematics, other curriculum areas and the real world. Discuss what

evidence of achieving the objective will look like. Record the objective and the assessment criteria on the board for adults and children to refer back to.

5 *Appropriate feedback.* Base comments on the learning objective, rather than administrative or presentation features. Do not give children marks or tell them the National Curriculum level that they are working at; this will reduce motivation and remove the focus from the learning. Clarke (2001) notes that even stickers or smiley faces will do this. Ensure they know how well they have met learning objectives and what they need to do next to make further improvements. Allow time for these further improvements to happen. Feedback can become part of the focus teaching in the main part of the lesson. All children should have the opportunity for focus work with you at some point over the week.

6 *Planning for assessment.* Include time to observe children, including listening to pair, small group or class discussions. Set appropriate tasks that allow a variety of responses from children (talking, writing, drawing, role-play, concept mapping, keeping a maths diary). Be flexible and prepared to adapt planning and teaching either during the lesson or following the lesson to address assessment information immediately. Allow for innovation.

7 *Questioning.* Plan open questions that will enable children to express their understanding. Use techniques enabling you to make whole-class assessments, such as the use of individual whiteboards. Ask thought-provoking questions and provide time for children to think about their response or discuss briefly with a partner: 'How do we know if a shape is a rectangle?' Be aware of possible misconceptions and deliberately use them to develop understanding: 'Some people think multiplying by 10 means adding a 0! How can we explain what really happens?'

8 *Self-assessment.* Children should make genuine assessments against learning objectives and see it as their responsibility to raise concerns about their understanding. Initially this should be done privately and public comparisons with other children must be avoided. Once children are confident they are learning in an atmosphere of trust, self-assessments can be used to pair children, thus developing each other's understanding further by questioning, challenging, explaining and justifying.

9 *Peer-assessment and peer-tutoring.* This can be modelled by using the questions that extend children's thinking from the *Mathematical Vocabulary* booklet (DfEE 2000). These could be displayed in the classroom as posters. They will be useful for children and adults working in the room, for example (p. 6), 'Can you think of another method that might have worked?' Giving developmental feedback to each other should become part of the normal class routine. Peer-tutoring can also be used when looking at test papers.

Greater emphasis needs to be placed on the importance of high quality formative assessment. This is the best way to raise children's understanding and attainment and to improve teaching.

References

Assessment Reform Group (1999) *Assessment for Learning: Beyond the Black Box*. Cambridge: University of Cambridge School of Education.

Black, P. and Wiliam, D. (1998) *Inside the Black Box: Raising Standards through Classroom Assessment*. London: School of Education, King's College.

Black, P. and Wiliam, D. (2002) *Working Inside the Black Box: Assessment for Learning in the Classroom*. London: School of Education, King's College.

Clarke, S. (2001) *Unlocking Formative Assessment*. Bristol: Hodder & Stoughton.

DfEE (Department for Education and Employment) (1998a) *Numeracy Matters: The Preliminary Report of the Numeracy Task Force*. London: DfEE.

DfEE (Department for Education and Employment) (1998b) *The Implementation of the National Numeracy Strategy: The Final Report of the Numeracy Task Force*. London: DfEE.

DfEE (Department for Education and Employment) (1999a) *Framework for Teaching Mathematics from Reception to Year 6*. London: DfEE.

DfEE (Department for Education and Employment) (1999b) *Auditing Mathematics in Your School*. London: DfEE.

DfEE (Department for Education and Employment) (1999c) *Professional Development Materials 1 and 2: Guide for your Professional Development, Book 2: Effective Teaching and the Approach to Calculation*. London: DfEE.

DfEE (Department for Education and Employment) (2000) *Mathematical Vocabulary*. London: DfEE.

DfES (Department for Education and Skills) (2001) *Using Assess and Review Lessons*. London: DfES.

Making sense of mathematics

Malcolm Swan

Introduction

This chapter is about children struggling to make sense of mathematics and how we might best assist them to overcome their misconceptions. Many teachers view misconceptions as things to be avoided or 'put right' as efficiently as possible through careful explanation. They look for ways of teaching that avoid misconceptions arising and believe that clear enough introductions might achieve this. This view of teaching is essentially a transmission one where the concepts are transmitted as clearly as possible to children. If they still do not understand, then the transmission is repeated more slowly and carefully until they do.

The view taken in this chapter is different. It begins by exploring the nature and causes of the mistakes that children make and tries to show that many so-called misconceptions are unavoidable, natural and may even be *necessary* stages in their development. An attempt will be made to show how we can welcome misconceptions as opportunities to engage children in learning through discussion, where different interpretations and ideas are shared, compared and worked on. From this viewpoint, learning is a collaborative enterprise in which children are seen as creative interpreters rather than passive imitators, and assessment plays a formative role – we make opportunities to interpret children's thinking and plan our own explanations in this light. In this chapter, the aim is to be practical. For a fuller discussion of the psychological theories underpinning these ideas, the reader is referred to Swan (2001).

Why children make mistakes

Children make mistakes for a variety of reasons. These include lapses in concentration or memory, hasty reasoning and a failure to notice important features of a situation. Such mistakes occur particularly when a child is under pressure or when learning has been based on memorizing a set of disconnected rote-learned rules.

Other mistakes, however, occur even when a child is calm, thoughtful and well-motivated. These are often symptomatic of some deeper problem. When we listen carefully to children's explanations, we find that many have alternative interpretations of mathematical ideas to the accepted ones. These are often called *misconceptions*, but more accurately they should be referred to as *alternative conceptions* as they are rarely 'completely wrong' – more often they are valid generalizations that are true in more limited circumstances. Let us look at a few examples.

Interpreting numbers

Children should never be regarded as 'blank slates'. When they first encounter a new idea, they need time to assimilate it and relate it to concepts they already possess. They build their own conceptual framework. When they first see a decimal, for example, they interpret it in terms of their earlier experiences with whole numbers, money, measurement and so on. Some avoid the unknown part, the decimal point, by simply ignoring it. Others treat the number as if it were two separate natural numbers with a dot in between as some form of separator. Thus 5.75 is read as 'five-hundred and seventy-five' or as two separate numbers 'five and seventy-five'. Others confuse the decimal point with other separators such as the 'r' in 9r2 (nine remainder two). One common interpretation is to view the decimal point as a 'dot' whose sole purpose is to separate a larger unit from a smaller one. This is understandable, when one considers that £5.75 is conventionally read as 'five pounds seventy-five pence' not as 'five point seven-five pounds'. Here the point separates a larger unit from a smaller unit and the digits either side of the point are interpreted as whole numbers referring to different units. It is little wonder therefore that some children interpret an answer like 12.125 metres as '12 metres 125 centimetres'.

Many children do not recognize the 'ten-ness' of a decimal. Thus they assume that if the number 8.59 is shown on a digital watch, then it is a decimal (because it looks like one), 8:59 is not (it has two dots), and if it has a flashing dot then it is ... sometimes! Later, as children have place value explained to them, usually in terms of fractions, new and more sophisticated misconceptions emerge. Some believe that 0.4 is greater than 0.62 because '0.4 is in tenths and 0.62 is in hundredths and tenths are bigger than hundredths' or because they know that decimals are another way of writing fractions and 1/4 is greater than 1/62. We have seen children move from believing that 'longer decimals are always bigger' (e.g. 0.75 > 0.8 because 75 > 8) to believing that 'shorter decimals are always bigger' (e.g. 0.62 < 0.4) as they begin to move away from ignoring the decimal point towards understanding place value. By the age of 15, most pupils are still unable to compare decimals reliably and with understanding.

It may be noted that such misconceptions are rarely corrected by practising algorithms as children usually produce answers to computations by dealing with the digits and decimal points independently. Digits are first evaluated and then the decimal point is inserted according to some rule (e.g. 'keep the points in line'). This contributes nothing to the meaning of decimals. Oral work is perhaps more likely to reveal alternative interpretations as children tend to retain the meaning of numbers when operating mentally and explanations are sought for.

Interpreting operations

When young children first encounter multiplication and division, these concepts are usually associated with the words 'times' and 'share'. The equation $6 \times 2 = 12$ is read as '6 times 2 makes 12' or '6 lots of 2 is 12' and $6 \div 2 = 3$ is read as '6 shared by 2 is 3'. Thus multiplication is interpreted as repeatedly adding a given quantity a given number of times and division is interpreted as sharing a given quantity into a given number of groups of equal size (partition). These concepts are usually reinforced through physical objects. From these elementary models, most children naturally create the generalizations that multiplication makes numbers bigger; division makes numbers smaller; you must always divide larger numbers by smaller ones (as '6 into 3 won't go') and so on. Such generalizations are natural, unavoidable and break down when they are applied to calculations involving fractions, decimals and negative numbers. Children are natural generalization-makers – when acquiring language, for example – and they do not need to be taught such things.

It is an interesting challenge to ask oneself, what *sense* does one make of calculations like 2.3×0.4, $17 \div 4.25$ or even $2.5 \div 3.6$? Where would one do such calculations? When some 13-year-old children were invited to find a context for $17 \div 4.25 = 4$ they found it extremely difficult and tried to force the question into a sharing problem. Here is one of the more successful attempts: 'We went carol singing. We made 17 pounds. One left early. There were 4 of us and we gave a quarter to the fifth who went early. We had 4 pounds each' (Swan 1983a).

As we encounter different types of number, our understanding of multiplication grows and develops. This understanding evolves from an understanding based on physical actions ('repeatedly adding', 'sharing') through more abstract meanings (such as 'multiplying by a rate') until much later we even expand the ideas to include operating on other mathematical objects (such as vectors). In this sense we constantly redefine and expand our interpretation of multiplication.

Conservation concepts

Children are natural pattern spotters. They notice that as some things change other things remain invariant. Sometimes perceptions are unreliable. Young children, for example, sometimes believe that when a line alters its position in

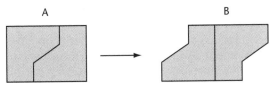

Figure 10.1 Rearranging a rectangle

space its length changes. This shows an inability to appreciate conservation of length. Similar conservation obstacles are encountered when children consider areas and perimeters. Many children think that the area will change when I cut a rectangle and rearrange the pieces, as shown in Figure 10.1.

Many also seem to believe that the area and perimeter are related in some way, so that if the area stays the same, then so must the perimeter. There are numerical conservation concepts to learn also – for example, the fact that the order in which we count a collection of objects does not affect the total number of them. When faced with the problem 'A litre of paint costs £8, how much will three litres cost?' many will recognize it as a multiplication problem and evaluate 3 × 8. If we change the numbers in the problem, however, children often believe that the operation must change. When the 3 is replaced by 0.75, then they may believe that the operation becomes division and this is reinforced by the feeling that 'division should make the answer smaller'. Such children do not recognize conservation of operation. (There is an interesting discussion point here, as when solving the two problems mentally we may well use different processes for calculation. When automating a process on a spreadsheet or later when using algebra we need to perceive such underlying structure.)

A look at the National Numeracy Strategy

Before considering just how misconceptions may be discussed and worked on in the classroom, it is interesting to consider the view taken by the National Numeracy Strategy (NNS). One laudable aim of the Strategy is to enable children to become *fluent* in mathematics. Clearly, we would all like our children to be able to immediately recall a name for a mathematical object like a 'square' or a number fact like 9 × 7 = 63, or be able to carry out a written subtraction procedure quickly and accurately without having to pause for thought. Learning for fluency involves *practice* until a stage is reached when one can perform the skill with little mental effort – indeed the mind may be elsewhere.

In the 'daily mathematics lesson' as defined in the *Framework for Teaching Mathematics from Reception to Year 6* (DfEE 1999), there is a strong emphasis on developing fluency, especially on remembering terminology and on oral and mental calculation. The *Framework* uses terms like 'remembering facts', 'sharpening skills' and 'practising calculations'. There is the repeated suggestion that lessons should be conducted at a 'brisk pace', especially during the oral 'starter'. Here, *'how did you get that?'* appears to be a more common question than *'can you explain what that means?'*

There is more to learning mathematics than developing fluency, however. Mathematics is also about developing *meaning*.[1] Fluency and meaning should be interrelated. When fluency is not underpinned by meaning, we are left with an assortment of unconnected rules and labels that are rapidly forgotten or misremembered. The teacher's task is not merely to explain meanings in everyday terms but also to help children to create *their own* meanings and links between mathematical ideas and other familiar concepts. This is not something that can happen 'at a brisk pace', but which needs time for *reflection* and *discussion* in which alternative interpretations are shared, compared and worked on. Unlike fluency, which may deteriorate with lack of use, when one creates meaning it is rarely forgotten, indeed it continues to grow and evolve.

In relation to the *Framework*, there seems to be an assumption that 'meaning-making' takes place during the middle, 'main' part of the lesson and 'where you have identified general errors or misunderstanding during the main part of the lesson, you might need a longer plenary to sort them out' (DfEE 1999: 15). The Strategy seems to have a view that misconceptions may be 'sorted out' much as a medical ailment may be sorted with the appropriate drug. If only teaching were so simple!

Questioning

To be fair, the *Framework* does emphasize the importance of giving pupils time to think and reflect when asking questions:

> Better numeracy standards occur when teachers question pupils effectively, including as many of them as possible, giving them time to think before answering, targeting individuals to take account of their attainment and needs, asking them to demonstrate and explain their methods and reasoning, and exploring reasons for any wrong answers.
>
> (DfEE 1999: 15)

There is an evident tension here between 'pace' and 'time to think'. Lessons should not be conducted at a uniform breakneck pace but have a rhythm. Quick-fire questioning for fluency should sometimes give way to unhurried periods for reflection and discussion, so that children can:

- examine their own ideas and confront inconsistencies;
- compare their own interpretations with those of other children and with accepted conventions.

Most lessons are about children seeking answers to specific problems. The natural questions to ask in this case are: 'What did you get?'; 'Could you describe how you got that?'; 'What should Sharon do next?' These questions are about process and product. In the lessons I am advocating, the questions will be more like:

- Can you tell us what this means to you – in your own words?
- Can you draw me a picture which will help me understand what you are saying?
- What is the same and what is different about these two things?
- If I change this, what else will change? What will stay the same?
- What does this remind you of?
- Can you make up another example like this?
- When is this true? When might it not be true?

Such questions as these need more considered responses.

Teaching for meaning

There has been a great deal of research on children's learning of mathematical concepts. In our own work at Nottingham we have evolved a particular teaching approach which does seem to generate the active learning of mathematical concepts. We begin by first outlining the design principles and then provide some examples.

1   *Uncovering the problem.* We start the lesson with a task that has the purpose of uncovering and making vivid children's pre-existing interpretations. We ask children to attempt a task on their own and to prepare themselves to explain their ideas. At this stage, we make no attempt to 'teach' anything new. This is also an assessment opportunity for the teacher.

2   *Creating an awareness that new learning is needed.* We then ask children to share ideas and try to make them aware of inconsistencies and disagreements in a non-judgemental manner. This can happen in several ways:

   - by comparing one child's response with that of another child;
   - by pointing out contradictions in what an individual child has just said;
   - by asking children to redo the task using a different method that leads to a different conclusion.

   If the task has been well chosen, this process will produce an unsettled state which we call 'cognitive conflict' as children begin to confront the inconsistencies and implications of their own beliefs. Notice that, so far, no teacher explanations have been offered. We are trying to create a strong desire to 'sort things out'. This stage can take time and should end with children puzzled and intrigued. As a teacher we hold our tongue and resist the temptation to explain, even when some children plead to be told 'who is right?' Some teachers leave an issue in suspense overnight, so that children go away discussing and arguing and come back the next day having had time to reconsider their ideas more carefully.

3   *Resolving the conflict.* We hold a whole-class discussion in order to 'resolve' the issue. Children are encouraged to reformulate their ideas in a non-judgemental atmosphere. *After* this, the teacher explains the 'mathematician's' viewpoint, acknowledging cases where this is just an arbitrary 'convention'.

4 *Consolidating learning.* We then consolidate learning by asking children to tackle further problems; by inviting students to create and solve their own problems; or by asking students to act the role of the teacher and mark a fictional piece of 'child's' work into which we have introduced some common errors. They really seem to enjoy getting out a red pen and writing advice!

The essence of this approach is that we try to create the 'itch' before we offer to 'scratch'. More conventional approaches usually offer explanations before children see the need for them. They also tend to try to smooth the path for children by *avoiding* errors and conceptual obstacles through carefully structured examples. The process described here *confronts* children with these things. There is a strong emphasis on oral explanation and this often generates intense, lively discussions focused on just one or two 'big ideas', which are pursued in depth.

An example

Such lessons need not be elaborate affairs. One began with the teacher simply asking children to complete two decimal number sequences on paper.

1) 0.2, 0.4, 0.6, —, —, —, —, —, — (Adding on 0.2 each time)
2) 0.05, —, —, —, —, —, —, — (Adding on 0.05 each time)

Most did as was expected, producing answers like 0.8, 0.10, 0.12, for the first question and 0.10, 0.15, 0.20 for the second. Some answered correctly, but these were a minority. After a short while, the class was stopped and children were asked to share their answers. This was done by 'counting round the room': 'Let's begin by counting up in 0.2s. Jane, you start . . . now Ben, you continue'. The children continued to make the errors and no comment was made by the teacher. Some more knowledgeable children looked a bit worried at this point and disagreements were voiced by them. The teacher asked for explanations but offered no judgement on who was right.

The teacher then asked the class to redo the questions by 'bouncing along number lines' and checking the sequences on a calculator (by pressing 0.2 + 0.2 =; + 0.2 =; + 0.2 =; . . .). They did this on paper, working in pairs (see Figure 10.2). The children now had three sets of answers. They were asked to write down what they noticed about their answers. There were many puzzled faces and discussions about the inconsistencies revealed.

A class discussion was then held and children were asked to report back on what they had noticed: 'I noticed that there is no such number as 0.10'; 'Instead of 0.10, the number line says 1'; 'I wrote 0.10 in question two. The calculator said I was wrong. It said 0.1. It said 0.15 for the next one though. I got 0.10, 0.15, 0.20, 0.25. The calculator got 0.1, 0.15, 0.2, 0.25. Are my answers right?' The discussion was messy at times, but the children were encouraged to respond to each other rather than expect answers from the teacher: 'Do you agree with Ben? Why?' After a while, when total curiosity was aroused, the teacher took a more active part in helping to resolve the issues.

Figure 10.2 'Bouncing along a number line'

The teacher told the class that we do not read 0.10 as 'nought point ten' because then it would sound bigger than 'nought point nine' and we know now that it really means just the same thing as 0.1. (If we enter '0.10 =' on the calculator, we get 0.1.) If we read 0.10 as 'nought point one nought' it will not sound bigger than 'nought point nine', and so on.

This discussion on the meaning of the decimal was followed by a consolidation activity in which children wrote about what they had learned and then generated their own sequences for others to continue and check using calculators. At the end the teacher checked through the work to see who had gained from the lesson.

When this approach was compared with an approach that began with explanations and was followed up with exercises, short-term gains were similar. Over the longer term, however, the discussion approach was more effective (Swan 1983b). This type of approach was also used when teaching other topics and similar results were found, both at primary and secondary levels (Bell *et al.* 1985).

Two types of activity that generate discussion

More recently, I have been investigating the types of task that are best suited to generating intensive discussions on mathematical concepts. Two types have emerged which seem particularly useful: collecting together equivalent representations of a concept and deciding whether given statements are always, sometimes or never true. Examples of each of these are illustrated below. If you think these are inappropriate for your class, then try to devise examples of your own! Further ideas for discussion starters may be found in Ryan and Williams (2000).

Collecting together equivalent representations of a concept

In coming to understand a concept (Sierpinska 1994: 56), a child has to:

- single it out and bring it to the forefront of attention (identification);
- see similarities and differences between this concept and other similar ones (discrimination);
- see general properties of the concept in particular cases of it (generalization) and begin to perceive a unifying principle (synthesis).

One type of activity that is particularly suitable for encouraging this process involves giving children a collection of cards and asking them to sort the cards

Decimals and fractions

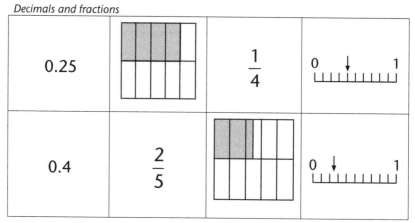

Figure 10.3 'Sorting cards' for decimals and fractions

Operations

$6 \div 3$	I share £3 among six people. How much does each person get?	$\dfrac{3}{6}$	2
$3 \div 6$	$\dfrac{6}{3}$	I share £6 among three people. How much does each person get?	0.5

Figure 10.4 'Sorting cards' for number operations

into sets where each set has the same meaning. The cards must be designed so that pupils have to discriminate between them very carefully. The focus of the activity is on the interpretation of representations and notation. Samples of sets of cards focused on the misconceptions discussed are illustrated in Figures 10.3 and 10.4 (these are just samples, the actual sets were bigger than this).

The first set was used to reveal and encourage discussion of the misconceptions that 'longer decimals are greater in value' and that '0.4 means 1/4'. It is also important for children to see that fractions can represent points on a number line as well as part/whole areas and that decimals can be used to represent areas.

The second set focuses on the common misconception that 'you cannot divide small numbers by larger ones' and that $6 \div 3 = 3 \div 6$. It also encourages children to consider the link between fractions and division.

Numbers: Always, sometimes or never true?

If you multiply a number by 10, you add a zero on the end.	Write down two numbers. The one with more digits is the bigger number.	If you add 1 to the top and bottom number of a fraction, the fraction gets bigger.
If you multiply the top and bottom number of a fraction by 2, the fraction gets bigger.	If you put a zero at the beginning of a number, it changes the size of the number.	If you put a zero in the middle of a number, it changes the size of the number.

Figure 10.5 'Sometimes, always, never' cards for numbers

Operations: Always, sometimes or never true?

If you add a number to 6 the answer will be greater than 6. $6 + y > 6$	If you take a number away from 6 the answer will be less than 6. $6 - y < 6$	If you multiply 6 by a number, the answer will be greater than 6. $6 \times y > 6$
It doesn't matter which way round you multiply two numbers, you get the same answer. $y \times z = z \times y$	It doesn't matter which way round you subtract two numbers, you get the same answer. $y - z = z - y$	It doesn't matter which way round you divide two numbers, you get the same answer. $y \div z = z \div y$

Figure 10.6 'Sometimes, always, never' cards for number operations

When creating sets of cards like this it is often a good idea to include some blank ones and leave some cards without partners. This encourages children to make up their own representations in words, symbols and pictures.

Always, sometimes or never true

A second type of activity involves giving a class a small number of statements on cards, all on a related theme, and asking the children to look at each one in turn and decide whether it is always, sometimes or never true. Children then have to try to justify their decision with examples, counter-examples and explanations and make a poster to present their reasoning. It is helpful if the cards contain statements which relate to common misconceptions. For example, some cards concerning numbers, number operations and areas and perimeters are illustrated in Figures 10.5, 10.6 and 10.7.

For the first two sets, children are encouraged to try different kinds of numbers: natural numbers, negative numbers, fractions and decimals. When children have decided if a statement is true for all numbers, just some numbers or is never true, they then paste the statement under an appropriate heading on the poster and write their reasoning around it. Calculators are used to test

Areas and perimeters: Always, sometimes or never true?

If you cut a piece out of a rectangle, you make its perimeter smaller.	If you cut a piece out of a rectangle, you make its area smaller.	If you cut a rectangle in half, you halve the perimeter.
Draw two rectangles. The one with the bigger area will have the longer perimeter.	A square and a rectangle have the same perimeter. The square has the greater area.	If you double the lengths of the sides of a rectangle, you double the area.

Figure 10.7 'Sometimes, always, never' cards for areas and perimeters

any theories that emerge. You may be able to challenge children further by asking them to find boundaries where statements change from being true to being untrue and illustrating these on number lines.

The statements in the third set work on the concepts of area and perimeter and in particular the misconception that they are related in some way. Children will need to generate their own drawings (easier on squared paper), and measure them to test statements. Examples that illustrate or refute statements are cut out and pasted onto their posters as before.

Managing discussion

Discussion-based activities are difficult for many children. They are often more concerned with getting through exercises quickly, or presenting work neatly than with discussing and reflecting on ideas. Expectations will need educating. Some children may be reluctant to share and learn from mistakes during plenary discussion, fearing ridicule. As teachers we need to work hard at creating a culture in which children feel comfortable talking about ideas without feeling judged and 'put down'.

A good introduction is crucial. As well as explaining what to do and how to do it, we need to explain *why* we want them to work in this way:

> This lesson is not about trying to cover lots of pages. It's not about working quickly. It's about trying to understand something new. In this lesson we are going to do a lot of talking. I would like you to work in pairs or groups of three. Take it in turns to pick up a card and explain why it matches another card. If you don't understand what your partner says, then challenge your partner to explain again. Take turns. Don't rush. I will ask some of you to explain your poster to the whole class so you must make sure you understand what you are doing.

It is helpful to model the discussion process with a few examples to get children started. Children often work better when the pairs are reasonably matched in ability, otherwise one tends to become a 'passenger'. While they work on their posters, I go round and encourage them to slow down (!), find more examples and explain more carefully: 'Have you tried using fractions? Decimals? Negative numbers?'; 'What makes you say that? Can you show me an example?'; 'Can you put what Craig just said into *your* words?'; 'Write down what you just said'.

It sometimes helps to ask someone from one pair to explain an idea to someone in another pair, but I try to hold back the authoritative 'answer'. As soon as this is supplied it terminates discussion. I just try to generate curiosity. After a while, not necessarily when everyone has finished, but when children all have some useful ideas to share, stop the class and hold a plenary. During this phase the teacher's role is to 'chair' the discussion, avoiding judgemental responses such as 'good answer' until the very end. (When one child hears 'well done' to another's response, she might think to herself 'that's not what I was going to say, so I'll keep quiet'.) Instead try to list all the ideas and save the explanations for the resolution part of the lesson when the teacher moves from 'chair' to 'explainer'.

Concluding remarks

It could be that some of the examples used here may not at first seem appropriate for very young classes or for classes with children of very limited attainment, and it is certainly the case that there is still some work to do before the above suggestions can be widely applied. The role of language, however, is crucial for all learning (see Higgins, Chapter 5). In mathematics, in particular, the predominant transmission culture in which the teacher explains, asks questions and offers examples needs to be rebalanced into a more collaborative culture in which the child takes on these roles. While practice for fluency will always be important (and rightly so), the current emphasis on quick-fire, mental and oral work should be accompanied by a similar emphasis on considered and thoughtful discussions of meaning. Children will not be able to explain things fluently to start with, but even tentative and inexplicit talk is a bridge towards richer understanding. As Vygotsky (1996: 218) once said: 'Thought is not merely expressed in words; it comes into existence through them'.

Note

1 We recognize that there is much more to learn in mathematics than is discussed in this chapter. We must also include, for example, problem solving *strategies* and an appreciation of *everyday applications* and *values*. These aspects of teaching also involve a range of classroom activity in which discussion plays an important part.

References

Bell, A., Swan, M., Onslow, B., Pratt, K. and Purdy, D. (1985) *Diagnostic Teaching for Long Term Learning: Report of ESRC Project HR8491/1*. Nottingham: Shell Centre for Mathematical Education, University of Nottingham.

DfEE (Department for Education and Employment) (1999) *Framework for Teaching Mathematics from Reception to Year 6*. London: DfEE.

Ryan, J. and Williams, J. (2000) *Mathematical Discussions with Children*. Manchester: University of Manchester Press.

Sierpinska, A. (1994) *Understanding in Mathematics*. London: Falmer.

Swan, M. (1983a) *The Meaning and Use of Decimals: Calculator-based Tests and Teaching Materials*. Nottingham: Shell Centre for Mathematical Education, University of Nottingham.

Swan, M. (1983b) *Teaching decimal place value: a comparative study of 'conflict' and 'positive only' approaches*. Paper presented at the 7th conference of the International Group for the Psychology of Mathematics Education, Jerusalem, Israel, Department of Science Teaching, Weizmann Institute of Science, Rehovot.

Swan, M. (2001) Dealing with misconceptions in mathematics, in P. Gates (ed.) *Issues in Mathematics Teaching*, pp. 147–65. London: Routledge Falmer.

Vygotsky, L. (1996) *Thought and Language*. Cambridge, MA: Massachusetts Institute of Technology Press.

S e c t i o n 4

INTERVENTION ISSUES

Ann Dowker, a research lecturer in the Department of Experimental Psychology at Oxford University, has various related research interests, one of which is the role of intervention in helping children with difficulties in numeracy. She argues that research suggests that arithmetical ability is not unitary but comprises several broad components and sub-components, and that weaknesses in any one of them can occur relatively independently of weaknesses in the others. She provides some historical background to interventions in arithmetic and outlines one of the specific intervention techniques associated with the National Numeracy Strategy (NNS): the Springboard programme. The author then describes, in some detail, two independently developed, individualized intervention programmes that address numeracy in young children and take componential approaches based on cognitive theories of arithmetic. These are the Mathematics Recovery programme, which was originally developed in Australia, and her own Numeracy Recovery programme. The chapter finishes with a look at some of the results from the latter programme and at some of the ensuing implications.

Valsa Koshy is director of the Able Children's Education Centre at Brunel University. In Chapter 12 she asks and answers three particular questions: what do we mean by the mathematically gifted; how do we identify them; and how do we ensure that we have effective strategies for provision? As part of her answer she discusses Krutetskii's list of attributes of mathematically gifted children and generates her own list of principles of provision. The chapter continues with a substantial section on planning for gifted children that includes points that need to be taken into consideration when designing and selecting activities for able mathematicians. Several practical examples are provided. The chapter engages us briefly in the acceleration/enrichment debate, and concludes with an example to illustrate the extent to which the more able child can be catered for within a three-part lesson structure.

Interventions in numeracy: individualized approaches

Ann Dowker

Individual differences in arithmetic in the general population are very great. The Cockcroft Report (DES 1982) pointed out that, in a typical class of 11-year-olds, there is likely to be a seven-year gap between the highest and lowest achievers in arithmetic. Some children and adults have a high degree of talent in, and often fascination with, numbers and arithmetic. At the other end of the scale, there is increasing awareness that many individuals have major difficulties with arithmetic, ranging from severe and global difficulties with all aspects of numeracy to mild specific problems which nevertheless interfere with coping with some important educational and/or practical tasks. Mathematics anxiety and even 'mathematics phobia' are relatively common problems.

There are a number of measures sometimes used to combat these problems. Children may be divided into different, supposedly more homogeneous groups ('sets') according to their mathematical ability and taught separately. They may be grouped within a class and given different activities. They may be given the opportunity to work individually, at their own pace, through textbooks, workbooks and worksheets, or computer materials. One potential risk with all of these measures is that children may be simply classed as 'good' or 'bad', 'fast' or 'slow', and their specific weaknesses and strengths may remain undiagnosed. Moreover, some of these measures may mean that 'less able' children are separated on a long-term basis from 'more able' children, with the risk both of children labelling themselves in self-fulfilling ways, and of their not being exposed to the stimulus of discussions with others at different levels of knowledge and understanding. Some of these risks would be reduced if targeted interventions brought children to a point where they could gain increased benefit from whole-class teaching, as well as increased ability and motivation to pursue the subject independently.

Thus far, the discussion has been about individuals who are 'high' or 'low' achievers in arithmetic; but that is an oversimplification of the actual situation. Experimental, educational and psychometric studies of children

(Ginsburg 1977; Dowker 1998) and adults (Geary and Widaman 1992), and studies of brain functions in people with and without brain damage, have provided overwhelming evidence that arithmetical ability is not unitary (see Dowker, Chapter 16). Its broad components include counting, memory for arithmetical facts, the understanding of concepts and the ability to follow procedures. Each of these broad components has, in turn, a number of narrower components: for example, counting includes knowledge of the counting sequence, ability to follow counting procedures in counting sets of objects and understanding of the principles of counting (e.g. that the last number in a count sequence represents the number of objects in the set, and that counting a set of objects in different orders will give the same answer).

Moreover, though the different components often correlate with one another, weaknesses in any one of them can occur relatively independently of weaknesses in the others. Weaknesses in even one component can ultimately take its toll on performance in other components – partly because difficulty with one component may increase the risk of the child relying exclusively on another component and failing to perceive and use relationships between different arithmetical processes and problems; and partly because when children fail at certain tasks they may come to perceive themselves as 'no good at maths' and develop a negative attitude to the subject. However, the components described here are not seen as a hierarchy. A child may perform well at an apparently difficult task (e.g. word problem solving) while performing poorly at an apparently easier component (e.g. remembering the counting word sequence). Though certain specific components may frequently form the basis for learning other specific components, they need not always be prerequisites. Several studies (e.g. Denvir and Brown 1986) have suggested that it is not possible to establish a strict hierarchy whereby any one component invariably precedes another.

The componential nature of arithmetic is important in planning and formulating interventions with children who are experiencing arithmetical difficulties. It is true that any sort of extra help in arithmetic may benefit children who are experiencing difficulties, but interventions that are focused on the particular components with which an individual child has difficulty are likely to be more effective than a 'one size fits all' strategy.

There has been an increased emphasis on numeracy in psychological and educational research and in educational policy and practice in Britain and other countries. There is, however, still a much smaller research base on numeracy development than on literacy development. There is agreement that far more research is needed on early mathematical development and that policy needs to be more informed by research (Thompson 2001).

The focus of this chapter will be on individualized intervention programmes with primary school children, which are based on analyses of their specific strengths and weaknesses. Certain important forms of intervention will not be discussed here. These include, for example, 'whole-school' approaches to raising overall numeracy standards in a school; and group-based interventions with preschool children from disadvantaged backgrounds, which aim to reduce the risk of numeracy difficulties developing later on. They also include projects aimed at improving numeracy, as well as other aspects of academic performance, by teaching (usually older) children more sophisticated general reasoning skills and strategies (e.g. Adey and Shayer 1994).

Interventions in arithmetic: some of the history

Some forms of individualized, component-based techniques of assessing and remediating mathematical difficulties have been in existence at least since the 1920s (Buswell and John 1926; Tilton 1947). On the other hand, they have never been used very extensively and there are many books, both old and new, about mathematical development and mathematics education which do not even refer to such techniques, or to the theories behind them.

If componential theories of arithmetical ability, and their applications to differentiated instruction and remediation in arithmetic, were already being advocated when our contemporary schoolchildren's grandparents were at school, why have they had comparatively little impact on theory and practice? Part of the reason is practical: in the overcrowded, under-resourced class-rooms that have been common in schools, it is difficult to diagnose individual strengths and weaknesses or to provide individualized instruction. Moreover, appropriate individualized instruction depends on appropriate selection of the components of arithmetic to be used in assessment and intervention. This is still an issue for debate and one which requires considerable further research. One of the main potential problems, which was more common in the past than nowadays, is to assume that the components to be addressed must necessarily correspond to specific arithmetical operations (e.g. treating 'addition', 'subtraction', 'multiplication', 'division' etc. as separate com-ponents). It is, of course, quite possible for children to have specific problems with a particular arithmetical operation. Nevertheless, it is an oversimplifica-tion to assume that these operations are likely to be the primary components of arithmetical processing. Current classifications tend to place greater emphasis on the type of cognitive process – for example, the broad distinctions between factual knowledge ('knowing that'), procedural knowledge ('knowing how'), conceptual knowledge ('knowing what it all means') and in some theories utilizational knowledge ('knowing when to apply it') (see e.g. Greeno *et al.* 1984). A potential danger of overemphasizing the different operations as separate components is that it may encourage children, and perhaps adults, to ignore the relationships between the different operations.

Another potential problem – again commoner in the past though still a danger nowadays – is looking at children's difficulties only in terms of procedural errors. It is, of course, important to investigate the strategies that individual children use in arithmetic, including those faulty arith-metical procedures that lead to errors. Nonetheless, diagnosing the incorrect strategies is not always the final step. There may be a conceptual reason why the incorrect strategy is acquired and maintained or there may be unperceived conceptual strengths which need to be noted and built on (Tilton 1947; Ginsburg 1977).

Interventions and the National Numeracy Strategy

The National Numeracy Strategy (NNS) (DfEE 1999) incorporates some intervention techniques for children who are struggling with arithmetic. The main intervention programme is the Springboard programme, used with children in Years 3 to 7 (7 to 12 years). The target group is children with relatively mild arithmetical difficulties (e.g. those who perform at Level 2C in standardized school tests at age 7. In this age group, Level 3 reflects superior performance; 2A above-average performance; 2B average performance; 2C below-average performance; Level 1 seriously weak performance; and Level W, or 'Working toward Level 1', very serious difficulties). The Springboard programme provides additional tuition for small groups of six to eight children as a supplement to the daily mathematics lesson that they experience with the whole class. Typically, it provides two 30-minute sessions which consolidate the work currently being taught in the daily mathematics lesson.

There appear to be no similar government-sponsored intervention programmes for children under 7 in Britain. This younger age group seems particularly important from this point of view, as the first two years of school are when much of the foundation is being laid for later mathematical learning. Identifying and intervening with difficulties at this stage has the potential to prevent children from developing inappropriate arithmetical strategies which may handicap them in later work, and from developing negative attitudes toward arithmetic.

Individualized intervention programmes with young children

Two independently developed, individualized intervention programmes which address numeracy in young children, and take componential approaches based on cognitive theories of arithmetic, are the Mathematics Recovery programme, designed by Bob Wright and his colleagues in Australia (Wright *et al.* 2000, 2002), and the Numeracy Recovery programme (Dowker 2001). There are some important differences between the two programmes. Notably, the Mathematics Recovery programme is much more intensive than the Numeracy Recovery programme, and places more emphasis on methods of counting and number representation. The Numeracy Recovery programme emphasizes estimation and derived fact strategy use. From a more theoretical point of view, the Mathematics Recovery programme places greater emphasis on broad developmental stages, while the Numeracy Recovery programme treats mathematical development, to a greater extent, as involving potentially independent, separately developing skills and processes. Despite these distinctive features, the two programmes have other important common elements besides being individualized and componential. Both are targeted at the often neglected early primary school age group (6- to 7-year-olds); both deal mainly with number and arithmetic rather than other aspects of mathematics; and both place a greater emphasis than most programmes on collaboration between researchers and teachers.

The Mathematics Recovery programme

This programme was designed in Australia by Bob Wright and his colleagues (Wright *et al.* 2000). In it, teachers provide intensive individualized intervention to low-attaining 6- and 7-year-olds. Children in the programme undergo 30 minutes of individualized instruction per day over a period of 12 to 14 weeks.

The choice of topics within the programme is based on the 'Learning Framework in Number', devised by the researchers. This divides the learning of arithmetic into five broad stages: emergent (some simple counting, but few numerical skills); perceptual (can count objects and sometimes add small sets of objects that are present); figurative (can count well and use 'counting-all' strategies to add); counting-on (can add by 'counting-on from the larger number' and subtract by counting down; can read numerals up to 100 but have little understanding of place value); and facile (know some number facts; are able to use some derived fact strategies; can multiply and divide by strategies based on repeated addition; may have difficulty with carrying and borrowing).

Children are assessed, before and after intervention, in a number of key topics. They undergo interventions based on their initial performance in each of the key topics. The key topics that are selected vary with the child's overall stage. For example, the key topics at the emergent stage are:

- number word sequences from 1 to 20;
- numerals from 1 to 10;
- counting visible items (objects);
- spatial patterns (e.g. counting and recognizing dots arranged in domino patterns and in random arrays);
- finger patterns (recognizing and demonstrating quantities up to 5 shown by number of fingers);
- temporal patterns (counting sounds or movements that take place in a sequence).

The key topics at the next, perceptual, stage are:

- number word sequences from 1 to 30;
- numerals from 1 to 20;
- figurative counting (counting-on and counting back, where some objects are visible but others are screened);
- spatial patterns (more sophisticated use of domino patterns; grouping sets of dots into 'lots of 2'; 'lots of 4', etc.);
- finger patterns (recognizing, demonstrating and manipulating patterns up to 10 shown by numbers of fingers);
- equal groups and sharing (identifying equal groups and partitioning sets into equal groups).

The key topics at later stages place greater emphasis on arithmetic and less on counting. Despite the overall division into stages, the programme acknowledges and adapts to the fact that some children can be at a later stage for some topics than for others.

There are many activities that are used for different topics and stages within the Mathematics Recovery programme. For example, activities dealing with temporal patterns at the emergent stage include children counting the number of chopping movements made with the adult's hands; producing a requested number of chopping movements with their own hands; counting the number of times they hear the adult clap; and clapping their own hands a requested number of times. Activities dealing with number-word sequences in fives at the counting-on stage include children being presented with sets of five-dot cards; counting the dots as each new card is presented; counting to 30 in fives without counting the dots; counting to 30 in fives without the cards; counting to 50 in fives without the cards; and counting backward in fives from 30, first with and then without the cards.

Children in the programme improved very significantly on the topics that form the focus of the problem: often reaching age-appropriate levels in these topics. The teachers who worked on the programme found the experience very useful. They felt that it helped them to gain a better understanding of children's mathematical development and used ideas and techniques from the programme in their subsequent classroom teaching.

The Numeracy Recovery programme

The Numeracy Recovery programme (Dowker 2001), piloted with 6- and 7-year-olds (mostly Year 2) in some primary schools in Oxford, is funded by the Esmee Fairbairn Charitable Trust. The scheme involves working with children who have been identified by their teachers as having problems with arithmetic. One hundred and seventy-five children (about 15 per cent of the children in the relevant classes) have so far begun or undergone intervention.

These children are assessed on nine components of early numeracy, which are summarized and described below. The children then receive weekly individual intervention (half an hour a week) in the particular components with which they have been found to have difficulty. The interventions are carried out by the classroom teachers, using techniques proposed by Dowker (2001).

The teachers are released (each teacher for half a day weekly) for the intervention by the employment of supply teachers for classroom teaching. Each child typically remains in the programme for 30 weeks, though the time is sometimes shorter or longer, depending on teachers' assessments of the child's continuing need for intervention. New children join the project periodically.

The interventions are based on an analysis of the particular sub-skills that children bring to arithmetical tasks, with remediation of the specific areas where children show problems. The components addressed here are not to be regarded as an all-inclusive list of components of arithmetic, either from a mathematical or educational point of view. Rather, the components were selected because earlier research studies and discussions with teachers had indicated them to be important in early arithmetical development, and because research had shown them to vary considerably between individual children in the early school years.

The components that are the focus of the project are:

1 counting procedures;
2 counting principles: especially the order-irrelevance principle that counting the same set of items in different orders will result in the same number; and the ability to predict the result of adding or subtracting an item from a set;
3 written symbolism for numbers;
4 understanding the role of place value in number operations and arithmetic;
5 word problem solving;
6 translation between arithmetical problems presented in concrete, verbal and numerical formats (e.g. being able to represent the sum $3 + 2 = 5$ by adding three counters to two counters, or by a word problem such as 'Sam had three sweets and his friend gave him two more, so now he has five' (see Hughes 1986);
7 derived fact strategies in addition and subtraction (i.e. the ability to derive and predict unknown arithmetical facts from known facts, e.g. by using arithmetical principles such as commutativity, associativity, the addition/ subtraction inverse principle, etc);
8 arithmetical estimation: the ability to estimate an approximate answer to an arithmetic problem and to evaluate the reasonableness of an arithmetical estimate;
9 number fact retrieval.

The assessments and interventions used for these components are described elsewhere (Dowker 2001). The assessment and intervention used for one of the components, derived fact strategies, will be described here as an example.

The assessment for this component involves giving children the Addition and Subtraction Principles Test developed by Dowker (1998). In this test, they are given the answer to a problem and then asked to solve another problem that could be solved quickly by the appropriate use of an arithmetical principle (e.g. they may be shown the sum $23 + 44 = 67$ and then asked to do the sum $23 + 45$ or $44 + 23$). Problems preceded by answers to numerically unrelated problems are given as controls. The children are asked whether 'the top sum' helps them to do 'the bottom sum', and why. The actual addition and subtraction problems involved vary in difficulty, ranging from those which the child can readily calculate mentally, through those just beyond the child's calculation capacity, to those too difficult for the child to solve. The particular derived fact strategies that are the main focus of this project are those involving commutativity (e.g. if $8 + 6 = 14$, then $6 + 8 = 14$); the associativity-based N + 1 principle (if $9 + 4 = 14$, then $9 + 5 = 14 + 1 = 15$) and the N − 1 principle (e.g. if $9 + 4 = 13$, then $9 + 3 = 13 − 1 = 12$).

The intervention for this component involves presenting children with pairs of arithmetic problems. The derived fact strategy techniques are pointed out and explained to them and they are invited to solve a similar problem. If they fail to do so, the strategies are demonstrated to them for single-digit addition and subtraction problems, with the help of manipulable objects, and of a number line, and they are again invited to carry out other derived fact strategy problems.

Some results from the Numeracy Recovery programme

The children in the project, together with some of their classmates and children from other schools, are given three standardized arithmetic tests: the British Abilities Scales Basic Number Skills sub-test (1995 revision), the Wechsler Objective Numerical Dimensions (WOND) test and the Wechsler Intelligence Scale for Children (WISC) arithmetic sub-test. The first two place greatest emphasis on computation abilities and the latter on arithmetical reasoning. The children are retested at intervals of approximately six months.

The initial scores on standardized tests, and the retest scores after six months of the first 146 children to take part in the project have now been analysed. Not all of the data from 'control' children are yet available, but the first 75 'control' children to be retested showed no significant improvement in standard (i.e. age-corrected) scores on any of the tests. In any case, the tests are standardized, so it is possible to estimate the extent to which children are or are not improving relative to others of their age in the general population.

The children in the intervention group have so far shown very significant improvements. (Average standard scores are 100 for the Basic Number Skills sub-test and the WOND Numerical Operations test, and 10 for the WISC arithmetic sub-test.) The median standard scores on the Basic Number Skills sub-test were 96 initially and 100 after approximately six months. The median standard scores on the WOND test were 91 initially and 94 after six months. The median standard scores on the WISC sub-test were 7 initially, and 8 after six months (the means were 6.8 initially and 8.45 after six months). Wilcoxon (non-parametric matched pairs) tests showed that all these improvements were highly significant. Indeed, the improvements on the WOND test (W = 632.85), the Basic Number Skills sub-test (W = 7064.5) and the WISC sub-test (W = 6385) were all significant at the 0.01 level.

One hundred and one of the 146 children have been retested over periods of at least a year, and have been maintaining their improvement.

The reactions of the teachers in the schools concerned have been very positive. They have expressed enthusiasm at the chance to work with children on an individual basis, and feel that the children are enjoying the project and are making considerable improvements. Some of them have said that involvement in the project is also giving them good ideas for general class-room arithmetic teaching. It may be noted that some of the principles of this intervention project were influenced by brain-based research on the components of arithmetic. It thus provides an example of how research on the brain can influence work on education.

General conclusions

It appears that individualized, component-based approaches to intervention can be highly effective. Further research may show whether different approaches to such intervention (e.g. age when intervention starts; degree of intensiveness) may be differentially appropriate to different groups of children. It would also be desirable to investigate the potential for similar types of intervention in areas of mathematics other than numeracy (e.g. geometry and measurement).

Acknowledgements

I am grateful to the Economic and Social Research Council (ESRC) and the Esmee Fairbairn Charitable Trust for financial support and to all the schools which have participated in the Numeracy Recovery intervention study and the research that led up to it.

References

Adey, P. and Shayer, M. (1994) *Really Raising Standards*. London: Routledge.
Buswell, G.T. and John, L. (1926) Diagnostic studies in arithmetic, *Supplementary Educational Monographs*, 30. Chicago: University of Chicago Press.
Denvir, B. and Brown, M. (1986) Understanding of concepts in low attaining 7–9 year olds. Part 1: description of descriptive framework and diagnostic instrument, *Educational Studies in Mathematics*, 17: 15–36.
DES (Department of Education and Science) (1982) *Mathematics Counts* (Cockcroft Report). London: HMSO.
DfEE (Department for Education and Employment) (1999) *Framework for Teaching Mathematics from Reception to Year 6*. London: DfEE.
Dowker, A. (1998) Individual differences in arithmetical development, in C. Donlan (ed.) *The Development of Mathematical Skills*. London: Taylor & Francis.
Dowker, A.D. (2001) Numeracy recovery: a pilot scheme for early intervention with young children with numeracy difficulties, *Support for Learning*, 16: 6–10.
Geary, D.C. and Widaman, K.F. (1992) On the convergence of componential and psychometric models, *Intelligence*, 16: 47–80.
Ginsburg, H. (1977) *Children's Arithmetic: How They Learn It and How You Teach It*. New York: Teachers' College Press.
Greeno, T., Riley, M. and Gelman, R. (1984) Young children's counting and understanding of principles, *Cognitive Psychology*, 16: 94–143.
Hughes, M. (1986) *Children and Number*. Oxford: Blackwell.
Thompson, I. (2001) Issues for classroom practice in England, in J. Anghileri (ed.) *Principles and Practice in Arithmetic Teaching*. Buckingham: Open University Press.
Tilton, J.W. (1947) Individualized and meaningful instruction in arithmetic, *Journal of Educational Psychology*, 38: 83–8.
Wright, R., Martland, J. and Stafford, A.K. (2000) *Early Numeracy: Assessment for Teaching and Intervention*. London: Paul Chapman.
Wright, R.J., Martland, J., Stafford, A.K. and Stanger, G. (2002) *Teaching Number: Advancing Children's Skills and Strategies*. London: Paul Chapman.

Nurturing mathematical promise

Valsa Koshy

Introduction

For more than two decades the challenge of meeting the needs of mathematically gifted children, with appropriately conceived teaching strategies and well-designed activities, has been drifting on the tides of educational thought. Straker's (1982: 7) assertion is that 'Gifted pupils have a great deal to contribute to the future well-being of society, provided their talents are developed to the full during their formal education. There is a pressing need to develop the country's resources to the fullest extent, and one of our most precious resources is the ability and creativity of all children'.

This call for action was followed by the Cockcroft Report (DES 1982), which reminded us that it is not sufficient for gifted children to be left to work through a textbook or a set of work cards; nor should they be given repetitive practice of processes that have already been mastered. The report emphasized that the view of able children being able to take care of themselves is misleading; although such children can probably take care of themselves better than the less able, this does not mean that they should be entirely responsible for their own learning. They need guidance, encouragement and the right kind of opportunities and challenges to fulfil their promise. The sentiments described within this report are at the heart of this chapter. The important issue is how we can provide the necessary guidance and support for these children. One effective way is through the empowerment of practitioners, which can be achieved by preparing them to be better informed, with an enhanced understanding of the nature of the challenge.

Although there have been various attempts over the last few years to implement effective strategies for educating gifted mathematicians, progress had been slow, until the government launched its 'Gifted and Talented' initiative in 1997. Within mathematics, developing a teaching programme had received much attention and a number of supporting documents had been issued to schools (DfEE 2000a, 2000b; QCA 2001). One of the major initiatives launched within the context of provision for gifted children was the introduction of World-Class tests by the Qualifications and Curriculum Authority (QCA) in mathematics and problem solving for pupils aged 9 and 13.

The developments described above have brought the debate about teaching gifted mathematicians to the forefront and it is hoped that the contents of this chapter will make a contribution to that debate. The aim of the chapter is to provide a framework of effective provision for mathematically gifted children, and with this in mind it focuses on two themes. First, it explores what we mean by the mathematically gifted and how we may identify gifted mathematicians. Second, it considers effective strategies for provision. Much of the content of this chapter is informed by the ongoing research and development work of the Able Children's Education Centre at Brunel University.

Who are the mathematically gifted?

There are no simple definitions which describe a mathematically gifted child, but it is useful to consider some issues relating to high ability in mathematics in order to gain a better understanding of how we may identify a promising mathematician. The question often asked is: does a child identified as *gifted*, using IQ tests or other assessment instruments, always show high mathematical ability? Not necessarily. The concept of giftedness as a single dimensional measure of intelligence has been challenged by many, and by Gardner (1993) in particular. Gardner describes ability in domain-specific terms and mathematical intelligence is one of a range of talents demonstrated by children. This subject-specific concept of intelligence is likely to be more useful when considering enhanced provision for children with mathematical promise.

Identifying mathematical talent

Identification of mathematical talent needs a fluid and iterative approach. Children's work needs to be observed in a range of contexts and at different levels of teacher direction in order to assess attributes of outlook and interest. As time passes, it should be possible to detect and gauge a child's emerging potential. While it is complex to construct a definitive list of attributes for identifying mathematical giftedness, it is useful to be familiar with what research says about the identification of mathematical promise.

Attributes of mathematically gifted children

Based on his observational studies, Krutetskii (1976) has provided a list of characteristics to guide both researchers and practitioners in the process of identifying mathematical talent. The following criteria proposed by Krutetskii have been validated by other researchers and educators (Koshy 2001), and could be used as a basis for observation of gifted mathematical behaviours. According to Krutetskii, mathematically gifted pupils are likely to:

- *Possess swiftness of reasoning.* Mathematically gifted children are able to follow various directions of mathematical thought. They are able to offer quick solutions to problems, including unfamiliar ones, by applying logic. They may behave as though they have innate cognitive ability to process information. It is common for these children to omit steps and not always be able to explain their methods.
- *Show ability to generalize.* This is another attribute demonstrated by mathematically gifted pupils. While working on a mathematical task an able mathematician is likely to perceive patterns and spot a general rule which can be applied to the task in hand and also be relevant to future mathematical work.
- *Have the ability to work with abstract ideas.* The mathematically promising child may pay little attention to given data and prefer to work within an abstract form.
- *Make use of the mathematical structure of a problem.* They are likely to recognize and categorize mathematical problems according to their structure.
- *Possess the ability to memorize relationships and principles of solutions from previous experiences.*
- *Think flexibly.* Krutetskii refers to this as *economy of thought.* Mathematically gifted children are able to switch from one method to another while solving problems, and, as they get older, develop strategies to find the clearest, most elegant and logical solution.

Lists or attributes like those presented above are useful for raising awareness. We cannot expect a pupil to exhibit all the above attributes, but she or he may demonstrate an appreciable number of them. Being aware of such a list of attributes should also enable us to reflect on the needs of such pupils and plan appropriate provision.

Some aspects to consider in the identification process

It is important to remember that children who possess high mathematical ability will only show this special talent if appropriate opportunities are provided. It is unlikely that pupils who are given a diet of only repetitive tasks and closed problems from textbooks would always show their true potential. Some children may also mask their ability for other reasons. For example, fear of being given 'more of the same' when set work is completed, being teased for being 'too clever', or being bored with the lessons and switching off completely, could all contribute to children hiding their potential ability. We also need to build in much flexibility within the identification process and be prepared to change our first judgements of pupils' mathematical ability. Gathering information from multiple sources such as tests, observations, parents' remarks, recordings and peer group comments can all help the identification process (Koshy 2001).

Identification

Provision

Figure 12.1 An identification/provision model

In this context, the recommendation of the National Numeracy Strategy (NNS) (DfES 2002) that we should target a larger cohort of pupils (35–40 per cent) rather than the top 5–10 per cent seems to be a sensible course to follow. This strategy of targeting a wider cohort of pupils was found useful within the *Mathematical Enrichment Project* (Koshy and Casey 2003), which was designed to select the best mathematicians from inner-city schools and provide an intervention programme for them. Teachers were asked to base their selection on observation of mathematical behaviours, motivation and experiences to identify mathematically promising pupils, rather than rely on standardized tests alone. Interestingly, many of the pupils who started with lower test scores in a pre-intervention test eventually did better in a post-test than pupils with higher initial scores. The designed enrichment programme seemed to have helped children to fulfil their potential.

Principles of provision

Identification and provision are discrete parts of a two-way process (see Figure 12.1). It may be that we notice a child's mathematical talent and plan appropriately challenging activities, making organizational arrangements accordingly. At the same time, it is also important to remember that it is easier to identify mathematically gifted pupils when they are working on rich mathematical tasks.

In setting out the following principles, three factors have been taken into account: the attributes of mathematically promising students; the mathematics curriculum; and the organization of teaching.

Mathematically gifted pupils need their talents to be acknowledged

This statement, of course, is true for all children, but in the case of a talented mathematician it is particularly important. It is quite common for teachers to avoid putting questions to an able group of children who have their hands up for nearly every question put to the class so the rest of the class will have a chance to contribute. From the point of view of the able child this can be upsetting. During an interview, Hamesh, an able 9-year-old told his teacher that he had stopped putting his hand up because 'no one ever took any notice'. He added that there was 'not much point in working hard in the class'.

Gifted mathematicians are capable of dealing with more advanced concepts

Most gifted children are quick learners. They are fast information processors and are capable of responding to a high level of cognitive challenge. Quite often they have already mastered what is planned for the rest of the class. Drill and practice types of lesson are less likely to appeal to these children. Most textbooks and ready-made photocopiable lesson plans are usually written with the average child in mind, and may not be suitable for the able child. Some kind of curriculum compacting will be necessary in these cases.

Gifted mathematicians need to be given time for extended tasks

Most gifted students in mathematics show persistence and stamina while carrying out investigations. They respond positively when they are given problems and investigations with open-ended outcomes. They may resent time constraints and imposed restrictions. The implication of this is that timed daily mathematics lessons need to be flexible for these children. Extension work may also be given as homework.

Able mathematicians benefit from communicating with able peers

In both learning new mathematics and sharing strategies, able pupils benefit from communicating with other children of similar ability or potential. In situations where they can spend time with other higher ability learners, their curiosity can be shared and complex questions, which may not be too well received within a mixed ability situation, can be pursued. Sharing ideas also enhances their conceptual understanding.

Mathematically able pupils are capable of being engaged in higher levels of thinking

Able children need to be provided with opportunities to analyze ideas, extract principles, reason and theorize. It would be an interesting exercise to look at a particular lesson plan or a page in a textbook and assess the level at which these processes are incorporated.

Planning activities

The QCA (2001) publication, *Working with Gifted and Talented Children*, a pack of resources designed to support the education of mathematically gifted children, includes a list of key principles to adopt when planning lessons. It is suggested that the way we plan should enable children to learn within the following dimensions:

- broader
- deeper
- faster
- independence
- reflection

There follows a list of questions that need to be taken into consideration when designing and selecting activities for able mathematicians. These are considered in the following sections.

Does the activity offer interest and challenge?

The word 'challenge' here is not intended to mean a 'more difficult' number operation. It means that the child can be given a task which is cognitively more demanding, but is presented in an interesting context. While routine problems that can be solved by set procedures are useful, they may not always involve a high level of challenge. Realistic problems such as 'design a bedroom' with a given amount of money and a few pages of a catalogue from which to select items, or 'if you won a free holiday for 1 million hours, how would you plan it?' are often motivating contexts and at the same time can generate open-ended solutions. Not all problems need to be in a real context. Pure mathematics problems which lead to generalizations also appeal to able children, who are often fascinated by patterns and can recognize and apply previously learned ideas.

Has the activity potential for different levels of outcome?

A familiar activity such as 'the handshakes problem' ('If everyone in this room shakes hands with everyone else – just once – how many handshakes will take place?'), when given to a mixed ability group, can generate solutions at different levels. For example, children may choose to use any of the following strategies:

- Draw pictures to represent handshakes; record answers for smaller numbers; and progress to a manageable number by counting the number of handshakes.
- Draw pictures to illustrate what happens and notice that the first person out of the total 20 shakes hands with 19 people, but the second person shakes hands with only 18 people as one handshake has already taken place. This strategy would lead to the calculation:

  $19 + 18 + 17 + 16 + 15 + 14 + 13 + 12 + 11 + 10 + 9 + 8 + 7 + 6 + 5 + 4 + 3 + 2 + 1 + 0 = 190$ handshakes

- Draw models and systematically record the results in a table:

Number of children	Number of handshakes
0	0
1	0

2	1
3	3
4	6
5	10
6 . . .	15 . . .

The sequence is the key to working out the problem. For seven people there would be 21 handshakes, for eight there would be 28 and so on. By continuing the sequence it can be worked out that there would be 190 handshakes for twenty people.

Some challenging questions put to an able group would lead them to further investigation.

- Is there a connection between the number of people and the number of handshakes?
- Can we think of ideas to help us to make a generalization which would work for any number of people?

Nine-year-old Jamie, a promising mathematician, offered the following explanation: 'Well, there are 20 people, each person must shake hands with 19 other people, as you don't shake hands with yourself. That means there would be 20 × 19 handshakes taking place. The total number of handshakes would only be half of that, because 2 people only need to shake hands once'. That, with the teacher's prompts and support, led to the generaliztion:

For n people, the number of handshakes would be:

$n(n - 1)/2$

Children like Jamie are likely to remember this situation and the rule, and use this experience in other situations which are structurally similar.

Does the activity provide opportunities for recording and reflection?

Research has shown that gifted children have high levels of metacognition that make them aware of their own thinking processes. Keeping mathematics diaries in which they record how a problem was solved or the direction selected for an investigation would make them reflect on their own thinking. Written comments could also include what children did, what they found challenging and how they felt about a particular piece of work. Such a diary not only provides a basis for the teacher and child to be engaged in talking about mathematics, it also becomes a portfolio of self-assessment. Nine-year-old Emma's work (see Figure 12.2) is an example of how her teacher, Jim, trained her class to record their thinking and progress.

Does the activity encourage problem solving skills?

There has been a resurgence of interest in problem solving within mathematics teaching. World-Class tests in problem solving are offered (QCA 2001) to

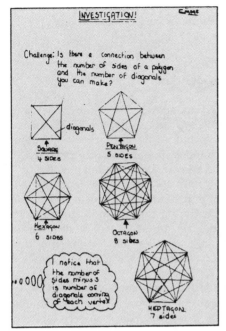

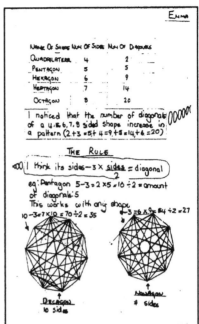

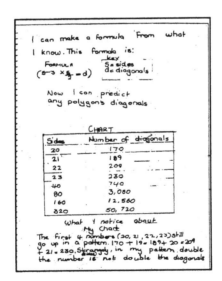

Figure 12.2 Emma's investigation

gifted children at ages 9 and 13. A NNS in-service pack emphasizes the role of problem solving for extending able pupils (DfES 2002). It recommends that children need to be trained in problem solving while pointing out that they do not appear to have secure problem solving strategies. Problem solving activities provide opportunities for all children – particularly the very able – to think, talk and write mathematics.

The acceleration versus enrichment debate

When considering provision, we need to address the issue of whether *acceleration* or *enrichment* is more effective as a strategy for provision. Support from the government for fast-tracking and early entry to GCSE examinations is based on the acceleration model. This move was criticized by a group of mathematics educators (UK Mathematics Foundation 2000: 7) as having: 'serious disadvantages for pupils' long term development [and needing to be] handled with great caution'. Enrichment for *added breadth* was recommended as a way forward in the documentation. This involved providing 'extension work which enriches the official curriculum by requiring deeper understanding of standard material (for example, by insisting on a higher level of fluency in working with fractions, ratio, algebra or in problem solving)'.

Among those who feel uneasy about the acceleration strategy is Fielker (1997: 9), who expresses his concern by asserting that: 'in this model pupils do not learn more about mathematics. What they do is merely learn the same mathematics sooner'. This strategy, according to Fielker, does not seem to fulfil the needs of the more able, who, he argues, deserve something better.

Sheffield (1999), the chairperson of the US Task Force looking into provision for mathematically promising students, urges us to drop the acceleration versus enrichment debate and suggests that we think about *depth* in mathematics. She offers a three-dimensional model for mathematically gifted pupils which is worthy of consideration (see Figure 12.3). She recommends that mathematically promising pupils should look not only at changing the rate or number of mathematical offerings but also at changing the depth or complexity of the mathematical investigations. Interestingly, Koshy (2001) found that many of the mathematical tasks offered to very able mathematicians involved both enrichment and acceleration in the sense that when pupils were motivated to carry out a complex and in-depth investigation they often sought new and more advanced knowledge from a higher level in the curriculum.

The NNS and the able mathematician

The main purpose of implementing the NNS in 1999 and issuing the *Framework for Teaching Mathematics from Reception to Year 6* (DfEE 1999: 2) was to help schools 'set appropriately high expectations for all pupils and understand how pupils should progress through the primary years'. The needs of able mathematicians are obviously included in this statement. At this point it is

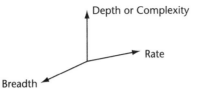

Figure 12.3 Sheffield's three-dimensional model

useful to make an analysis of the structure and requirements of the *Framework* in the context of educating mathematically able children. Such an analysis shows both the positive features of the *Framework* and, at the same time, raises some aspects of concern with regard to provision for able pupils. These are now briefly presented.

Mathematical content

The *Framework* offers clear and specific guidance on mathematical content. The progression that is built into it helps with planning. It also helps the teacher to gauge children's mastery of facts, knowledge and understanding at a certain level and move them on to appropriate tasks. Children who are potentially very able quite often do not possess numerical fluency and a repertoire of skills due to lack of experience. In such cases, in spite of their high potential ability, they are unable to carry out investigations and solve problems. Using the *Framework* teachers can monitor any gaps in their knowledge and take action. Also, for teachers who feel they do not have the necessary subject knowledge, the explanations of mathematical content in the *Framework* are very helpful.

Some words of caution are necessary at this juncture. If the *Framework* is followed strictly within the recommended year groups without careful monitoring, it is possible that children who may already know much of the content might get frustrated and feel that mathematics is boring, resulting in their being turned off the subject.

Calculations

The *Framework* stresses the importance of flexibility in the use of algorithms and gives a high profile to mental and oral mathematics. All children, and this includes mathematically able children, need to develop effective strategies for mental calculations. As it cannot be taken for granted that an able child would automatically be competent and fluent in mental calculations, the development of greater fluency and speed of calculation can assist the child in carrying out challenging mathematical tasks without having to struggle with arithmetic calculations. Managing mental mathematics sessions becomes more challenging as children get older with a widening range of ability and experiences, and it is essential that teachers involve differentiated activities and teaching styles in these sessions.

Teaching strategies

The NNS provides guidance with timings of the daily mathematics session and a list of features of *good direct teaching*. The advantage of a timed structure is that it provides a built-in faster pace which helps able children. This is because many of them are fast learners and do not need a great deal of time to learn new ideas.

As with all good intentions, there are also some concerns about the timed structure of the lessons. Able mathematicians who are capable of extended work may not respond to a three-part lesson, especially when the lesson focuses on something they already know. Many of these pupils enjoy mathematics and may like to spend more uninterrupted time on tasks. Flexibility is therefore needed in the use of a strictly timed sequence for every day of the week.

The daily mathematics lesson

The NNS recommends two approaches for extending able pupils (see DfES 2002). The first is to use challenges and investigations and the second is to extend the work planned for the rest of the class by asking more challenging questions that involve thinking at a deeper level.

So, how can we ensure that we maximize learning during the three-part mathematics lesson? The following examples of lessons were observed by the author on her visits to two schools as part of a research project.

Mental and oral starter

For their mental and oral session, Eileen started her 'What is my mystery number?' activity with her 6-year-olds. She described the activity as being pitched at 'average level' for her class. She asked the children to work out the mystery number from the following clues:

> I am thinking of a number;
> It is lower than 40;
> It is higher than 26;
> If you count in fives you will land on that number;
> It is an odd number.

After some discussion, the class worked out the mystery number (35). Then Eileen gave activity sheets to different groups with different clues and asked them to find the mystery number. The clues on the able group's sheet read:

> It is an odd number;
> It is a multiple of 3 and 7 (discuss what a multiple is);
> It is between 60 and 100.

Number of jumpers	1	2	3	4	5	6	7
Cost of jumpers	10	20	30	40	50	60	70
Left over money	95	85	75	65	55	45	35
Exact number of T-shirts bought (without remainders)	–	–	–	5 can be bought	–	–	–

Figure 12.4 Amy's answer

Jason thinks he can make a quadrilateral with four acute angles and drew this shape.

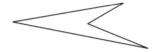

Is he right? Study the shape above and see if you agree with him. Write down your reasons for your decision.

Figure 12.5 Jason's quadrilateral

The main part of the lesson

Andy, a Year 4 teacher, introduced the following problem solving activity to his class:

Natalie bought T-shirts for £13 each and some jumpers for £10 each. She spent a total of £105. How many of each did she buy?

He asked the children to solve this problem and be able to justify their answer to satisfy the conditions given in the problem. They could use any type of recording and then share the solutions. The following solution was offered by the able group who responded to what the class was shown in the previous week on *drawing tables* for solving problems. With trial and improvement methods and their teacher's prompts most of the children worked out a correct solution. It seemed that the able group quickly grasped the usefulness of systematic recording, as can be seen in Amy's work (see Figure 12.4).

Helen, a Year 5 teacher, planned a series of activities for teaching her class about angles. On a particular day when the rest of the class were working in groups discussing obtuse and acute angles, a challenging extension was given to the able group. She had asked all the children whether it was possible to make a quadrilateral with four acute angles and most of them said it was impossible because the total of the four angles of a quadrilateral is 360 degrees. She asked the able group to solve the question illustrated in Figure 12.5.

Plenary

During the plenary session, Andy asked his children to share their methods of problem solving. They showed an impressive range and variety of strategies. He also asked them to join in solving a simple similar problem to reinforce the usefulness of a table in problem solving.

In her plenary session, Helen asked her able group to share their explanations and used this opportunity to introduce them to another idea – interior and exterior angles. She asked them to find out the size of the interior angles of a regular hexagon for homework.

Conclusion

So years have gone by, and the 'gifted' seeds of the Cockcroft Report are finally on more fertile ground. Support from the NNS and an emphasis on problem solving have provided the climate for growth in provision for mathematically gifted children. The issues explored in this chapter, it is hoped, will reduce the drift in planning appropriate provision for our most able mathematicians and guide teachers towards a more enriched course, contributing to whole-school improvement by focusing on mathematical promise. As Joseph Renzulli, an expert in gifted education in the USA, always says at the opening of all his speeches: 'a rising tide lifts all ships'.

References

DES (Department of Education and Science) (1982) *Mathematics Counts* (Cockcroft Report). London: HMSO.

DfEE (Department for Education and Employment) (1999) *Framework for Teaching Mathematics from Reception to Year 6*. London: DfEE.

DfEE (Department for Education and Employment) (2000a) *National Literacy and Numeracy Strategies: Guidance on Teaching Able Children*. London: DfEE.

DfEE (Department for Education and Employment) (2000b) *Mathematical Challenges for Able Pupils in Key Stages 1 and 2*. London: DfEE.

DfES (Department for Education and Skills) (2002) *Supporting More Able Pupils in Year 5* (course tutor's pack). London: DfES.

Fielker, D. (1997) *Extending Mathematical Ability Through Whole-class Teaching*. London: Hodder & Stoughton.

Gardner, H. (1993) *Multiple Intelligences*. New York: Basic Books.

Koshy, V. (2001) *Teaching Mathematics to Able Children*. London: Fulton.

Koshy, V. and Casey, R. (2003) Developing mathematically promising students by empowering teachers, *The Research Journal for the National Association for Gifted Children*, 7(1): 22–28.

Krutetskii, V.A. (1976) *The Psychology of Mathematical Abilities in School Children*. Chicago: University of Chicago Press.

QCA (Qualifications and Curriculum Authority) (2001) *Working with Gifted and Talented Children (Key Stages 1 and 2)* (video and in-service pack). London: QCA.

Sheffield, L. (1999) The development of mathematically promising students in the Unites States, *Mathematics in School*, 28(3): 15–18.

Straker, A. (1982) *Mathematics for Gifted Pupils*. Harlow: Longman.

UK Mathematics Foundation (2000) *Acceleration or Enrichment: Serving the Needs of the top 10% in School Mathematics*. Birmingham: School of Mathematics, Birmingham University.

INFORMATION AND COMMUNICATION
TECHNOLOGY ISSUES

Helen J. Williams is a freelance educational consultant with a particular interest in early years mathematics, and in Chapter 13 she and Ian Thompson make a case for using the calculator to teach mathematics to children in Key Stage 1. They begin by setting the ongoing calculator debate in a historical context and by looking briefly at some of the research evidence concerning the use of calculators in primary schools. They consider the limitations of the National Numeracy Strategy (NNS) calculator policy and its effect on the use of calculators in primary schools, and argue that restricting calculator use to older children deprives the younger child of some important early learning experiences. The main part of the chapter focuses on examples of activities that have been used successfully with Key Stage 1 children, and draws on the work of nursery, Reception and Year 1 children to illustrate that using a calculator can develop mathematical thinking in youngsters, and can be a catalyst for discussing numbers.

One of Steve Higgins' research interests is effective teaching and learning with a particular focus on mathematics and the use of information and communication technology (ICT). In Chapter 14 he begins by providing an overview of some of the research on primary mathematics and ICT, focusing particularly on evidence of the impact of computers in the classroom on mathematical attainment. He provides details of three case studies to help illustrate the extent to which ICT can be effectively integrated into mathematics lessons. In two of these the teachers used ICT to target specific mathematics objectives that they had identified as capable of benefiting from a clear focus and increased time. In the third study mathematical activities were chosen that would develop the use of mathematical talk through collaborative discussion of mathematical tasks in small groups. The chapter concludes with some implications for classroom teachers.

Calculators for all?

Helen J. Williams and Ian Thompson

Introduction

This chapter begins with an outline of the history of the place of calculators in primary mathematics education, and then uses mainly Key Stage 1 examples to support the point of view that calculators can be an effective tool for learning about number. The argument concerning the extent to which calculators should be used in mathematics lessons has been a long-standing one. A seminal article by Girling in 1977 significantly raised the level of the debate by defining basic numeracy as 'the ability to use a four-function calculator sensibly': a definition very different from that given in the *Framework for Teaching Mathematics from Reception to Year 6* (DfEE 1999).[1] Twenty years after the appearance of Girling's article a Numeracy Task Force was established by the Secretary of State for Education and Employment, David Blunkett, 'to develop a national strategy to raise standards in order to reach the Government's national numeracy targets by 2002' (DfEE 1998a: 4). Included in this brief was a request to look at the calculator issue.

A press release on 8 July 1998 (353/98) announcing the publication of the Numeracy Task Force report *The Implementation of the National Numeracy Strategy* (DfEE 1998b) stated, erroneously, that the report would include 'a ban on the use of calculators by children up to the age of eight and restricted use throughout the remainder of primary school'. This incorrect interpretation was picked up by most of the press, who on the release of the preliminary report earlier in January had had quite a field day. For example *The Times* headline on 22 January 1998 had said 'Calculators out in drive to raise standards' (O'Leary 1998), and the *Daily Mail* had suggested that 'The Education Secretary at long last acknowledged one of the great mathematical truths: that children plus calculators equals disaster' (Halpin 1998). This interpretation was reinforced in an article the following day by David Reynolds (1998), Chair of the Numeracy Task Force, who said 'Calculator usage should, we believe, be restricted until the age of eight or nine'. Five years earlier, a report (Ofsted

1993) had pointed out that calculators were being used in only 10 per cent of primary lessons, and so the press reports in 1998 provided a legitimate excuse for many teachers to perpetuate their minimal use of calculators.

It is difficult not to believe that the Department for Education and Employment (DfEE) press release was a deliberate exercise in disinformation. For, despite David Blunkett's attempts to put the record straight in the *Times Educational Supplement* (*TES*) (10 July) with the blunt statement 'We're not banning calculators', and members of the Numeracy Task Force 'denouncing the Government's press machine' (*TES*, 24 July), the damage had already been done. This helps to explain the observation on the Office for Standards in Education (Ofsted) website (Ofsted 2002) that: 'Despite its potential value, the use of the calculator is not a regular feature in the teaching of the daily mathematics lesson'.

Research evidence

The Task Force had also been charged with ensuring that their recommendations took account of national and international evidence. So what does the research evidence concerning calculator use actually say? The School Curriculum and Assessment Authority's (SCAA) *The Use of Calculators at Key Stages 1–3* (SCAA 1997) and Ofsted's *Recent Research in Mathematics Education 5–16* (1995) both suggest that there is no evidence to support the claim that the use of calculators has a negative effect on children's understanding of number or on their ability to calculate in their head or on paper. In fact, the subheading of the chapter on calculators in the latter publication is '*Open access to calculators does not lead to dependence, and can improve pupils' numeracy*'. In a similar vein, Ofsted's *The Teaching and Learning of Number in Primary School* (1993: 11) states unequivocally that 'There was evidence that using a calculator as an aid to learning enhanced the pupils' understanding of number'.

Two different illogical arguments are used to make banning or seriously restricting calculator use in lower primary school seem reasonable: one relates to our performance in international surveys and the other to the relationship between mental calculation and calculator usage. The latter argument will be dealt with later.

It does appear to be the case that England fares worse, particularly on number tasks, than many of the countries that participate in international surveys, and some people argue that the reason for this poor performance is our over-reliance on calculators. However, this over-reliance is questionable given Ofsted's (1993: 11) comment that: 'The skills of using a calculator were neglected in a high percentage of the schools; in only a tenth of the lessons seen were calculators used.' It is also interesting to note that in the Third International Mathematics and Science Survey (TIMSS), Singapore, with the highest teacher-reported frequency of calculator use, performed better than every other country.

Calculators in the National Numeracy Strategy

The *Framework for Teaching Mathematics from Reception to Year 6* (DfEE 1999: 8) provides contradictory advice about the use of calculators. On the one hand it suggests that they 'offer a unique way of learning about numbers and the number system, place value, properties of numbers, and fractions and decimals'. And yet, given that children in Key Stage 1 learn about these topics, it seems strange to read later that 'schools should not normally use the calculator as part of Key Stage 1 mathematics, but should emphasise oral and mental calculation'. It is little wonder that, given this 'official' exhortation and the biased media presentation of the Task Force report, Ofsted (2000: 18) reported that 'Overall, however, teachers remain uncertain about when and how often to use calculators as part of their daily mathematics lesson'.

The reason given by the British Educational Communications and Technology Agency (Becta) (2001) for discouraging the use of calculators at Key Stage 1 is that children at this stage are still developing skills such as mental calculation, rounding and checking results, all of which are necessary for using calculators effectively. This betrays a fundamental misunderstanding of the role the calculator plays in helping the young child understand number and think mathematically. It falsely assumes that all these skills have to be well-developed prior to children using calculators effectively, and ignores the fact that using calculators can help the development of these very skills at all ages and key stages.

The *Framework Supplement* contains a detailed list of the skills and techniques of calculator use that children in Years 5 and 6 need to acquire. The following skills are taken from this list (some have been slightly modified or broken down into sub-skills), and it is suggested that there is no reason why they could not be taught to children in Key Stage 1:

- understand the words 'calculator', 'display', 'key', 'enter', 'clear', 'constant';
- clear the display before starting a calculation;
- use the [+], [−], and [=] keys to calculate with realistic data;
- use the constant function to generate multiples of any given number;
- make the calculator count forwards or backwards in multiples of a number from a given starting point;
- recognize a negative number output by using the constant function to count backwards;
- begin to select the correct key sequence;
- have a feel for the approximate size of an answer.

It is worth noting that this list of skills fails to address how teachers can use calculators to enhance children's numerical knowledge and understanding. In relation to this, we believe that there are two main areas where calculators are at their most effective in the learning of mathematics, and these apply to all key stages:

- as a calculating aid in solving problems: to 'free' children from mundane calculations, allowing them to concentrate on the processes they need to employ to solve a problem; to help them 'keep their eye on the ball';
- as a teaching aid: a rich piece of equipment that can be used to illuminate and model how our number system works.

Often, these areas overlap.

In fact, the National Numeracy Strategy (NNS) (see DfEE 2001: 87) argues similarly, suggesting that: 'For this purpose, [as a teaching aid] it [the calculator] may be used at appropriate times in any year group'. However, even in *Developing Mathematics in Years 4, 5 and 6* (DfEE 2001), a five-day course designed to strengthen the mathematical knowledge of Key Stage 2 teachers, the amount of time devoted to the calculator as a teaching aid is just 15 minutes, whereas 135 minutes are allocated to developing teachers' own calculator skills and to discussing ways of helping children tackle the type of questions appearing on Paper B, the calculator paper of the Key Stage 2 National Curriculum tests. While paying lip-service to the role of the calculator as a teaching aid there is very little material in the course devoted to this crucial aspect.

Classroom activities in Key Stage 1

The remainder of this chapter focuses on examples of activities for children in Key Stage 1 that exemplify the acknowledgement in the Task Force's final report (DfEE 1998b) that 'used well, calculators can be an effective tool for learning about numbers' while at the same time challenging the misconceived statement that 'schools should not normally use the calculator as part of Key Stage 1 mathematics' (DfEE 1999: 8).

Calculators can positively affect children's willingness to explore and discuss numbers

Calculators attract children because children are naturally inquisitive. Young children need opportunities to play with calculators freely, exploring their own ideas, just as they need opportunities to play with any piece of structured mathematical equipment. The justification for this is twofold:

- spontaneous activity can tell teachers much about the child's level of number confidence and number knowledge;
- children's play helps to embed and extend their developing ideas about number.

It is important to provide pencil and paper, 'to help you keep track of what you are finding out'. Children's jottings reveal their ability to do the following (all the examples, unless otherwise stated, are from Year 1 children):

- *Read and write a range of numbers accurately.* In Figure 13.1 the child identified her telephone number, her age and her two-digit door number

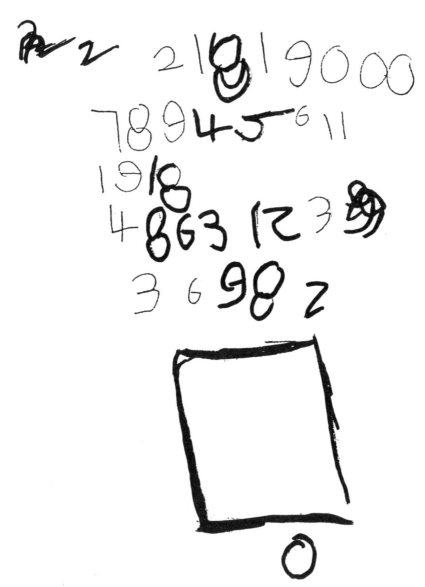

Figure 13.1 A Year 1 child identifying her age, telephone number and door number

among others. The nursery child in Figure 13.2 identified his telephone number (can you find 372110?) and had a sustained conversation with his friend about the difference between the digits 8 and 0. As children play with

Figure 13.2 A nursery child writing his telephone number

their calculators they gradually progress from reading strings of single-digit numbers to reading two- and three-digit numbers.

- *Recognize a number or counting pattern.* Both children in the following two examples (Figures 13.3 and 13.4) showed interest in repeating patterns after making these with other apparatus. This is an example of calculators extending and supporting other mathematical resources in children's learning.

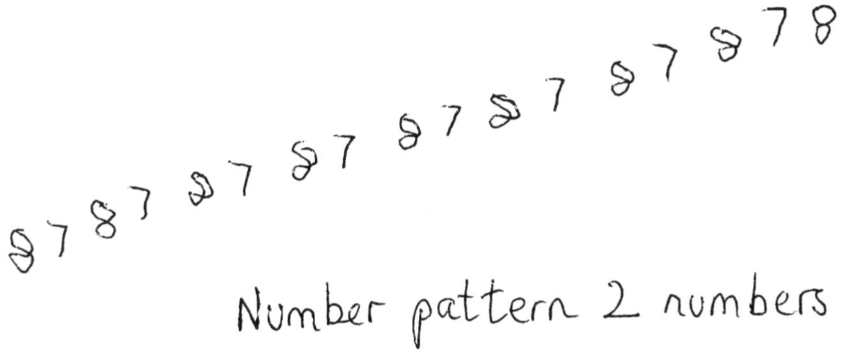

8 7 8 7 8 7 8 7 8 7 8 7 8 7 8 7 8 7 8 7 8

Number pattern 2 numbers

Figure 13.3 Generating a repeating pattern

- *Use the function keys with understanding.* In Figure 13.5, the Year 1 child argued that 'Twenty one-hundred and thirty one-hundred is fifty two-hundred because 20 and 30 make 50'. Although not all of her calculations are correct she was able to talk about those she was sure about and those she was unsure about.

Calculators can be used to stimulate mental calculation

One of the great strengths of a basic four-function calculator is that it has a constant function. Children characterize this as the calculator 'counting'. By entering a simple key sequence to generate repeated addition (0 + 1 = = = usually works) or subtraction (5 – 1 = = =), children can make the calculator count up and down in steps of different sizes. The calculator is being used to verify their mental and oral counting, as illustrated in Figures 13.6 and 13.7.

A key objective for children in Year 1 is to count on and back in ones from any small number. With the calculator set up as an 'add one' machine a preliminary activity involves the children counting with their eyes closed while pressing the equals key, occasionally checking to see whether they have said the same number that the calculator shows. When young children are asked to continue the count from a given number they often have to start from the beginning each time. They are at the developmental stage of treating the counting numbers as an 'unbreakable string'. To give them practice at naming the next number without starting from 1 (a prerequisite for finding a sum by counting on), children can be asked to enter their age and find out how old they will be in, say, three years' time by pressing the equals key three times. The next stage is to have them read aloud the numerals appearing in the display as they press. This activity gives them practice at the double count involved in the counting-on strategy: children have to continue the count from a given starting number while also keeping a tally of the actual numbers spoken.

There are many other early Key Stage 1 activities where calculators can be used to stimulate such mental calculation – the grid shown in Figure 13.8 also

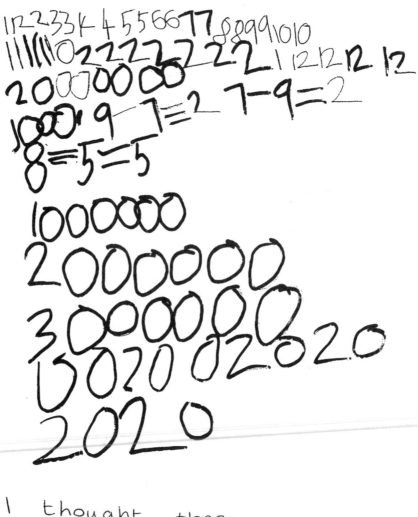

Figure 13.4 Generating repeating patterns

involves young children in checking conjectures. In this activity the children shade the numbers they can make 'appear' by using the function keys – for example, to colour 12, a child might enter $10 + 2 = 12$, $6 + 6 = 12$, or any other appropriate number sentences.

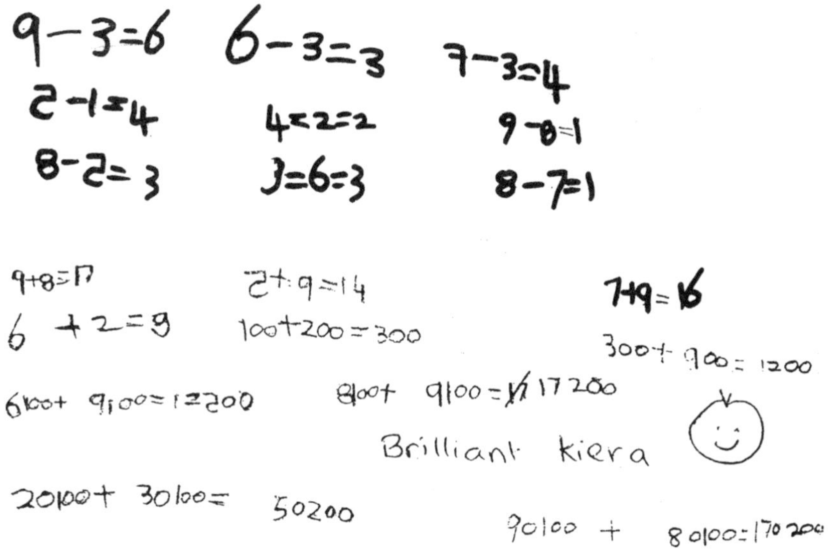

$9-3=6$ $6-3=3$ $7-3=4$
$2-1=4$ $4=2=2$ $9-8=1$
$8-2=3$ $3=6=3$ $8-7=1$

$9+8=17$ $2+9=14$ $7+9=16$
$6+2=9$ $100+200=300$
                                          $300+900=1200$
$600+900=1200$ $800+9100=17200$
                    Brilliant kiera ☺
$2000+3000=$ 50200
                            $9000 + 80100=170200$

Figure 13.5 Using the function keys with understanding

In the example shown in Figure 13.9, children are asked to choose a number to write in the box, and then find four numbers, one for each corner, that add up to their number in the middle. Although they have access to a calculator, they have to do the calculations in their heads. The calculator is again being used to check their ideas. Of course, this task does not require calculators to be used, but if they are available children definitely become more adventurous in their choice of numbers. This is an example of the calculator 'freeing' the child to work on some mathematics. This activity is easily differentiated – for example, in Key Stage 2 children can be asked to choose a fraction or an amount of money to go into the box.

The phrase 'using a calculator for checking' can be interpreted in two different ways: for checking calculations and for checking conjectures. Many years ago Johnson (1978) argued that using calculators to check pencil and paper calculations is an abuse of calculators: they should have been used to perform the calculation in the first place. And yet Ofsted (1993) showed that this was the most common use for them. A more enlightened interpretation of 'checking' involves children in making conjectures (educated guesses), using their calculators to check these conjectures, modifying them where necessary. For example, in the work illustrated in both Figures 13.3 and 13.4 it is the child that has done all the hard work, not the calculator. There are many games involving pairs of children where one child uses a calculator to check their opponent's mentally-calculated answer (it is usually in their interest to do this!). Checking is meaningless unless some sense is made of the check.

Counting 2's.

2 4 6 8 10 12 14
16 18 20 22
24 26 28 30

lovely ☺

10 11 12 13 14 15 16 17 18

Figure 13.6 Counting in twos with a calculator

By the time children reach Year 2 they are expected to be able to add and subtract a single-digit number to or from a number in the teens or the twenties by bridging through 10 or 20 as appropriate. For example, 16 + 7 would be found by reasoning that '16 + 4 is 20 and 20 plus the remaining 3 is 23', and 24 – 6 would be calculated by arguing that '24 – 4 is 20 and 20 take away the remaining 2 is 18'. Bridging through the next multiple of 10 is a very powerful strategy for children to use in Year 4 when they have to find the sum of, or

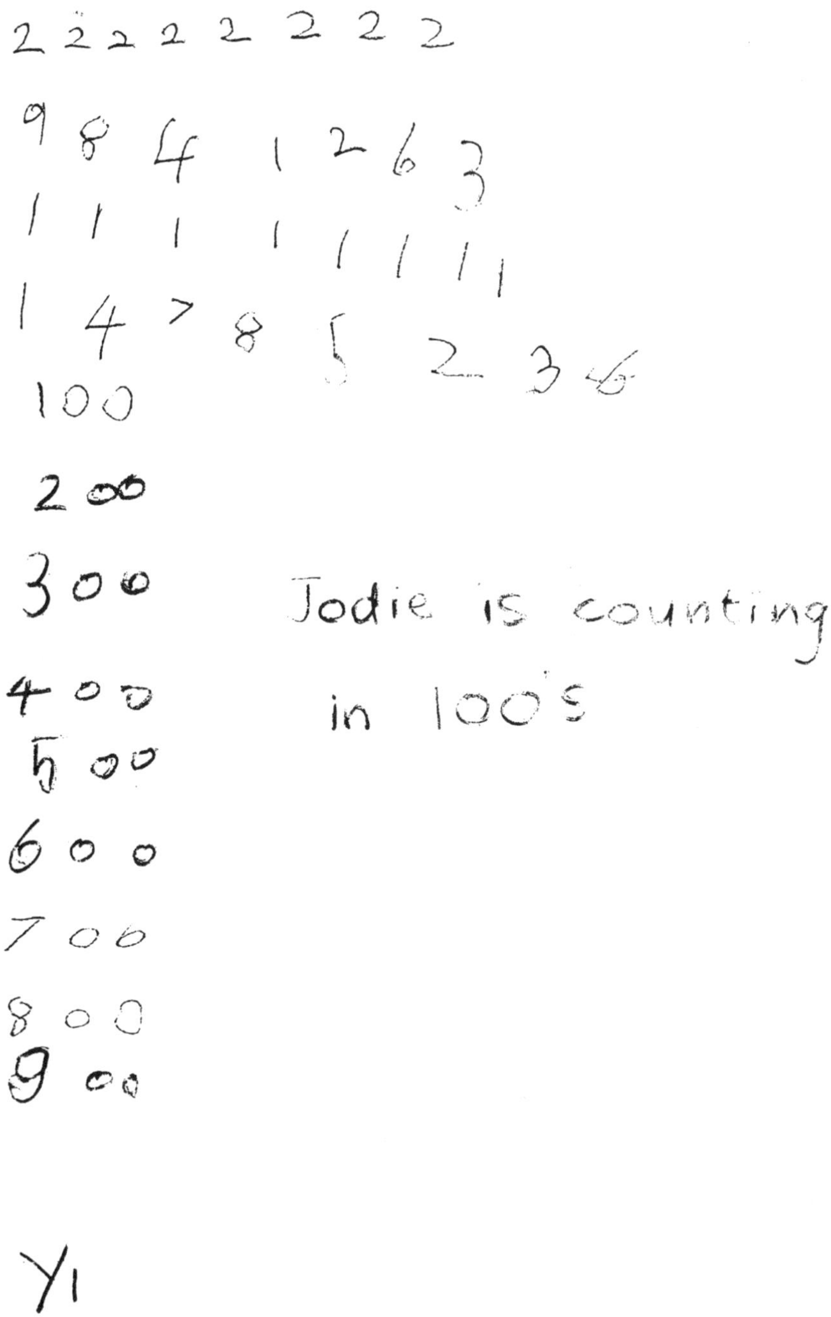

2 2 2 2 2 2 2 2

9 8 4 1 2 6 3
1 1 1 1 1 1 1 1
1 4 7 8 5 2 3 6

100

2 00

3 00

Jodie is counting

4 00

in 100's

5 00

6 0 0

7 0 0

8 0 0

9 00

Y1

Figure 13.7 Using the calculator to support counting in hundreds

0	1	2	3	4
5	6	7	8	9
10	11	12	13	14
15	16	17	18	19
20	21	22	23	24

Figure 13.8 A calculator activity grid

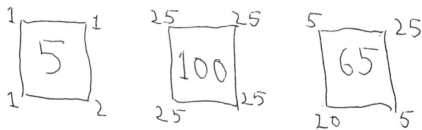

Figure 13.9 The 'box' game

difference between, any pair of two-digit numbers, either with or without the support of an Empty Number Line (ENL). Nearly all of the calculation strategies that involve an ENL (see Rousham, Chapter 3) involve jumping to the next (or previous) multiple of 10. Children should be taught the pre-requisite skills needed to carry out this strategy effectively, and yet commercial schemes usually fail to give sufficient attention to these prerequisites or to the bridging strategy in general.

To be able to use bridging effectively children must be able to do the following:

- quickly recall complements in 10 or in 20;
- split any single-digit number into its various partitions;
- appreciate the result of adding a single-digit number to 10 or 20 (and later to any multiple of 10);
- recognize what to subtract from a teen or twenties number to reduce it to a multiple of 10.

The following activity (see Figure 13.10) involves the use of a calculator to help in the development of some of these skills. The task is to write in the squares the number and the operation necessary to get from one circle to the next. So, in the case of movement from the first circle to the second the child would

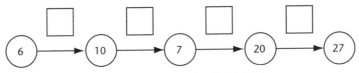

Figure 13.10 A calculator activity to practise 'bridging'

write '+ 4': the complement in 10 of 6. To move from the second to the third circle the child would have to find the complement in 10 of 7, and so on. The children are practising (or perhaps learning) complements and bridging. The calculator checks the accuracy of the mental calculation in each case and provides immediate actionable feedback. The blank grid can be modified to provide suitable differentiation within the class, or to use later with larger multiples of 10.

Calculators stimulate discussion about large numbers

Children are interested in large numbers. Observations of children exploring the calculator keys suggest that they often ask an adult to read a full display, getting excited about the result. They are interested in making larger and larger numbers and over time begin to show some understanding of what it is that makes a written number 'larger' or 'smaller'. The calculator can also arouse children's interest in negative and fractional numbers. After exploring how a calculator 'counts backwards', a 7-year-old was heard to ask if the negative numbers and the positive numbers meet anywhere around the back of the world. Just as children are exposed to unusual and exciting words through literature, so they can be exposed to exciting numbers through calculators.

In Figure 13.11 a Reception child has recorded some large numbers in her calculator display, which she asked an adult to 'read' to her. It was a challenge for her to use this paper record to re-enter the same numbers, correctly oriented: a valuable lesson about how we read and write numbers.

Additionally, for a multi-digit number to appear correctly in the display, it must be entered correctly – i.e. the larger-value digit before the smaller. As they enter '143', the children see each digit move into position according to its value. A Reception child had written 15 as 51 and so his teacher reminded him 'Can you write your 15 starting with the 1?' This he did, writing the 1 first, but on the *right-hand side of the 5*. Using a calculator, entering the 1 first would have shown a correctly-oriented 15.

Calculators aid children's understanding about how our number system works

The calculator is invaluable in developing the young child's understanding of place value. At the end of Year 2 children are expected to have a firm grasp of three-digit numbers. Using a calculator to explore adding, for example,

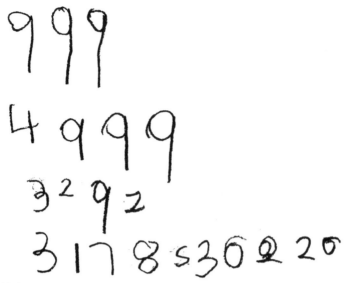

Figure 13.11 A Reception child recording large numbers

100 and 40 and 3, reveals how this is correctly recorded – i.e. 143 rather than 100403. This activity supplements the use of place value cards (arrow cards) which are often used for developing young children's understanding of this important concept. It also links to a powerful Key Stage 2 place value game where children are invited to 'remove' the digits in three- or four-digit numbers by using the subtraction key. For example, one child might enter 4753 and ask another to reduce each digit in turn to zero. Subtracting 7 rather than 700 will give the answer 4746 instead of the required 4053. Once again, the calculator provides important feedback to help children assess the extent to which they have been successful.

An appreciation of important place value principles of our numeration system can be developed (see Thompson, Chapter 15) by asking children to multiply various numbers by 10 and then discuss their findings. Repeated multiplication by 10 and later, in Key Stage 2, repeated division by 10, demonstrate how the digits move around the decimal point to make numbers of various sizes.

Calculators link the world outside the classroom to that within it

Using calculators as part of their role-play helps children practise using a calculator in an appropriate context, such as shopping. It forms links between the classroom and the world outside, where calculators are in everyday use. Teachers can model how to use a calculator when working out the solution to a problem such as how much two bars of chocolate and one toothbrush will cost in total.

Conclusions

The use of calculators in primary schools has long been the focus of controversy. The NNS, which could have taken the opportunity to articulate effective calculator practice at both key stages, instead advocated the illogical position that children should use them efficiently at Key Stage 2, without being allowed to use them at Key Stage 1. Perhaps evidence stating that calculator use continues to be inefficient in Key Stage 2 mathematics may be one result of not using them at all in Key Stage 1. What we need is to encourage enlightened teacher debate about the effective and ineffective use of calculators in all classrooms.

Note

1 The definition of numeracy given in the *Framework for Teaching Mathematics from Reception to Year 6* (DfEE 1999: 4) is as follows:

> Numeracy is a proficiency which involves confidence and competence with numbers and measures. It requires an understanding of the number system, a repertoire of computational skills and an inclination and ability to solve number problems in a variety of contexts. Numeracy also demands practical understanding of the ways in which information is gathered by counting and measuring, and is presented in graphs, diagrams, charts and tables.

Acknowledgements

Part of this chapter originally appeared in the article 'Calculators and KS1' by Helen Williams, in *Micromath*, a journal of the Association of Teachers of Mathematics (18/2, summer 2002: 34–6).

References

Becta (British Educational Communications and Technology Agency) (2001) Calculator activities for primary schools from BECTa, *Micromath*, 17(3): 20–34.
DfEE (Department for Education and Employment) (1998a) *Numeracy Matters: The Preliminary Report of the Numeracy Task Force*. London: DfEE.
DfEE (Department for Education and Employment) (1998b) *The Implementation of the National Numeracy Strategy: The Final Report of the Numeracy Task Force*. London: DfEE.
DfEE (Department for Education and Employment) (1999) *Framework for Teaching Mathematics from Reception to Year 6*. London: DfEE.
DfEE (Department for Education and Employment) (2001) *Developing Mathematics in Years 4, 5 and 6: The Five-day Course*. London: DfEE.
Girling, M.S. (1977) Towards a definition of basic numeracy, *Mathematics Teaching*, 81: 4–5.

Halpin, T. (1998) Labour turns the tables to bring back sums by rote, *Daily Mail*, 22 January.

Johnson, D.C. (1978) Calculators: abuses and uses, *Mathematics Teaching*, 85: 50–6.

Ofsted (Office for Standards in Education) (1993) *The Teaching and Learning of Number in Primary School*. London: Ofsted.

Ofsted (Office for Standards in Education) (1995) *Recent Research in Mathematics Education 5–16*. London: Ofsted.

Ofsted (Office for Standards in Education) (2000) *The National Numeracy Strategy: The First Year*. London: Ofsted.

Ofsted (Office for Standards in Education) (2002) *Teaching of Calculation in Primary Schools* (HMI 461), http://www.ofsted.gov.uk/publications/index.cfm?fuseaction= pubs.summary&id=2313.

O'Leary, J. (1998) Calculators out in drive to raise standards, *The Times*, 22 January.

Reynolds, D. (1998) Maths plan that adds up, *The Times*, 23 January.

SCAA (School Curriculum and Assessment Authority) (1997) *The Use of Calculators at Key Stages 1–3*. London: SCAA.

Does ICT make mathematics teaching more effective?

Steve Higgins

Introduction

This chapter has three main aims: first, to present an overview of some of the research on primary mathematics and information and communication technology (ICT); second, to present case studies from research which aimed to improve attainment in mathematics; and third to outline some implications for classroom teachers. The chapter draws on a number of projects, in particular the literature review for the British Educational Research Association (BERA) professional user review of the impact of ICT on teaching and learning in schools, the outcomes of a Teacher Training Agency (TTA) funded project on effective pedagogy for the use of ICT in numeracy and literacy in primary schools (Moseley *et al.* 1999) and a project funded by the Nuffield Foundation examining the impact of effective collaborative discussion on mathematics and science (Mercer *et al.* 2002). The recommendations also try to take into account the changing picture of mathematics in primary classrooms as a result of the impact of the various national educational strategies in England. The particular focus of this chapter is mathematics in primary schools, with an emphasis on numeracy. It includes references to other aspects of mathematics such as shape and space, and data handling, though the issue of calculators is not covered (see Williams and Thompson, Chapter 13). The review concentrates on the evidence of the impact of computers in the classroom on mathematical attainment rather than the possible impact or use of a wider range of information technologies that are also found in schools.

The research

There is relatively little hard evidence for any beneficial effects of ICT on mathematics in the primary age range. Indeed, internationally there is a suggestion of the possible negative effects of computers on mathematics attainment (from Israel and from the most recent analysis of data from the Third International Mathematics and Science Survey – TIMSS). Some caution is therefore called for at this broad level as to where and how ICT might have an impact. Two main issues can be identified. The first is the modest effect of ICT compared with other researched interventions, and the second is the almost negligible effect of the provision and use of ICT generally.

There has been extensive research into computer-assisted instruction (CAI) and computer-based learning. Some major reviews of this work have been undertaken. One study (Fletcher-Flynn and Gravatt 1995) into the effectiveness of CAI limited the studies it examined to those that took place between 1987–1992 and identified almost 400 reports of research that met this criterion. The impact of the use of computers was then combined statistically to identify the overall impact. In this meta-analysis the mean effect size was relatively small (.24) for the five years in question but increased for more recent studies analysed (.33). This kind of improvement would move an 'average' class of pupils from fiftieth to about fortieth in a list of 100 classes ranked in order of attainment. This suggests two things: first, it is possible that the beneficial impact of computers may be increasing, and second ICT only produces relatively small improvements. Other forms of educational interventions, such as peer tutoring, reciprocal teaching and homework, for example, all produce greater average impact. In a study of the effect of different types of study skills interventions the average effect size was .57 (Hattie *et al.* 1996); this would move a class from fiftieth to the top 30. A study of the effect of thinking skills or metacognitive approaches (Marzano 1998) indicates the average impact of this type of intervention would move a class into the top 20 (an effect size of .72).

The IMPACT2 study (Harrison *et al.* 2002) found no link between level of resources for ICT and either reading or mathematics marks at Key Stage 1. At Key Stage 2 there was a significant, but very weak, association between ICT resources and pupil attainment. This indicated that the provision of resources and ICT equipment was at least 99.5 per cent independent of pupil performance at Key Stage 2 (no correlation coefficient exceeded .07). A weak link between high computer use and pupil attainment was reported in a TTA study in England (Moseley *et al.* 1999: 82), though the authors did not interpret this as a causal link, but rather that more effective teachers (and more effective schools) tended to use more innovative approaches, or tended to use the resources that they had more effectively.

What works?

This same study, however, also reported dramatic impact on pupil attainment in its 16 development projects in primary schools. The average gain on standardized tests was 2.8 months' progress per month of the project in mathematics (and 5.1 months per month for literacy). The report states, however, that these gains do not prove that ICT will raise attainment, but that 'teachers can raise levels of pupils attainment when they use ICT to support their teaching in literacy and numeracy' (Moseley *et al.* 1999: 6). In these projects the use of ICT was planned to have an impact on particular areas of pupils' learning and the development work involved working closely with the class teachers over an intensive period. These projects did not use control groups, but the consistent and significant increase in the attainment of pupils in mathematics suggests that where ICT is targeted at specific areas of learning, with a clear rationale for its use from research (about ICT, pedagogy and professional development) it can have a positive effect. Two case studies from this project illustrating how ICT can be used to support the teaching and learning of mathematics can be found later in the chapter.

Grouping

Computers can be used individually, in small or large groups or by the teacher with the whole class. Each approach has been shown to be effective, though there are some differences in approach and in outcomes. Individuals perform better than groups when carrying out drill and practice activities (Jackson and Kutnick 1996). However, computers can also be used effectively to support pupils' talk when they work in small groups on collaborative tasks (Wegerif *et al.* 1998) and even 'directive' software can support discussion and reasoning. However, teachers need to teach pupils how to interact with each other when using the computer collaboratively (Dawes *et al.* 2000). When ICT is used to promote discussion in small groups and in whole-class settings this can help to develop pupils' thinking and understanding. This includes learners' mathematical thinking, their individual reasoning, their creativity through Logo programming, and specifically their mathematical attainment (see also Higgins, Chapter 5 for some issues relating to talk and effective discussion in mathematics classrooms).

Feedback

Feedback from a computer can improve pupils' learning. Computer 'marking' of work in simple practice tasks and more sophisticated integrated learning system (ILS) programs have all produced evidence of improved pupil attainment. Feedback can, however, take very different forms and the quality of response is important in a tutoring or ILS program as pupils can be learning merely how to get the best help from the system (Balacheff and Kaput 1996). This research indicates that effective use of computer feedback in mathematics needs monitoring to ensure that the pupils are learning what they are supposed to learn. In mathematics tutoring programs, for example, feedback usually only provides the number of correct responses or the total scores of performance. This type of feedback does not help pupils to correct their errors, other than by trying again. Most software does not offer formative feedback that might help pupils to identify how they could improve. It therefore assumes that they are motivated to learn and that they know what they are supposed to be learning. This is often not the case as pupils simply want to complete the task or 'win' the game on the computer.

Practice

A key factor contributing to pupils' improved attainment when using ICT is the fact that they spend more time working at or practising the skills being studied and tested. Many pupils enjoy using computers and one benefit of them may also be the combination of such motivation and the increased practice of particular tasks. Computers can therefore help by increasing the amount of time pupils spend on particular activities, by increasing their motivation and engagement when doing these activities and by providing practice at an appropriate level. There is evidence of the impact of ICT in this area from a wide range of studies including simple programs with a particular focus such as learning about negative numbers in mathematics (Hativa and Cohen 1995) as well as more complex ILS programs which have all shown some evidence of improved pupil attainment. Some researchers have suggested that pupil practice is a crucial factor in any improvement in pupils' attainment (Underwood and Brown 1997). Use of ICT can clearly be effective in improving pupils' performance in this way. However, such positive results do not help a teacher to decide if the use of ICT is efficient, as other methods or approaches (e.g. reciprocal teaching or peer tutoring) may similarly increase the amount of time pupils spend actually engaged in learning particular skills.

Representing and manipulating information

ICT is a powerful tool for presenting or representing information in different ways. This can be in different forms (such as numbers and pictures, or tables and graphs) or by enabling changes to be shown dynamically, as in mathematical modelling. Information can be manipulated easily on a computer so that a pupil can make changes and evaluate the effect of those changes. Observing changes in a graph when changes are made to the table of numerical information on which the graph is based, or by manipulating an algebraic formula and observing how a graph of that function changes on a computer or graphical calculator can develop pupils' understanding of mathematical relationships. Computer tools can help students or teachers manipulate complex data sets, and this can provide a context for discussion to develop mathematical understanding (Cobb and McClain 2002).

The aim of the case studies that follow is to illustrate how ICT can be effectively integrated into mathematics lessons. In the first two examples the teachers used ICT to target specific mathematics objectives which they had identified should benefit from clear focus and increased time. In the third case study mathematical activities were chosen that would develop the use of mathematical talk through collaborative discussion of mathematical tasks in small groups. Evidence from research into children's learning of mathematics, the effective use of ICT and research into effective teaching and learning were used to plan and shape all of the interventions. In addition, each teacher was offered support or training to develop the skills needed so that their use of the technology was an efficient use of teaching time.

Case study 1: developing counting skills with Reception pupils

This project focused on developing counting skills with 4–5-year-old pupils (Moseley *et al.* 1999). The pupils created counting pictures, using a children's drawing and painting program, by drawing and stamping collections of objects to make pictures on the screen. The activities were designed to complement other numeracy activities and to act as a focus for discussion between the researcher and the teacher. The development work took place over two terms with two different classes of pupils. The results from the standardized testing suggest that the teacher was able to use ICT effectively as part of her teaching to support the development of her pupils' counting skills. Using detailed knowledge of how young children learn to count and the errors that they commonly make was an important feature of the development work in ICT and mathematics.

When planning activities the teacher liked to make links between different activities and to draw out connections for the children: 'they might need work on number recognition, or using number lines, and it isn't always linked. But usually we do something that is to do with counting, a counting rhyme or acting out a song which is linked to other activities'.

At the beginning of the summer term, some pupils were making errors in reciting the number names accurately (particularly numbers from 13–19 and at the decade transitions such as 29–30), some had inaccurate touch counting skills and strategies which led them to give an incorrect total at the end of a count and some were also unable to identify the correct written number to go with a number name with numbers up to 20. The teacher saw ICT as enabling her to tackle these issues more effectively than she had been able to do with previously available software which focused only on numeral recognition: '[it] was quite different from anything I've used before, [which] had been very closed'. The teacher found the diagnostic information from the baseline test very useful. It gave her detailed information about the particular counting errors that specific pupils were making. In addition to the work using ICT she planned other numeracy activities to address pupils' particular difficulties. The teacher wanted pupils to be able to practise specific aspects of counting and therefore emphasized different counting skills with different children. The software has the facility to let children stamp a variety of pictures onto the screen thus allowing them to work on the different aspects of counting that had been identified in the initial assessment.

The teacher thought that having pupils create mathematical pictures, and count out loud as they did so, enabled them to use the ICT more independently. They were able to create a variety of pictures over a period of several weeks. This matched a number of the teacher's mathematical objectives for the term, such as using their counting vocabulary, improving the reliability of their counting, teaching them more systematic counting strategies and helping them to recognize and use numerals: 'We didn't have much in the way of numeracy materials, whereas using [ICT] has really helped, and the children have used a lot more mathematical language'.

A target group of five pupils was identified that the teacher thought would benefit from the ICT work, together with a control group of three others. A standardized test was used as pre- and post-intervention. The target pupils all showed that their counting and number ability had improved. They had also improved relative to the other three pupils (an average 8 point gain in age-standardized score compared with an average gain of 1 point for the control group). This development work was repeated in the autumn term with the teacher's next class, but without a control group. The class made impressive gains. Their age-standardized score improved by an average of 15 points in just over two months.

It is clearly not possible to claim that the pupil score improvements were directly due on either occasion solely to the ICT activities, especially as the teacher used the information from the standardized test to inform her planning more broadly. However, the results do suggest that carefully planned and structured ICT activities with clear mathematical objectives can play an effective role in improving pupils' counting skills.

Case study 2: developing understanding of decimals with 8–9-year-olds

In this case study, the teacher wanted to introduce her class to decimal notation and initially chose to do this using the context of money (Moseley *et al.* 1999). However, this is challenging as many pupils see £3.24 not as a single number of pounds but rather as two closely related numbers: three pounds and, separately, 24 pennies. This leads to the common error of writing the amount as £3.24p. The result is that for teachers of 8–9-year-olds, this becomes an unnecessarily difficult hurdle when teaching decimal number, so one of the teacher's main concerns was the issue of how meaningful the pupils would find such decimal numbers. Given that she eventually wanted her pupils to be able to order and even calculate with decimal numbers, she felt that it was important to use numbers where the pupils could draw some understanding from the context.

After discussing the issue with the research team, she agreed to try using time as the medium rather than money – time measured through the use of ICT. The activity used a laptop computer connected to a pressure-mat sensor. This allowed the children to generate times in seconds to two places of decimals. The equipment enabled two different types of activities to be timed, each of which needed different interpretations as to which was the 'best'. The first activity required the children to stand on the pressure mat and jump in the air before landing on the mat again. The times for these standing jumps were typically .43 or .37 seconds. Here, the 'best' time was the biggest number – the longest time in the air. The second activity exploited the portability of the equipment as the children used the ICT as a timing gate. They took it out into the playground and ran from one side to the other and back again. As they set off, they trod on the mat starting the timer. It stopped when they returned and trod on it again. Here the 'best' time was the smallest number – the shortest time taken.

The teacher chose to use the ICT equipment for two reasons. The first was to generate 'real' numbers which the children could understand from the context in which they were produced. The second was as a stimulus to get the children thinking about what 'best' meant and about using decimals in a specific context to achieve this. Using the ICT also had an effect upon the choices related to her expectations of the children. She had not done a lot of work on decimals with previous Year 4 classes. This, she thought, might have been related to her own needs as well as those of the children: 'I found decimal fractions quite difficult for a lot of children. It may be the fact that I didn't expect them to take it much further was part of my problem as well. The e-Mate [the pressure mat] stimulated their interest to learn and understand beyond my expectations. I would never in my wildest dreams have thought they would cope with this'. Not only was there a global shift in her expectations of what the whole class could achieve, but she also reported some changes for individuals.

The pupils completed a mathematics test before and after the intervention. The results indicate that their average age-standardized scores rose from 8 years and 4 months to 9 years and 5 months. This gain was achieved in four months. The test did not specifically look at using decimals, although it was a component of the test. While again it is important not to attribute this gain solely to the ICT activities, it seems reasonable to suggest that they will have played a part in developing specific mathematical skills and understanding. In addition, it also seems reasonable to assume that ICT will also have played a part in the more general increase in the pupils' confidence and attitude.

Case study 3: developing mathematical thinking through collaborative discussion

Many of the activities in the Nuffield project described in Chapter 5 used ICT (Mercer *et al.* 2002). Two mathematics activities were developed using experimental software called the Elicitation Engine which encouraged pupils to sort and classify numbers and shapes by finding similarities and differences. Other mathematics activities were based on existing software. Three lessons were created using software developed for the National Numeracy Strategy's (NNS) training materials. These aimed to develop pupils' understanding through activities such as identifying patterns in number grids (using the program Monty), combining numbers (Playtrain) and using monetary calculations (Toyshop). Other mathematics-related ICT activities also used widely available software. One of these (Hurkle, a version of the popular game 'battleships') involved grid references and coordinates. Another used an on-screen version of a 3 × 3 magic square to present a problem for discussion.

Children worked in small groups at the computer, usually in threes, and discussed possible solutions before agreeing what to do. Earlier work by the Open University team on children working together at the computer

(Wegerif *et al.* 1998) had concluded that software which supports and sustains discussion should provide:

- challenges and problems that have meaning for the children, and which provide a range of alternative choices that are worth discussing – such challenges should engage the children with the content of the software rather than its interface;
- a clear purpose or task which is made evident to the group and which is kept in focus throughout;
- on-screen prompts to talk together, reach agreement and ask for opinions and reasons;
- resources for discussion, including information on which decisions can be based and opportunities to review decisions in the light of new information;
- no features that encourage individuals to take turns, 'beat the clock' or work competitively;
- buttons, multi-choice answers or the use of audio input to minimize typing during the 'flow' of a task.

The results, as discussed in Chapter 5, showed that the children in the experimental classes gained significantly better scores in mathematics than those in control classes. The impact of the intervention was equivalent to moving a class from fiftieth position in a league table of 100 schools into the top 30 (an effect size of .59). The role of the computer in this research was to help to frame or structure the pupils' talk according to the outlined principles above.

Conclusion and implications

ICT provides a wealth of tools for teachers to use, either for themselves to present and demonstrate or for pupils, individually or in a group. Such technological tools can be explicitly designed for use in educational contexts (such as a mathematics teaching program or an overhead projecting calculator), or they can be equipment and software also used in other contexts (such as word processors and spreadsheets, or interactive whiteboards). The choice of when and how to use such technologies in teaching and learning is complex. The evidence above clearly indicates that it is *how* ICT is used that makes the difference.

Knowledge of, and experience with, computers is not enough to enable teachers to make the best use of ICT in the classroom. Effective adoption of computers within the classroom takes time, and this might be as long as a year, even with the support of an experienced team. In addition, the way in which teachers' skills, beliefs and practices are related is complex and this affects the way they choose to use ICT and how effective they are at using it (Higgins and Moseley 2001).

The final issue is that ICT changes rapidly and new innovations offer new possibilities for teaching and learning. These not only open up new techniques to teach the existing curriculum more effectively or more efficiently but can also change the nature of that curriculum. This might entail changes to the content of what is taught, such as has happened in aspects of data handling and with the importance of developing a 'feel' for number when routine calculations can be completed so easily electronically.

To summarize, the implications for teaching are to:

- Identify clear objectives that will benefit from an increased focus: what are the challenging topics or ideas in mathematics that ICT can best support?
- Determine which aspect of ICT is most likely to help achieve these objectives: will gains be achieved through a powerful presentation of an idea, or particular feedback from mathematical software, or increased practice at particular tasks, or because of the way that computers can represent or manipulate mathematical information?
- Decide how the children are to be grouped: will the pupils be challenged though whole-class presentation and question and answer; will they benefit from individual practice; or will mathematical discussion help and, if so, how will they be taught to discuss and collaborate effectively?

References

Balacheff, N. and Kaput, J.J. (1996) Computer-based learning environments in mathematics, in A.J. Bishop, K. Clements, C. Keitel, J. Kilpatrick and C. Laborde (eds) *International Handbook of Mathematics Education*. Dordrecht: Kluwer.

Cobb, P. and McClain, K. (2002) Supporting students learning of significant mathematical ideas, in G. Wells and G. Claxton (eds) *Learning for Life in the 21st Century*. Oxford: Blackwell.

Dawes, L., Mercer, N. and Wegerif, R. (2000) Extending talking and reasoning skills using ICT, in M. Leask and J. Meadows (eds) *Teaching and Learning with ICT in the Primary School*. London: Routledge.

Fletcher-Flynn, C.M. and Gravatt, B. (1995) The efficacy of computer-assisted instruction (CAI): a meta-analysis, *Journal of Educational Computing Research*, 12: 219–42.

Harrison, C., Comber, C., Fisher, T., Haw, K., Lewin, C., Lunzer, E., McFarlane, A., Mavers, D., Scrimshaw, P., Somekh, B. and Watling, R. (2002) *IMPACT2: The Impact of Information and Communications Technologies on Pupil Learning and Attainment*. Coventry: Becta.

Hativa, N. and Cohen, D. (1995) Self learning of negative number concepts by lower division elementary students through solving computer-provided numerical problems, *Educational Studies in Mathematics*, 28: 401–31.

Hattie, J., Biggs, J. and Purdie, N. (1996) Effects of learning skills interventions on student learning: a meta-analysis, *Review of Educational Research*, 66(2): 99–136.

Higgins, S. and Moseley, D. (2001) Teachers' thinking about ICT and learning: beliefs and outcomes, *Teacher Development*, 5(2): 191–210.

Jackson, A. and Kutnick, P. (1996) Groupwork and computers: task type and children's performance, *Journal of Computer Assisted Learning*, 12: 162–71.

Marzano, R.J. (1998) *A Theory-Based Meta-Analysis of Research on Instruction*. Aurora, CO: Mid-continent Regional Educational Laboratory.

Mercer, N., Wegerif, R., Dawes, L., Sams, C. and Higgins, S. (2002) *Language, Thinking and ICT in the Primary Curriculum: Final Project Report to the Nuffield Foundation.* Milton Keynes: Open University.

Moseley, D., Higgins, S., Bramald, R., Hardman, F., Miller, J., Mroz, M., Tse, H., Newton, D., Thompson, I., Williamson, J., Halligan, J., Bramald, S., Newton, L., Tymms, P., Henderson, B. and Stout, J. (1999) *Ways Forward with ICT: Effective Pedagogy using Information and Communications Technology in Literacy and Numeracy in Primary Schools.* Newcastle upon Tyne: University of Newcastle upon Tyne.

Underwood, J. and Brown, J. (1997) *Integrated Learning Systems: Potential into Practice.* Oxford: Heinemann.

Wegerif, R., Mercer, N. and Dawes, L. (1998) Software design to support discussion in the primary classroom, *Journal of Computer Assisted Learning*, 14(3): 199–211.

Section 6

RESEARCH ISSUES

This final section looks at the work of three different types of researcher/research body: the individual (Chapter 15); the dedicated research team working on a large project (Chapter 17); and the wider research community – in this case the cognitive neuroscience community (Chapter 16).

In Chapter 15 Ian Thompson uses some of the findings from a Nuffield-sponsored research study to support his contentious views on place value. By combining these findings with a historical account of the development of the notion of place value he constructs an argument for a reconceptualization of the concept. He then attempts to support this argument by analysing those aspects of place value that are in evidence when children calculate using a range of mental strategies for the four basic operations; when they make use of the range of informal written strategies exemplified in the *Framework* and related National Numeracy Strategy (NNS) training materials; and when they perform standard written algorithms. Practical suggestions are made in the final section in the hope that they might contribute towards improving the teaching of this difficult concept.

Ann Dowker is Research Fellow for the Organization for Economic Co-operation and Development (OECD) Network on Brain, Development and Numeracy. In Chapter 16 she discusses some of the work being done in a specific non-educational area of research: the branch of psychology known as cognitive neuroscience. She provides a succinct synopsis of aspects of this work that might help cast light on our understanding of the difficulties that some children experience in learning basic arithmetic. She explains some of the procedures used to study the functions and activities of areas of the brain and considers the extent to which certain general educational theories are legitimated or contradicted by these studies. The author also considers several specific cases of individuals presenting dissociations between different components of arithmetic, and draws some conclusions for those involved in teaching mathematics to young children.

Chapter 17, the final chapter, is by Margaret Brown and Alison Millett: Director and Senior Research Fellow, respectively, of the Leverhulme Numeracy Research Programme, a five-year programme to investigate the causes of, and possible remedies for, low attainment in numeracy. In this chapter the authors focus specifically on a related Nuffield-sponsored project, as this allows them to compare the test results of a substantial number of Year 4 children in 1997/8 with those of a similar number of Year 4 children in 2001/2, on the same test and in the same schools. This generates some fascinating and unexpected results, particularly when the data are analysed in terms of comparisons between the mean scores on the two sets of results for different groups in the population. This chapter constitutes a fitting conclusion to the book.

Place value: the English disease?[1]

Ian Thompson

Introduction

In a discussion paper published by the School Curriculum and Assessment Authority (SCAA) (later to become the Qualifications and Curriculum Authority – QCA) Askew and Brown (1997: 4) state that: 'There is considerable evidence that understanding of place value in both whole numbers and decimals is limited for many pupils even in Key Stage 3'. The accumulated experience of the many teachers who have struggled to teach place value to children of different ages would no doubt confirm their findings.

Because we are very familiar with the conventions of place value we tend to forget that this particular concept was a very late arrival in the development of number notation. The seemingly simple notion of using a limited number of symbols, 0 to 9, combined with the innovatory idea of allocating meaning to the *position* of these symbols in a number caused a revolution in the development of numerical calculation. As Ifrah (1998: 399) succinctly states: 'Nowadays this principle seems to us to have such an obvious simplicity that we forget how the human race has stammered, hesitated and groped through thousands of years before discovering it, and that civilisations as advanced as the Greek and Egyptian completely failed to notice it'.

The main barrier to the Romans inventing place value was their written number system: try adding XII to LVI or multiplying CXXI by V. It is also quite amazing that medieval Europe did not succeed in developing any form of place value notation, despite the fact that this was not only at hand in visual form on the counting board, where counters were placed in columns and moved from one to the other, but was also heard daily in the spoken number sequence (for example, '*two thousand, six hundred and seventy-four*'). The fact that it took such a long time for mankind to invent this important idea signals the fact that it is going to prove to be a difficult concept for children to understand.

Research findings

Thompson and Bramald (2002) interviewed 144 children (48 in each of Years 2 to 4 from eight primary schools) in an attempt to explore their understanding of place value. One of the nine questions the children were asked was the following (the words in italics are those spoken by the researcher):

Can you read this number to me? (Show card with 16 written on it)
Please take 16 cubes out of the box
Can you show me with the cubes what this part (6) of the number means? (Circle the 6 with the back of a pen)
Can you show me with the cubes what this part (1) of the number means? (Circle the 1)

American researchers interviewing a similar-sized sample and using the same question found that not a single child in Grade 1 (Year 2) correctly showed ten cubes to the interviewer when the 1 was circled, whereas 54 per cent of the Year 2 children in the English sample did. In a different American study with older children, 20 per cent of those in Grade 2 (Year 3) obtained the correct answer, and in Australia 44 per cent of a sample of children of the same age were successful on a similar task. In Thompson and Bramald's sample of Year 3 children, an impressive 77 per cent were successful.

A different question in the English study asked the children to calculate 25 + 23 mentally and to explain how they did it. Over three-quarters were correct and 91 of the 144 children (63 per cent) used a partitioning strategy, splitting 23 into 20 and 3 in order to do the calculation. Both of these results: 77 per cent of Year 3 children successful on the '16 cubes' question and 63 per cent of the whole sample using partitioning to find the sum of two two-digit numbers correctly might lead one to conclude that English children have an excellent grasp of the difficult concept of place value. But is this actually the case? A brief look at the children's answers to two other interview items might help us get nearer to answering this question.

After discussing a picture of a car dashboard showing a mileage of 6299 the children were asked what the milometer would show after the car had travelled one more mile. Only 24 per cent were correct. Another question asked the children to say how the value of several cubes had changed after they had been physically moved by the researcher from the 'ones' to the 'tens' column on a base-10 board. Only 10 per cent were correct (this rose to 28 per cent when they were asked the follow-up question *'How many times bigger is it now?'*). Since both of these questions address important aspects of place value, how do we reconcile an average of 70 per cent success on the '16 cubes' question with a mere 10 per cent success on the 'base-10 board' question? One possibility is that the two questions are testing different concepts.

A closer look at Thompson and Bramald's findings suggests that if you take the view that a child who can be said to understand place value would be expected to be able to give correct answers to both the milometer and the base-10 board questions, then only 4 per cent (4 per cent!) of their sample do actually understand the concept. Comparing this 4 per cent with the 63 per

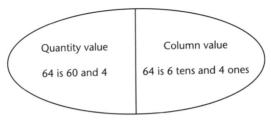

Figure 15.1 A suggested model for place value

cent who used partitioning to correctly add two-digit numbers, it would seem reasonable to assert that *an understanding of place value is not essential for mental calculation with two-digit numbers*: a statement that would appear to contradict everything that English primary mathematics educators have ever argued for over the years. For example, in a very influential book from the 1970s, Williams and Shuard (1976: 120) advised that: 'as soon as numbers greater than ten need to be written the first introduction to the structure of our notation has to be made'. They then proceeded to recommend a range of grouping and abacus activities designed to develop an awareness of this structure. A look at any commercial primary mathematics scheme, old or new, will show that this has traditionally been, and to a certain extent still is, the standard recommended approach to the teaching of two-digit numbers.

If we follow this advice, it means that we are introducing the concept of place value at the same time as the 'awkward' teen numbers. So, just as children are struggling to make sense of the confusing set of names we give to these numbers, we burden them with one of the most sophisticated concepts in early mathematics. It must be difficult enough for a 6-year-old who is trying to discern some pattern in the number names to have to wrestle with the fact that even though 23 is read as 'twenty-three', 13 is read as 'thirteen'. In the latter case not only is the number read from right to left, with the 3 named first, but the 3 has actually become 'thir' and the 10 has become 'teen'. Adding an extra layer of sophistication on top of this – namely, that the 1 goes in the 'tens' column and the 3 goes in the 'units' column – must surely only confuse children even more.

One possible explanation for the wide disparity in the success rates on the questions discussed above lies in Thompson's (2000) argument that it is possible to identify two distinct characteristics, or sub-concepts, in what we normally call 'place value': *quantity value* and *column value* (see Figure 15.1). The former concerns knowing that 64 is '60' and '4', and is the aspect tested in the 'successful' '16 cubes' and the two-digit mental addition questions. Whereas the latter involves knowing that 64 is '6' in the tens column and '4' in the ones column, and is related more closely to those aspects tested in the 'unsuccessful' milometer and base-ten board questions.

The following sections look respectively at mental strategies, informal written methods and standard algorithms in an attempt to provide further evidence to justify the importance of acknowledging the separate *quantity value* and *column value* aspects of place value. For a more detailed consideration of these procedures see Thompson, Chapter 2.

Children calculating mentally

Consider the following examples of mental strategies used by young children for each of the four basic operations and think about the aspects of place value knowledge that are utilized in each case:

- *John, aged 9 (35 + 27): Well, 30 and 20 is 50 . . . 5 and 7 is 12 . . . add 50 and 12 makes 62.*
- *Sophie, aged 9 (54 – 27): 54 take 20 is 34 . . . and 34 take 4 gives me 30 . . . if I take the 3 from the 30 I've got 7, I mean 27.*
- *Elizabeth, aged 8 (28 × 5): 140 . . . I put 20 times 5 would be 100 and 8 times 5 is 40 . . . because I know tables and that's how I found out.*
- *Emma, aged 8 (46 ÷ 2): 23 . . . half of 40 is 20 and half of 6 is 3 . . . plus 20 and 3 is 23.*

Addition

When adding 35 and 27 John has treated the 35 as 30 + 5 and the 27 as 20 + 7; he has *partitioned* both numbers into multiples of 10 and the remaining ones; he has added these parts separately; and the two answers have been combined to give a final total. John's explanation of his strategy includes no mention of 'carrying a 10'; no 'treating the 30 and 20 as three tens and two tens'; no 'adding the 3 to the 2'; and no 'putting milk bottles on the doorstep'.

Subtraction

Sophie uses a different strategy from John, and deals with 54 – 27 by subtracting suitable 'chunks' of 27 from 54. Initially she subtracts 20, which gives her 34, and then she takes away the 7 in two chunks using a 'bridging' strategy: the 4 is removed first as this conveniently takes her down to 30 – a 'friendly' multiple of 10 – and she then uses her knowledge of 'complements in 10' to subtract the final 3. There is no 'exchanging a 10 for ten ones'; no 'borrowing a 10 and paying back'; and no thinking of the 5 in 54 as 'five tens' which can then be changed into 'four tens and ten ones' if necessary.

Multiplication

In order to multiply 28 by 5 Elizabeth has partitioned the 28 into 20 and 8. The partial products 20 × 5 and 8 × 5 have been calculated separately and then added together to give the final total. Once again the 2 in 28 is treated as 20 not as 'two tens', and after calculating 8 × 5 Elizabeth does not 'put down the 0 and carry the 4'.

Division

When finding $46 \div 2$ Emma sensibly treats division by 2 as equivalent to halving. Like Elizabeth she deals with the multiples of 10 and the ones separately, first halving the 40 and then the 6 before combining the two interim answers. At no time does she appear to contemplate 'dividing the 2 into the 4 and then into the 6': an action premised on a column value interpretation of the 4 in 46.

It is important to observe that, irrespective of the operation involved, the aspect of place value that underlies each of the strategies is *quantity value*. No mention is made of 'the tens place' or 'the hundreds column' in the children's explanations of their strategies. In fact, there is no attempt whatsoever to work with or even think in terms of columns, and no treating the digits in the numerals as individual digits: a strategy often used by children when they try to adapt the standard written algorithms for mental calculation. There is no evidence of any child visualizing multi-digit numbers as the concatenation of separate digits set out in different columns. Each child treats the numbers involved in a holistic way: quantity value takes precedence over column value. Research by Thompson and Smith (1999) showed that quantity value rather than column value understanding was used for the mental addition and subtraction of two-digit numbers by almost all of the 144 children in their sample. Mental calculation necessitates an understanding of quantity value, but what is the situation when informal written methods are used?

Informal written calculation

The following examples are taken from those sections exemplifying 'informal' written strategies for the basic operations in the Supplement of examples of the *Framework for Teaching Mathematics from Reception to Year 6* (DfEE 1999). The recommended algorithm for addition is described as 'Adding the most significant digits first', and one of the examples given for Year 3 is:

$$
\begin{array}{r}
67 \\
+24 \\
\hline
80 \\
11 \\
\hline
91 \\
\hline
\end{array}
$$

This algorithm constitutes an almost exact model of the partitioning mental strategy described above: the digits are treated as quantities; they are added from the left according to their significance; they provide a good first approximation to the answer; and there is no 'carrying' (a procedure that necessitates an understanding of column-based place value).

The following subtraction algorithm is illustrated in the *Framework* (DfEE 1999: 45, example Y123) alongside an equivalent empty number line (ENL) procedure:

```
  783
 -356
    4   to 360
   40   to 400
  300   to 700
   83   to 783
  427
```

The basic principle underpinning this method is to build up to the next multiple of 10 and then to the next multiple of 100. Quantities rather than digits are added at each stage.

An informal method for multiplication, recommended for Year 4 children, is:

```
   23
   ×7
  140   20 × 7
   21    3 × 7
  161
```

Given that quantity value is used in the calculation, there is actually no reason why the algorithm needs to be set out vertically in columns – other than to prepare children for the standard algorithm for multiplying pairs of two-digit numbers in Year 5!

The recommended informal method for division in Year 4 involves subtracting chunks of the divisor from the number being divided. The calculation $96 \div 6$ is illustrated as follows:

```
6)96
 -60   10 × 6
  36
 -36    6 × 6
   0
Answer 16
```

This 'chunking' procedure demands good estimation skills and the ability to make effective use of addition, subtraction and multiplication knowledge. In this example, as in the case of the other three operations, an understanding of quantity value would seem to be more useful than column value.

Standard (or compact) written methods

Standard algorithms for each of the four basic operations are detailed in Chapter 2. Figure 15.2 illustrates a selection of some of the well-documented errors that children make when performing these algorithms. As you consider them, ask yourself which aspect of place value has been misunderstood in each case.

In example (a) the child has forgotten to 'carry' the 1 (10), and the sum of

(a) 327	(b) 327	(c) 75	(d) 42
+218	+218	−27	×34
5315	581	52	128

Figure 15.2 Some common arithmetic errors made when using compact methods

7 and 8 has been written in the units column, whereas in example (b) the child has remembered to carry, but, having correctly calculated 7 + 8, has said to herself '15', and has then probably carried the 'fif' and put down the 'teen' (the 1). Example (c) illustrates the most common subtraction mistake, known as the 'smaller from larger' error. In each column the smaller digit is subtracted from the larger. It is unfortunate that the minus sign can be interpreted in so many different ways: 7 − 4 can be read as '7 take away 4' (i.e. from left to right) or '4 from 7' (right to left). This means that some children will use the interpretation that makes the single digit subtraction possible, so 4 − 7 is read as '4 from 7'. In example (d) the child has generalized from the column procedures associated with addition: she has multiplied the two digits in the left-hand column and has then done the same with the digits in the other column.

Many of these errors are due to children working with multi-digit numbers as a set of digits to be operated on individually: what Fuson (1998: 50) calls the 'numbers as a concatenation of single digits conceptual structure'. The children appear to have failed to understand the basic principles of column value and its related notation. This could be because of too early an introduction to compact or standard algorithms which, in contrast to the informal methods described earlier, involve the more sophisticated column value concept.

Place value in government publications

The *Framework* (DfEE 1999: 8) emphasizes the importance of place value by making it one of the Key Objectives in the Y123 number strand: 'Know what each digit in a number represents and partition a number into a multiple of 10 and ones (TU) or a multiple of 100, a multiple of 10 and ones (HTU)'. It is unfortunate, however, that this appears to blur the distinction made in this chapter between quantity value and column value: 'multiples of 10' refers to the former, whereas 'HTU', with its implicit reference to columns, alludes to the latter. This blurring of the two concepts can be found elsewhere in the document and its related publications. For example, the section on resources in the *Framework* emphasizes the importance of number lines, number tracks and hundred squares, recommending Dienes base-10 apparatus with an accompanying caveat. Also, each time an example such as 'Say what the digit 3 in 364 stands for' is given the document consistently provides an answer in quantity value terms, such as 'It represents 300'. However, despite this, the phrase 'represent on an abacus' – a very formal, and quite sophisticated representation of the column aspect of place value – appears in Years 1, 2 and

3. As Ifrah (1998: 560) says: 'To sum up, it was by rejecting the abacus that Indian scholars discovered the place value system'.

In Section 3 of the *Framework*, 'Yearly Teaching Programmes and planning grids', the Year 2 programme for teaching place value and ordering states that children should be taught to 'Know what each digit in a two-digit number represents, including 0 as a place holder, and partition two-digit numbers into a multiple of ten and ones' (DfEE 1999:10). The first half of this objective is in bold type, making it a *Key Objective*. The fact that 0 was invented by the Indians *after* the development of the place value system suggests that the concept of '0 as a place holder' is dependent upon, and more sophisticated than, an understanding of the concept of column value. I would argue that the place holder concept is far too sophisticated for Year 2 children.

A similar lack of clarity in the interpretation of place value is evident in publications emanating from the QCA. For example, the QCA's definition of place value (1997: 3) includes the sentence: 'In the numeral 62, the 6 has the value 60 and the 2 has the value 2'. This is a quantity value definition. However, an earlier report on the 1995 National Curriculum tests (SCAA 1995: 27) discussed a specific place value question ('*How many tens in 45?*') and criticized a child who gave a quantity value answer instead of a column value one. The document takes a fairly pedantic stance pointing out that: 'A common error was to write forty instead of 4'. Whilst accepting that, given the actual wording of the question, the child's answer is 'technically' incorrect, one could take an even more pedantic stance and argue that the SCAA's own answer is just as incorrect as there are actually 4.5 tens in 45!

Conclusion

Many European countries give little or no emphasis to what we have traditionally called place value (and what in this chapter is called column value) (Bierhoff 1996). It is also interesting to note that The Netherlands was the most successful European country in the primary mathematics section of the Third International Mathematics and Science Survey (TIMSS) and yet the Dutch make little or no mention of place value in what might be considered their equivalent of our National Curriculum (Freudenthal Institute 2001).

One argument being made in this chapter is that mental calculation strategies are based on the quantity aspect of place value, whereas standard (or compact) procedures are based on the column aspect. Consequently, given that the *Framework* recommends that standard written algorithms need not be taught until Year 4, teachers should not be in a rush to teach this aspect of place value. Obviously, once they have made the decision to teach more compact vertical written algorithms, teachers will have to ensure that connections have been made between quantity value and column value. The increased maturity of the children, along with their more developed number sense, will make it easier to integrate the two concepts. For example, one explicit connection is to be found in the language and meaning of the ten times table: $7 \times 10 = 70$ can be read as 'seven tens are 70'. This particular articulation represents the fundamental connection between the two concepts – namely, that '70' can be interpreted as 'seven tens', and that either of these two interpretations can be used as befits the situation.

The implications for the teaching of the ideas discussed in this chapter are that, as children progressively learn about two- and three-digit numbers, teachers should concentrate on developing their overall number sense. An understanding that 54 means five tens and four ones (or units) is just one small part of this. Children also need to develop a general awareness that 54 is (or could be):

- just over a half of 100;
- a number between 50 and 60;
- the position almost halfway between 50 and 60 on a number line;
- a house or bus number;
- the page that follows page 53 in a book (and precedes page 55);
- the age of their teacher (who will be 60 in six years time);
- the amount of money in their pocket when they have five ten-pence pieces and four pennies;
- the distance covered when just past the halfway mark in a 100-metre sprint.

Activities that concentrate on the development of these aspects of number sense need to be incorporated into lessons. They could easily replace activities found in commercial schemes that focus on:

- grouping games;
- discussion of numbers in terms of 'tens and units';
- constructing numbers using base-10 equipment;
- representing numbers on an abacus;
- working with columns headed T and U in exercise books.

Hopefully, if we as teachers become less obsessed about place value and more passionate about the development of number sense, our children will develop much more confidence and competence in mental and written calculation.

Note

1 This is the name given to place value by a Dutch mathematics educator.

References

Askew, M. and Brown, M. (1997) *The Teaching and Assessment of Number at Key Stages 1–3.* London: SCAA.

Bierhoff, H. (1996) *Laying the Foundation of Numeracy: a Comparison of Primary School Textbooks in Britain, Germany and Switzerland.* London: National Institute for Economic and Social Research.

DfEE (Department for Education and Employment) (1999) *Framework for Teaching Mathematics from Reception to Year 6*. London: DfEE.

Freudenthal Institute (2001) *Children Learn Mathematics: a Learning-Teaching Trajectory with Intermediate Attainment Targets for Calculation with Whole Numbers in Primary School*. Utrecht: Freudenthal Institute.

Fuson, K.C. (1998) Pedagogical, mathematical and real-world conceptual support nets: a model for building children's multi-digit domain knowledge, *Mathematical Cognition*, 4(2): 147–86.

Ifrah, G. (1998) *The Universal History of Numbers*. London: Harvill Press.

QCA (Qualifications and Curriculum Authority) (1997) *Mathematics Year 4 Assessment Unit: Place Value*. London: QCA.

SCAA (School Curriculum and Assessment Authority) (1995) *Report on the 1995 Key Stage 2 Tests and Tasks in English, Mathematics and Science*. London: SCAA.

Thompson, I. (2000) Teaching place value in the UK: time for a reappraisal? *Educational Review*, 52(3): 291–8.

Thompson, I. and Bramald, R. (2002) *An Investigation of the Relationship Between Young Children's Understanding of the Concept of Place Value and their Competence at Mental Addition* (Report for the Nuffield Foundation). Newcastle upon Tyne: University of Newcastle upon Tyne.

Thompson, I. and Smith, F. (1999) *Mental Calculation Strategies for the Addition and Subtraction of 2-digit Numbers* (Report for the Nuffield Foundation). Newcastle upon Tyne: University of Newcastle upon Tyne.

Williams, E.M. and Shuard, H. (1976) *Primary Mathematics Today*. London: Longman.

Brain-based research on arithmetic: implications for learning and teaching

Ann Dowker

Since, however, man is the most plastic of all beings, the order of his development is subject to great modification. This is especially true of his mind. Unlike other machines, the brain is always in process of construction, always being modified and never completed . . . Every time the mind does a thing it becomes a different mind. The question is often asked whether certain things are native or acquired. The answer is in almost all cases, 'They are both'.

(Kirkpatrick 1908: 8–9)

Now my brains are on power!
(Jake, aged 7, after completing an arithmetical estimation task)

There are many ways in which the functions of the human brain can be, and have been, studied. For a long time, it has been possible to study the structure of the brain at autopsy; more recently it became possible to study it in living people undergoing surgery; still more recently, it has become possible to examine it through brain scans. Such studies by themselves do not, however, tell us what the different parts of the brain *do*.

The two commonest ways of studying the functions and activities of different areas of the brain are:

1 *Studying patients who are known to have suffered damage to specific areas of the brain, and investigating which functions are lost or impaired.* This has been one of the most important ways of gaining information about brain functions. There are certain limitations to such studies: in particular, people with brain damage may be unusual in other ways besides the specific damage that is being investigated. For example, they may have known or undetected damage or disruption to other parts of the brain besides the area being studied; additionally, other parts of the brain may have compensated for the damage by taking over functions that they do not usually serve.

2 *Functional brain imaging.* In recent years, it has become increasingly possible to 'image' the brain in action: to discover the areas of the brain that are particularly active at a given time. The different methods of brain imaging

are all based on the fact that blood flow is greatest to the more active areas in the brain; and those areas therefore take up more oxygen, use up more glucose, and show more electrical activity.

The oldest, easiest but least precise method of finding out the relative activity level of different parts of the brain relies on levels of electrical activity. This is the electroencephalograph (EEG) which involves placing electrodes on the scalp and recording their activity. This technique has been used for the last 70 years, with increasing refinements over time. It is particularly useful in measuring differences in brain activity at different times (e.g. comparing the sleeping state with the waking state). It is less accurate in pinpointing the areas of the brain that are particularly active when specific functions are being carried out. Nevertheless, the EEG and its variants are sometimes used for the latter purpose in situations where other forms of functional brain imaging are difficult or undesirable: for example, with small children.

More sophisticated forms of functional brain imaging include positron emission tomography (PET) and magnetic resonance imaging (MRI). The technical details of these techniques are outside the scope of the present chapter. Briefly, both are methods of measuring relative differences in oxygen uptake by different parts of the brain. PET involves injecting either glucose or water containing radioactive oxygen atoms: this results in oxygen-consuming parts of the brain emitting gamma rays which strike sensors and make it possible to build up an image of the brain indicating the relative activity levels of different areas. MRI relies on the fact that the level of oxygen in haemoglobin affects its magnetic properties, and uses a magnetic field to investigate where the blood is taking up most oxygen.

What general theories are endorsed or contradicted by studies of the brain?

Studies of patients with brain damage, functional brain imaging studies and other forms of brain-based research converge in indicating the following:

- Different areas and networks within the brain have different degrees of involvement in different functions.
- It is not, however, usually the case that one very circumscribed 'bit' of the brain 'does' a single function. Most functions involve several parts of the brain – sometimes close to one another, sometimes far apart – which operate in parallel and interact with one another in a very complex way.
- The two hemispheres of the brain are to some degree specialized for different functions: for example, in most people, the left hemisphere is the one mainly responsible for language and the right hemisphere is mainly responsible for most spatial skills.
- Theories that the left hemisphere is 'the logical hemisphere' and the right hemisphere 'the creative hemisphere' are, however, oversimplified and misleading. Apart from the fact that logic and creativity are not mutually

exclusive, most activities that could be described as logical and/or creative involve the activity of multiple areas of both sides of the brain.

- As Kirkpatrick pointed out in 1908, and as has been confirmed by much recent research (Karmiloff-Smith 1997), the brain is continually changed and influenced by experience. The fact that an activity or skill is influenced by the functioning of particular parts of the brain does not mean that it is purely innate and cannot be influenced by external experiences. Though few people have yet carried out brain imaging studies with children, Posner and McCandliss (1999) recently carried out some PET scans of 10- to 12-year-olds with and without dyslexia. They found that, after some training, the dyslexics not only improved in their reading, but their brain scans when reading became more similar to those of good readers.

Areas of the brain that are responsible for arithmetic

A lot of work, both with 'normal' individuals and with patients, supports the view that there are areas and networks in the brain that are particularly important for arithmetic. Some of the most striking evidence comes from the study of patients who either showed extreme arithmetical disabilities despite normal language and general intelligence, or normal arithmetical performance despite severe disabilities in other areas.

For example, 'Signora Gaddi' was described by Cipolotti et al. (1991). She suffered a stroke affecting the left parietal cortex. She had no lasting problems with language, reasoning or memory, but had severe difficulties with all aspects of number. She could only deal with numbers up to 4 if she was permitted to count them. She could not count beyond 4 or in any way deal with numbers beyond that point.

There are also a few reports of patients who show the reverse pattern to Signora Gaddi. They suffer from dementia affecting most mental functions, but can still do arithmetic. One such patient, 'Mr Bell', was studied by Rossor et al. (1995). It turned out that the left parietal lobe – the area damaged in the case of Signora Gaddi – was one of the few areas in the left hemisphere that was undamaged in Mr Bell's case. Brain imaging studies with typical individuals have also shown that the left parietal lobe is heavily involved in arithmetic though, as we shall see, not all aspects of arithmetic rely on exactly the same areas.

Brain damage and dissociations between different components of arithmetic

The study of patients who have become dyscalculic (unable to cope with some or all aspects of arithmetic) as the result of brain damage has provided us with some of the most striking evidence that arithmetical ability is not 'all or nothing', or even a hierarchy of skills that can be placed in a consistent order from 'easiest' to 'most difficult', but is made up of a wide variety of components which can function relatively independently. (This is so even if we consider *only* arithmetic; of course, mathematics as a whole includes a far wider variety of components.) Such findings are consistent with educational studies which indicate that there is no consistent hierarchy of skills in normal arithmetical development (Denvir and Brown 1986).

This evidence is gained from the study of what are commonly termed 'dissociations' in such patients – i.e. impaired functioning of one component while another is preserved. Double dissociations, where one patient shows impaired performance in one component but not in another (e.g. can add but not subtract) while another shows the reverse (e.g. can subtract but not add), are particularly important for establishing the potential independence of different components.

By now there has been considerable research on such dissociations – for example, see summaries by Dehaene (1997) and Butterworth (1999). Patients can indeed demonstrate single and double dissociations between different arithmetical operations (addition, subtraction, multiplication and division); between oral and written presentations; and between reading and writing numbers and using them for calculation.

On a more abstract level, the study of patients with brain damage provides evidence for the broad distinction that the developmental psychologists Greeno *et al.* (1984) proposed between three major components of mathematical knowledge: factual, procedural and conceptual knowledge. Factual knowledge means 'knowing that' (e.g. remembering such number facts as '2 + 2 = 4' and the multiplication tables). Procedural knowledge means 'knowing how' (e.g. remembering how to 'borrow' when subtracting or how to perform long multiplication). Conceptual knowledge means 'knowing what it all means' (e.g. understanding the relative values of numbers and such arithmetical principles as the commutativity of addition and multiplication, and the inverse relationships between addition and subtraction, and between multiplication and division). Some patients can remember the facts but not the procedures; some remember the procedures but not the facts; some can remember both but have trouble with the underlying concepts; some have trouble with facts or procedures or both but understand the concepts well (Warrington 1982; Delazer 2003).

Another important form of dissociation, discussed extensively by Dehaene (1997), is that which is sometimes found between exact calculation and estimation. Some people, for example, cannot give the exact answer to a sum such as 9 + 3, but can tell that it is closer to 10 than 20. Exact calculation seems to be more affected than estimation by damage to the left parietal cortex.

Functional brain imaging and the components of arithmetic

Recently, the evidence from patients has received increasing support from functional brain imaging studies of people without brain damage – for example, a study by Dehaene *et al.* (1999). Different aspects of arithmetic seem to make different demands on different parts of the brain.

While different studies disagree as regards the details of brain organization for arithmetic, most suggest that the parietal cortex is involved on both sides of the brain, with a bias toward the right, in approximate arithmetic and comparisons of the relative values of numbers. Exact calculation is a predominantly left hemisphere function, involving predominantly the parietal cortex, but also several other areas.

Brain imaging studies so far appear to confirm the findings with patients that indicate that:

- there is a particular area – the left parietal cortex – that seems to be particularly involved in at least some types of arithmetic.
- Most forms of arithmetic involve the functioning of more than one part of the brain.
- Different components of arithmetic can emphasize different areas and networks within the brain, supporting the view that these different components of arithmetic can function in separate ways, and that people could be much better at one component than at others.

The findings that different arithmetical tasks make demands on different parts of the brain do not necessarily mean that individual differences in 'normal' people's performance in these tasks are related to differences in the functioning of these parts of the brain, or the ways in which they are connected. It is, however, noteworthy that both children and adults in the general population can show discrepancies between different aspects of arithmetic which are almost as great as the dissociations found in some patients.

For example, a study of individual differences in arithmetic in a group of 213 unselected children between 6 and 9 years of age has demonstrated that children can show very marked discrepancies (Dowker 1995a, 1998) – For example, between arithmetical calculation procedures and use of arithmetical principles such as commutativity; between calculation and arithmetical estimation; between arithmetical estimation and quantity estimation; and between the ability to read numbers and to compare their magnitudes.

Dowker (1995b) studied adults from the general population who have varying degrees of arithmetical difficulties. For example, Claire is a woman in her late 20s, who is educated to Masters degree level. Although she was very successful at academic subjects that depended on verbal skills, and particularly good at languages, she experienced a lot of difficulty with school mathematics, and at the age of 10 was described by her school as being of 'remedial' standard in this subject. At that age, she was given the Stanford Binet IQ test and almost solved the Superior Adult arithmetical reasoning problem about the yearly growth of a tree – except that, after working out a correct solution strategy, she calculated 37 + 13 as 39. When given the WAIS IQ test as an adult, she obtained a verbal IQ score of 132 and a performance IQ of 110. Her scaled score on the arithmetic sub-test was 13, suggesting above-average arithmetical reasoning. Her definitions of arithmetical operations are very sophisticated – for example, '[addition is] sort of self-explanatory. It's to make more of something by adding something to it. Unless you're adding minus numbers. If you add a minus number, you make less of the positive number.' However, she performed considerably less well than Hitch's (1978) less highly educated participants in most of his tests of whole-number, fraction and decimal arithmetic. For example, she could not do any addition sums that involved carrying. In these respects – good arithmetical reasoning and definitions of arithmetical operations, combined with poor calculation – her performance was quite similar to that of Warrington's (1982) dyscalculic patient D.R.C. who underwent many of the same tests. Warrington used the case of D.R.C. to demonstrate that calculation and arithmetical reasoning can be markedly discrepant in patients. Claire, and many other adults and children, show that such discrepancies also occur in individuals without brain damage. It is not clear to what extent they are caused by internal factors versus environmental factors: there is likely to be an interaction between these.

Thus, the evidence indicates that marked discrepancies often occur not only between arithmetic and other abilities but between different components of arithmetic. Moreover, such discrepancies are not confined to patients but are readily observable in the general population, both among children (Ginsburg 1977; Dowker 1998) and among adults. As suggested by studies of patients, different cognitive abilities, even within the same domain, such as arithmetic, can show considerable functional independence. However, the evidence contradicts the view, sometimes implied by studies of patients, that these cognitive abilities are things that one either does or does not have, and that most people do possess but some patients lack. Rather, they show continuous variation in the general population, both in children and adults.

Developmental dyscalculia: do some children have inborn brain-related deficits in arithmetic?

Children are less likely than adults to suffer the accidents and diseases, such as strokes, that can cause localized brain damage; but some children do suffer brain damage from such accidents and diseases. There are also some genetic disorders which can affect arithmetic more than some other functions. For example, children with Turner syndrome tend to have normal general intelligence with specific deficits in arithmetic and some spatial abilities.

Most children with arithmetical difficulties do not, however, have obvious brain damage or genetic disorders. Some have had limited educational opportunities or have been badly taught; some have emotional or medical problems that are affecting their learning; in some cases the arithmetical difficulties are clearly associated with language difficulties or more general learning difficulties. However, this still leaves many children who are much worse at arithmetic than at other academic skills, and who are doing worse at arithmetic than others who have had the same educational opportunities and have been taught in the same ways. Such problems are often described as 'developmental dyscalculia' by analogy with dyslexia. As in the case of dyslexia, the term does not imply that such children need to have diagnosable brain abnormalities: there are various estimates of the frequency of developmental dyscalculia, with some recent studies suggesting an incidence of about 6 per cent; though of course the frequency will depend on how strict the criteria are for diagnosis.

As stated above, most such arithmetical difficulties can be seen as representing the lower end of performance on a continuum for one or more arithmetic-related abilities. However, some children do appear to have more fundamental disturbances of arithmetical development.

For example, some people with developmental difficulties in arithmetic demonstrate difficulties in the recognition of even very small quantities. Butterworth (1999) studied one adult without known brain damage who had always had difficulty with arithmetic. Among other difficulties, he could not recognize two or three dots without counting them. Similar difficulties were observed in some children who had arithmetical difficulties associated with Turner syndrome.

Though more research in the area is desirable, it does not appear likely that most individual differences in arithmetic in the general population are caused by differences in ability to recognize small numbers. There are very few people who cannot recognize quantities up to 3 without needing to count them. Among 146 children who were selected for a numeracy recovery intervention programme – i.e. children who were considered by their teachers to be particularly weak at arithmetic, and who usually performed poorly on standardized tests – none showed an inability to distinguish between such small quantities (see Dowker, Chapter 11). However, even though such problems may be rare, it is important to be alert to the fact that they do sometimes occur.

The extent to which developmental arithmetical difficulties may be related to malfunctions of the same brain areas as in adult dyscalculic patients remains to be studied. There are fundamental differences between developmental and acquired disorders (Karmiloff-Smith 1997). There is some evidence that among children who were born very prematurely, those with arithmetical difficulties have smaller left parietal lobes than those without such difficulties (Isaacs et al. 2001). It is damage to this part of the brain which most often causes arithmetical difficulties in adults.

Conclusions

Though far more is known than a few years ago about the ways in which the brain is specialized for arithmetic, much remains to be learned, especially as regards children. We do know that certain parts of the brain, most notably the left parietal lobe, are particularly active in calculation tasks, and that damage to this area may result in calculation disorders. We know that different components of arithmetic can be selectively damaged in brain damaged patients and that brain imaging studies can show different brain areas being predominantly activated for different types of arithmetical task. Finally, and very importantly, we know that the brain can be influenced by experience and learning.

The most important conclusions for education are:

- Some children have severe and selective arithmetical disabilities: it is important to be alert to these, and, if possible, to screen for them.
- Marked discrepancies between different components of arithmetic are possible and indeed frequent. Assessment, intervention and, where practically possible, teaching techniques should take individual patterns of strengths and weaknesses into account.

References

Butterworth, B. (1999) *The Mathematical Brain*. London: Macmillan.

Cipolotti, L., Butterworth, B. and Denes, G. (1991) A specific deficit for numbers in a case of dense acalculia, *Brain*, 114: 2619–37.

Dehaene, S. (1997) *The Number Sense*. London: Macmillan.

Dehaene, S., Spelke, E., Pinel, P., Stanescu, R. and Tsivkin, S. (1999) Sources of mathematical thinking: behavioural and brain imaging evidence, *Science*, 284: 970–4.

Delazer, M. (2003) Neuropsychological findings on conceptual knowledge of arithmetic, in A. Baroody and A. Dowker (eds) *The Development of Arithmetical Concepts and Skills*. Mahwah, NJ: Erlbaum.

Denvir, B. and Brown, M. (1986) Understanding of number concepts in low attaining 7 to 9 year olds, 2, *Educational Studies in Mathematics*, 17: 143–65.

Dowker, A.D. (1995a) Children with specific calculation difficulties, *Links*, 2: 7–12.

Dowker, A.D. (1995b) Marked discrepancies between abilities in normal subjects. Paper presented to British Neuropsychology Society Annual Conference, London, 5 April.

Dowker, A.D. (1998) Individual differences in normal arithmetical development, in C. Donlan (ed.) *The Development of Mathematical Skills*, pp. 275–302. Hove: Psychology Press.

Ginsburg, H.P. (1977) *Children's Arithmetic*. New York: Teachers' College Press.

Greeno, T., Riley, M. and Gelman, R. (1984) Conceptual competence and children's counting, *Cognitive Psychology*, 16: 94–134.

Hitch, G.J. (1978) The numerical ability of industrial apprentices, *Journal of Occupational Psychology*, 51: 163–76.

Isaacs, E., Edmonds, C., Lucas, A. and Gadian, D. (2001) Calculation difficulties in children of very low birthweight, *Brain*, 124: 1701–7.

Karmiloff-Smith, A. (1997) Crucial differences between developmental cognitive neuroscience and adult neuropsychology, *Developmental Neuropsychology*, 13: 513–24.

Kirkpatrick, J. (1908) *Fundamentals of Child Study*, 2nd edn. London: Macmillan.

Posner, M. and McCandliss, B. (1999) Brain circuitry during reading, in R. Klein and P. McMullen (eds) *Converging Methods of Understanding Reading and Dyslexia: Language, Speech and Communication*. Cambridge, MA: MIT Press.

Rossor, M., Warrington, E. and Cipolotti, L. (1995) The isolation of calculation skills, *Journal of Neurology*, 242: 78–81.

Warrington, E.K. (1982) The fractionation of arithmetical skills: a single case study, *Quarterly Journal of Experimental Psychology*, 34A: 31–51.

Has the National Numeracy Strategy raised standards?

Margaret Brown and Alison Millett

Introduction: the Leverhulme Programme and related studies

The National Numeracy Strategy (NNS) (DfEE 1999) and its predecessor the National Numeracy Project, were a response to concern fed by press reports of poor performance in questions testing number in England in relation to other countries.

Another response to this concern was a generous offer by the Leverhulme Trust to fund a long-term research programme which would investigate the causes of, and possible remedies for, this low attainment, so as to inform future national policies. In the event though, it was overtaken by the rapid implementation of the NNS.

The Leverhulme Numeracy Research Programme began at King's College London in September 1997 and lasted until 2002, but it had been designed well before the 1997 election and prior to the proposal for a national strategy. The NNS was formulated during 1997/8, and introduced into schools in England in the school year 1999/2000, the third and middle year of the five-year Leverhulme programme. We had to modify the research design to take account of the implementation, and although the Leverhulme research was not designed to evaluate the NNS, we do have some evidence which can shed light on its effects.

In particular, as part of the Leverhulme Numeracy Research Programme we conducted a longitudinal study of numeracy learning in two cohorts (year groups) of pupils between 1997/8 and 2001/2. The children in our youngest cohort moved from Reception to Year 4 during this time, while the children in the older cohort moved from Year 4 to Year 8 (although we have only partial data in Reception and in Year 7, and none in Year 8). This means that coincidentally we have a sample of about 1300 pupils in the older cohort, complete year groups from 35 schools, tested towards the start and end of Year 4 in 1997/8 (two years before the national implementation of the NNS in 1999/2000) and a similar number of pupils from the younger cohort in the same 35 schools again tested towards the start and end of Year 4 in 2001/2 (two years after the implementation). All assessments were made on the same test.

The schools are from four diverse local education authorities (LEAs) in different parts of England. Within each LEA, ten schools were originally selected to represent different types of school according to five criteria (size, faith, test results, value added, intake characteristics). The tests used were part of a series, one for each year group, which contained many common items. They have been developed at King's over 25 years to assess key steps in numeracy learning. Items are read out by teachers, and children write answers in pre-designed test booklets. We also visited all the schools every year, both to observe lessons in each class as the pupils moved through the years, and to interview teachers, mathematics coordinators and head teachers about their views and practices. Alongside this large-scale study were five case study projects, mainly involving schools in the large-scale study. These concentrated respectively on teaching and learning numeracy in classrooms; professional development through NNS Five-day courses; school action on numeracy, triggered by the Office for Standards in Education (Ofsted) inspections and the NNS; home and school numeracy practices; and a cognitive acceleration mathematics intervention (Primary CAME) in Years 5 and 6.

At King's we also carried out a one-year extension, 'The Impact of the NNS: Comparing Pupil Attainment and Teaching in Year 4 before and after the Strategy's Introduction', funded by the Nuffield Foundation, which has provided a detailed analysis both of the Year 4 results and of the Year 4 lessons to help to evaluate the effects of the NNS. This chapter also reports on work from that project. Our views are also informed by results from two other projects which provide data which evaluates aspects of the NNS: Mental Calculation: Interpretations and Implementation (Askew et al. 2002) and Evaluation of the Implementation in Pilot Schools of the Numeracy and Literacy Strands in the KS3 Strategy (ATL) (see Barnes et al. 2003).

The effects of the NNS on attainment

When we compared the test scores for October and June in Year 4 in 1997/8 and in 2001/2 across the period of the implementation of the NNS, we found an average gain in pupils' results (or equivalently in the mean percentage of pupils answering each item correctly) of about 3 per cent. This is the equivalent of just over two months' development, as shown in Table 17.1. This difference is highly statistically significant, although probably disappointing to some who expected that the NNS would cause a large increase in attainment.

Looking at individual schools' results, about two thirds (66 per cent) of our schools (23 out of 35) had higher results in our tests in 2001/2 than they had in 1997/8; the remaining 34 per cent (12 of the 35 schools) had lower results. This is true whether the comparison is taken at the start or at the end of Year 4, although the sets of schools were not identical in both cases.

Table 17.1 Mean student score in Leverhulme Year 4 tests before and after the NNS (data from same 35 schools with n > 1290 pupils for each test)

	October	June
1997/8	52%	62%
2001/2	55%	65%
Rise	3%	3%
Equivalent	2 months	2 months

Table 17.2 National test results showing percentages of pupils reaching Level 4 in mathematics and science at Key Stage 2 (Year 6), 1997–2002

	Maths	Science
1997	62	68
1998	59*	69
1999	69	78
2000	72	84
2001	71	87
2002	73	86

* Mental arithmetic tests were introduced for the first time in 1998; it is suggested that this accounts for the drop in performance.

These results, although disappointing, are broadly in line with improvements of 4 per cent reaching Level 4 in national test results at Key Stage 2 (Year 6) between 1999 at the start of the Strategy and 2002, two years later (see Table 17.2). This table shows that there was a large increase in the national mathematics test results between 1998 and 1999 in the year *before* the NNS was introduced, which was attributed to early introduction of the NNS by the Secretary of State for Education at the time; however, our observations in schools suggest that it was more likely due to a combination of recovery from a fall the previous year due to the introduction of mental tests, and more focused test preparation for Key Stage 2 tests. (The science results in Table 17.2 show a similar increase between 1998 and 1999 and a greater overall increase, although there was no science strategy.)

There is clearly a problem in using high-stakes tests to compare standards over the period 1997–2002 when there was increasing pressure on schools. The Leverhulme results have the advantage that they are based on a single previously developed test for which children do not receive any specific preparation. Reasons for the overall change in test scores are discussed in a later section. In the next two sections we will look to see whether the changes affect some children more than others.

Table 17.3 Mean percentage scores for different attainment groups for June Leverhulme Year 4 tests before and after the NNS (data from same 35 schools with n > 1290 pupils for each test)

	June 1998	June 2002
Highest 5%	90	92
Highest 25%	82	85
Middle 50%	63	67
Lowest 25%	39	41
Lowest 5%	25	23

Children in different attainment groups

It might have been expected that the range of variation in pupils' attainment would have decreased with the introduction of more whole-class teaching, and this was certainly the stated intention of the first director of the NNS. However, the variation in results between the lower and higher attainers has actually increased.

The reason for this can be seen in the data when the comparison between the mean scores in the Year 4 results in June 1998 and June 2002 is made for different groups in the population, as shown in Table 17.3. The greatest improvements are made during the period of the NNS by the middle 50 per cent of pupils. The lowest 5 per cent show a small decline in performance. This corresponds closely to reports from secondary teachers in the evaluation of the Key Stage 3 pilot (Barnes *et al.* 2003) that while average and higher attainers have higher standards than previously, standards are lower among the lowest attainers.

Both observation of lessons, especially as part of the case study work, and interviews with children suggest that low attaining pupils derive little benefit from the whole-class teaching episodes, and the topic of the lesson does not always correspond to their areas of greatest need. Some high attainers also expressed to us their frustration at their progress being held back by the whole-class teaching emphasis, which tends to be pitched at the needs of the middle of the group.

The result is therefore that attainment has become further polarized. When we looked at the progress of each cohort on particular items it became clear that it takes between five and seven years between the time when the highest attaining children can give a correct response and when almost all children can. Table 17.4 and Figure 17.1 illustrate this in regard to two items which were included in all year groups.

This long period between the year group when the highest attainers are successful and when the lowest attainers are successful demonstrates the need for more formative assessment and greater differentiation of provision to satisfy the needs of both extreme groups, and helps to explain why the greater

Table 17.4 Progression in percentages of children successful in selected items which were tested in October and June for all year groups (older cohort in italics) (n > 1290)

Item description	Yr 1		Yr 2		Yr 3		Yr 4		Yr 5		Yr 6	
	Oc	Ju	Oc	Ju	Oc	Ju	Oc	Ju	Oc	Ju	Oc	Ju
Bags of 10 apples: 4 bags & 3 apples?	6	28	35	59	62	75	72	83				
							80	*85*	*77*	*80*	*81*	*92*
Write 1 less than 200	2	11	19	52	59	77	82	91				
							76	*82*	*87*	*94*	*95*	*97*

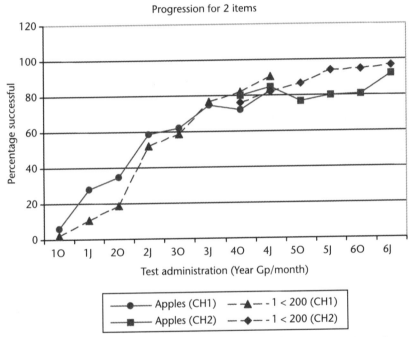

Figure 17.1 Progression in percentages of children successful in selected items which were tested in October and June for all year groups (CH1 is younger cohort) (n > 1290)

uniformity of provision has benefited mainly the middle 50 per cent of the attainment band.

Effects of gender, class and ethnicity

Table 17.5 shows that the performance of Year 4 girls is slightly lower than that for Year 4 boys, and also that it increases less during the implementation of the

Table 17.5 Mean scores for boys and girls in Leverhulme Year 4 tests before and after the NNS (data from same 35 schools with n > 1290 pupils for each test)

	Boys	Girls
June 1998	62%	61%
June 2002	66%	63%

Table 17.6 Mean percentage scores for groups of children with different ranges of deprivation index by postcode for June tests in 1998 and 2002

	June 1998	June 2002
Least deprived 25%	68	71
Middle 50%	61	65
Most deprived 25%	56	61

NNS. Thus the girls' overall performance is a little behind the boys' in 1998, but the gap has widened in 2002 after the introduction of the NNS, although both sexes made small gains. Analysis of the different attainment groups by gender shows that the group that has gained most are the middle 50 per cent of boys (with a gain of 6 percentage points), while the group that has gained least are very low-attaining girls. The reasons for such differences seem likely to be related to the increasing predominance of mental over written work (which seems to favour boys) and more emphasis on public performance, over which low-attaining girls who were interviewed expressed their anxiety.

The story in relation to social deprivation seems rather more optimistic than that for attainment groups and gender. We divided the sample into four equal groups in order of deprivation according to their postcodes. It should be borne in mind that the resulting data is less accurate than other data presented in this chapter, not only because of the unreliability of the deprivation values, but also because in order to keep the sample over 1000 we could not afford to control so tightly for pupils and schools. Thus the sample for these comparisons includes all children with valid postcodes participating in a particular test at the appropriate times, which explains the differences in overall results between this and other tables. It can be seen from Table 17.6 that because of greater gains between 1998 and 2002 for the most deprived group, the differences in mean scores between children living in the most and least deprived areas narrow slightly between 1998 and 2002. It is difficult to explain this but it seems possible that more equitable curriculum access may have helped the more deprived groups. However, concerns remain about the associations between deprivation and attainment – for example, the distribution of boys with the top 5 per cent of scores is even more polarized in 2002 than in 1998, with half the group coming from the least deprived 25 per cent and none from the most deprived 25 per cent.

Those children who achieve very high scores but come from the most deprived areas tended to be of Indian ethnic origin, with English as a second language but with both parents at home and not receiving free school meals. The girl with this sort of background in our study sample for the focus project on home-school relations was living in poor temporary accommodation with parents who were recent immigrants; her father had a degree in statistics but was initially unemployed and later worked as a minicab driver until he had improved his English; both parents did many informal mathematical activities with their daughter at home.

We have not compared the Year 4 data for other social groups between 1998 and 2002, but within the Year 4 data for 2002, children receiving free school meals are on average about one school year behind those who do not receive free school meals, those living with single parents are on average about five months behind, and children of white European, Chinese and Indian descent are about one school year *ahead* of children of black African or Caribbean descent, with the Pakistani group in an intermediate position. Clearly these ethnic differences are not independent of the data on deprivation indices.

How do we explain the small overall gain?

The overall increase of 3 per cent in Year 4 results on our test might be attributed to a different curriculum, or to changes in teachers or teaching (a different teaching style, more confident teachers after considerable training, or some combination of these).

A different curriculum

Differences in increase between items assessing different skills and understandings suggest that the increase seems most likely to be due to the different curriculum emphases introduced by the NNS. The overall increase is likely to be simply the consequence of a new curriculum which favours the type of mental strategies which are predominantly assessed in the Leverhulme tests. If the tests had been wider tests of mathematics then it is very possible that there would have been no overall change in attainment.

Table 17.7 shows (cryptically) the five test items which have the greatest improvements between 1997/8 and 2001/2, together with the three multiplication fact items and two items with the greatest reductions. The two items with the greatest improvement relate to the number line, and all other items except one relate to counting and recording with larger numbers. The remaining item, '$\Rightarrow 143-86$', is one which asks children to deduce the answer to $143-86$ given that the sum $86 + 57 = 143$, and thus tests application of the inverse relation between addition and subtraction. All these aspects are strongly emphasized in the NNS, supporting the contention that the increase is due to curriculum change.

Table 17.7 Differences in percentage success for some Year 4 items between 1997/8 and 2001/2 (n > 1290)

| | | October | | June | |
		1997	2001	1998	2002
Items with largest increases	Label – 2	26	47	42	71
	Label 267	44	63	58	72
	1 > 1099	23	37	37	56
	Write 2100	55	71	68	84
	1 < 2100	45	60	60	74
	=> 143 – 86	22	36	36	50
Multiplication fact items	4 × 5	86	83	89	89
	7 × 8	31	26	48	48
	9 × 9	50	43	64	66
Items with largest decreases	4(5) + 3	77	70	84	80
	4(10) + 3	80	72	85	83

In contrast to this are the multiplication fact items where there is little change at the end of the year and even some decrease in October results between 1997 and 2001, although this may be due to later testing in some schools in autumn 1997. (Teachers were asked to repeat all items so the percentage correct includes children who were able to quickly derive the answer as well as those who could immediately recall it.)

One of the items showing most decrease, '4(5) + 3', is one in which children are shown a picture of a box of five cakes and asked how many there would be if there were four similar boxes and three loose cakes, and a similar item using bags of ten apples and three loose apples '4(10) + 3'. These items, and others in which there is little change, concern word problems which are much more rarely encountered in the NNS than in previous curriculum materials, which often emphasized work in 'real' contexts (see Askew, Chapter 7). Nevertheless, by the end of Year 4 there is little difference in performance between 1998 and 2002. These results correspond broadly to reports from secondary teachers who agree that standards of mental calculation have increased, but children are less able to apply operations to problems in context (Barnes *et al.* 2003).

Generally in Year 4, performance on addition and subtraction items has improved most (+6 per cent on average), excluding items where these operations are set in real-world contexts where there has been a very small decline. Items testing numbers and the number system test have also improved (+5 per cent on average). The categories of items where there has been an average decline in facility are those testing multiplication and division (– 4 per cent), and ratio and proportion (– 2 per cent).

These results therefore indicate that some understandings and skills have been strongly affected by the change in curriculum which occurred as part of the implementation of the NNS in 1999/2000, whereas in many curriculum areas there has been little effect from a major systemic reform. The much greater use of number lines seems to have had the most significant effect, whereas expected changes in some basic skills (e.g. knowledge of multiplication facts) have not emerged.

Changes in teachers and teaching

We have not yet completed our analysis of the content and style of the Year 4 lessons in order to categorize changes between 1997/8 and 2001/2, so this section has to be based on the team's broad impressions of changes in teaching based on about 70 lessons observed in each cohort in each year of the study, together with interviews with each of these teachers, head teachers and mathematics coordinators.

It is certainly the case that teachers have without exception welcomed the NNS and told us how much they valued clear guidance from several different sources: the *Framework* and examples, the medium-term plans, local consultants visiting the school, observing lessons taught by leading mathematics teachers, sessions and support from the school mathematics coordinator and, in some cases, Five-day courses and/or lesson plans provided by the NNS. They reported feeling much more confident about knowing what mathematical ideas they were teaching and how to teach them, and felt no longer dependent on published textbook schemes. In a few cases we observed the same teacher teaching Year 4 in 1997/8 and in 2001/2, and increased confidence was evident in those lessons. However, we did also note growing dependence on new commercial schemes, published to fit the NNS, over the period of time since it was introduced.

The most serious complaints that some teachers expressed were that they often felt that children would benefit from more lessons on a topic before moving on, although they appreciated that the topic would soon be revisited. They felt that slower children in particular suffered from never having time to grasp anything properly (and the results shown above suggest that this might well be the case). In a small number of cases topics, especially in Years 5 and 6, were felt to be too difficult, especially for classes with many lower-attaining pupils. During 2001–2 we found some teachers trusting their own judgement more and becoming more flexible about both the three-part lesson and the curriculum. Many teachers complained about the additional work, especially in the first year, before new textbooks were published which were closely related to the *Framework*; this absence required them to search laboriously for suitable activities and examples.

It was our perception that lessons had become more lively, pacey and interactive over the course of the four years; however it was difficult in classroom observation to be sure that the new teaching styles were actually producing better learning. Some children felt that lessons were *too* pacey and that they did not get time, either within one lesson or across a sequence of lessons on one topic, to consolidate properly. Teachers were clearly working hard but not all children were, with frequently changing activities providing opportunities for distraction. The public nature of lessons meant that some children were concentrating on establishing or maintaining status, and not revealing their ignorance, rather than on learning mathematics.

The percentage of Year 4 teachers who taught the whole class for a significant part of every lesson rose from 60 per cent in 1997/8 to 100 per cent in 2001/2; however, median gains in the class average score between October and March were very slightly lower in 1997/8 and 1998/9 for those who taught the whole class together every lesson than for those who did so less frequently. The finding that the frequency of whole-class teaching makes little difference is not out of line with other findings – for example, in the earlier *Effective Teachers of Numeracy* study (Askew *et al.* 1997) we had also found no effects of class organization, and indeed our most effective out of 75 teachers *never* taught the whole class together for mathematics.

In another study (Askew *et al.* 2002) it was noted that mathematics lessons in 2001/2 were still mainly *procedural*, relating to ways of *doing* mental calculation. There were very few lesson episodes which could be termed *strategic*, in the sense of discussing *how* to make decisions (e.g. how to decide between different methods, or operations). Thus it may be that while the formats of lessons had changed, the style of the interactions between teachers and children had not.

In a study project we also observed the effect of the Five-day NNS courses on individual teachers, their subject knowledge, attitudes and classroom practices, and their pupils' mean gains. Although some teachers valued the Five-day courses in terms of their own knowledge and confidence, and the observations suggest some changes in classroom practice were made, once again no effect was found in relation to pupils' gains. Teachers attributed greater effects on practice to in-school training and working with the *Framework* document itself.

Evidence from the case study project looking at whole-school factors and their effect on change suggested that the presence of six constructs was important in facilitating the introduction of reform that led to improvements in attainment: the *enthusiasm* of the mathematics coordinator and their *clarity of vision* about successful ways of working with colleagues; a situation of *balance* between the head teacher and coordinator whereby each respected the other's role and expertise; *appropriate resourcing* of the coordination role that included time out of the classroom for the co-ordinator; the use of *outside expertise*; and *consistency of views* within the school community.

Conclusions: the way ahead

This evidence thus suggests that curriculum change is more effective than changing the way teaching is organized in producing learning gains, but that overall changes are unlikely to be very dramatic (and if they are, may well be superficial). Some further changes which seem likely to be beneficial are listed below:

- more work on applied problem solving (not just contrived word problems);
- more formative assessment, more differentiation and more teaching assistants to assist teachers in adapting the *Framework* to the needs of their pupils, especially to addressing the specific problems of lower attainers, and to a lesser extent higher attainers;
- more time on some single difficult topics, both within lessons and across groups of lessons;
- a greater focus on strategic discussions;
- more sustained teacher professional development – for some teachers (especially mathematics coordinators) outside the school, and for others within the school using release time of the mathematics coordinator.

We are pleased to report that several of these have already been pursued by the Primary Strategy.

References

Askew, M., Brown, M., Rhodes, V., Johnson, D. and Wiliam, D. (1997) *Effective Teachers of Numeracy, Final Report*. London: King's College.

Askew, M., Bibby, T., Brown, M. and Hodgen, J. (2002) *Mental Calculation: Interpretations and Implementation, Final Report*. London: King's College.

Barnes, A., Venkatakrishnan, H. and Brown, M. (2003) *Strategy or Strait-jacket? Teachers' Views on the English and Mathematics Strands of the Key Stage 3 National Strategy*. London: Association of Teachers and Lecturers.

DfEE (Department for Education and Employment) (1999) *Framework for Teaching Mathematics from Reception to Year 6*. London: DfEE.

Index

PRINCIPLES AND PRACTICES IN ARITHMETIC TEACHING
INNOVATIVE APPROACHES FOR THE PRIMARY CLASSROOM

Julia Anghileri (Ed.)

The teaching of arithmetic in the primary school has traditionally been dominated by a focus on standard algorithms and this approach is now being questioned. Curriculum changes are taking place that promote the development of mental strategies, and provide more opportunities for children to develop their own ways of working. This book shows contrasting influences for change as leading mathematics educators from the USA, the UK and the Netherlands identify the way research is used to develop different classroom practices. In England, changes are taking place through a *National Numeracy Strategy* which is set to raise standards in every primary classroom while in the Netherlands, *Realistic Mathematics Education* introduces innovative approaches such as use of an 'empty number line' to support the teaching of mental strategies. This book explores why we teach in different ways, challenges orthodoxy, and sets the agenda for learning from each other.

Contents

224pp   0 335 20633 6 (Paperback)   0 335 20634 4 (Hardback)

ISSUES IN TEACHING NUMERACY IN PRIMARY SCHOOLS

Ian Thompson (Ed.)

This timely book provides a detailed and comprehensive overview of the teaching and learning of numeracy in primary schools. It will be particularly helpful to teachers, mathematics co-ordinators and numeracy consultants involved in the implementation of the National Numeracy Strategy. It presents an accessible guide to current British and Dutch research into numeracy teaching. Leading researchers describe their findings and discuss implications for practising teachers. The projects include studies of effective teachers of numeracy and ICT and numeracy, an evaluation of international primary textbooks, assessment, using and applying mathematics, and family numeracy. The book also includes chapters on pedagogy, focusing on the teaching of mental calculation; the transition from mental to written algorithms; the place of the empty number line; and the use of the calculator as a teaching aid. Most chapters include practical suggestions for helping teachers develop aspects of their numeracy teaching skills.

Contents
Section 1: Numeracy: issues past and present – Swings of the pendulum – Numeracy matters: contemporary policy issues in the teaching of mathematics – Realistic Mathematics Education in the Netherlands – The National Numeracy Project: 1996–99 – Section 2: Curriculum and research project issues – Primary school mathematics textbooks: an international comparison – Using and applying mathematics at Key Stage 1 – Family numeracy – It ain't (just) what you do: effective teachers of numeracy – ICT and numeracy in primary schools – Section 3: Assessment issues – Choosing a good test question – Context problems and assessment: ideas from the Netherlands – Section 4: Pedagogical issues – Getting your head around mental calculation – The empty number line as a new model – Written methods of calculation – Issues in teaching multiplication and division – The pedagogy of calculator use – Index.

224pp   0 335 20324 8 (Paperback)   0 335 20325 6 (Hardback)